Sidney's Poetic Development

Sidney's Poetic Development

NEIL L. RUDENSTINE

HARVARD UNIVERSITY PRESS

Cambridge   Massachusetts

1967

For my mother and father

Preface

❦

THERE IS A moment in Sidney's *Arcadia* when King Basilius, frustrated in all his attempts to win favor from the Lady Cleophila, cries out in anger and indignation:

> But alas what a Cruelty ys this, not onely to torment, but to thincke the Tormentes lighte! . . . And wth like Cruelty are my wordes breathed oute from a flamy hart accounpted as Messingers of a quyett mynde. Yf I speake no thing, I choke my self, and am in no way of Releef; yf simply, neglected; yf Confusedly, not understood; yf by the bending together all my inward powers, they bringe forthe any Lyvely expressing of that they truely feele, that ys a Token forsoothe, the thoughtes are apte to too muche Leysure. Thus ys sylence desperate, folly punisshed, and witt suspected.[1]

Scarcely any passage could put more succinctly the plight, not only of lovers, but also of poets in Sidney's era. The problem, very simply, was how to make one's protestations of love convincing or persuasive, and the ordinary difficulties of such a venture were compounded by a great number of factors. Several centuries of what might be generally termed Petrarchan love poetry had all but exhausted the language, forms, and strategies which the troubadours, the *Romaunt de la Rose,* and the creators of the *dolce stil nuovo* had made popular. The game of love had become only too familiar, too routine, too conventional in a pejorative sense. Basilius, in the *Arcadia,* has an arsenal of timeworn phrases and tactics; and Cleophila is cold in her replies and sophisticated in her various means of self-defense.[2] Each knows thoroughly the gambits of the other. In such circumstances, ladies will find it difficult to distinguish true lovers from false, and courtiers—even kings—may fail to gain a hearing. Assuming Basilius' love to be genuine, how is he to give it convincing expression?

The poet writing within the Petrarchan tradition might, of course, side-step this problem, but Sidney himself clearly felt unable to do so. Rather, he deliberately made an issue of it and took considerable pains in the *Apologie for Poetrie* and the *Astrophel and Stella* (as well as in the *Arcadia*) to suggest a solution. In effect, he defined the kind of style Basilius ought to have used in his approaches to Cleophila, and he offered, by way of example, several versions of it in his own work. Many critics have dealt with this question of Sidney's style, and while their comments are difficult to summarize briefly, the main outlines of their conclusions can be sketched. The tendency has been to characterize Sidney—at least the Sidney of the *Apologie* and of the *Astrophel*—as one or another kind of rebel against Petrarchan modes. An older generation of commentators saw him protesting against "convention" on behalf of "sincerity." More recently, the terms have changed but the argument is not so very different: Sidney came to distrust Ciceronian "ornament" and in fact argued for the use of a "plain" style, rather as Jonson, Donne, and Bacon were to do several years later. At the very least, all the critics agree on two points. The poetry of the *Arcadia* and that of *Astrophel* differ radically from one another, and Sidney must therefore have changed his ideas about style in mid-career. He proposed two quite different ways of solving Basilius' dilemma, and the second—that of *Astrophel*—was infinitely superior to the first.[3]

The present study takes issue with such views, and it attempts to ground its conclusions in a detailed consideration of nearly all of Sidney's poetry and a selection of the prose.[4] In essence, it discovers a pattern of unbroken continuity in Sidney's poetic development. It argues that the *Arcadia*'s underlying principles of style are precisely those of the *Apologie* and *Astrophel*; in addition, it suggests that the experiments with a dramatic style in the *Arcadia* and the *Certain Sonnets* lead directly to the verse of *Astrophel*. In short, it stresses the fundamental unity and inner consistency of Sidney's œuvre. It is not that the work lacks change and "development" altogether, but that these are different in kind from what has been generally suggested.

They can best be described (as Chapter Ten proposes) in terms of the rhetorical concept of energia, which Sidney discusses in the *Apologie*. The consequence of such a view is generally to emphasize the technical aspects of Sidney's growth as a poet: his invention of a new English metrics, his adaptation and refinement of different styles to suit different genres, and his imaginative transformation of the lyric—in particular the sonnet—into the supple, dramatic instrument of expression it becomes in *Astrophel*.

If this study is primarily concerned with problems of style and technique, however, it views such matters as much as possible in the context of Sidney's larger meanings. Although it focuses essentially upon the development of Sidney's poetry, it also draws freely upon Sidney's prose materials whenever these seem relevant to a further understanding of the verse. No systematic study of the *Old Arcadia* is offered, and very little is said about the *New Arcadia*, but selections from both works (as well as from the *Apologie for Poetrie* and other prose pieces) are used to illuminate different aspects of the verse. The opening chapters, for instance, are devoted to Sidney's correspondence with Hubert Languet, to the relation between that correspondence and the *Old Arcadia*, and to a broad consideration of Petrarchan love themes as they appear in either the prose or the poetry of Sidney's earliest writings. Sidney's debate—if it may be called such—with Languet is seen as an analogue of similar debates in the *Old Arcadia*, the *Apologie for Poetrie*, and the *Astrophel and Stella*. It is the cornerstone for all that follows, an important introduction to both the style and the substance of Sidney's writing as a whole.

I am very much indebted to several people who have helped me in my study of Sidney. Professors Douglas Bush and Harry Levin read an early version of this book, and offered me sympathetic criticism. Mr. John Buxton, of New College, Oxford, first encouraged me to write on Sidney, and his erudition has saved me more than once from embarrassing errors and omissions. Professor Anne Davidson Ferry read the entire manuscript with all the care and rigor I could have desired, and many of her suggestions have been silently and gratefully incorporated in the following pages.

I*

x   PREFACE

I would like to thank the Clarendon Press, Oxford, for permission
to quote at length from William Ringler's *The Poems of Sir Philip Sidney*,
and the Cambridge University Press for similar permission to quote
from Albert Feuillerat's *The Complete Works of Sir Philip Sidney*. My
own study of Sidney is particularly indebted not only to Mr. Ringler's
excellent text of Sidney but also to his establishment of a reliable
chronology of Sidney's writings.

I have profited from the friendly interest as well as from the different kinds of valuable help given to me from time to time by
Professor John H. D'Arms, Miss Rachel Jacoff, Professor Irvin
Ehrenpreis, and Professor Piers Lewis. Mrs. Nora B. Anthony of the
Harvard University Press has suggested numerous corrections and
alterations which I have very willingly made. Finally, my quite
unpayable debt to David Kalstone is writ small in the footnotes and
large in a great many parts of the text which follows.

N.L.R.

Harvard University
November 23, 1966

Contents

Sidney's Poetic Development

CHAPTER I

Sidney and Languet

❦

IN THE AUTUMN of 1580, Philip Sidney ended a long sojourn at Wilton, the Countess of Pembroke's country house. A letter to his brother Robert, sent from Leicester House and dated October 18, suggests the extent of his renewed involvement in the life of London and the court. Robert was traveling and studying on the Continent, and Sidney wrote:

> My time, exceedingly short, will suffer me to write no more lei-surely: Stephen can tell you who stands with me while I am writing. Now (dear brother), take delight likewise in the mathematicals; Mr. Savile is excellent in them. . . . Arithmetic and geometry, I would wish you well seen in, so as both in matter of number and measure you might have a feeling and active judgment; I would you did bear the mechanical instruments, wherein the Dutch excel. I write this to you as one, that for myself have given over the delights in the world, but wish to you as much, if not more, than to myself. . . . My toyful books I will send, with God's help, by February, . . . [1]

Sidney, in his letter, has the air of a man who relishes, a little self-consciously, the idea of being busy again. He refers more than once to his "great haste," and adds that "my eyes are almost closed up, overwatched with tedious business" (Pears, 202). Drake has just returned, Portugal is counted as lost, and Sidney complains that the English sit idle and "look on at our neighbours' fires." Languet had years before charged him with the fact that "you English, like foxes, have slunk out" of the great religious struggles of Europe (Pears, 63). Sidney, in 1580, seems anxious to redress the balance, and he obviously longs for a greater commitment on Elizabeth's part to the

Protestant cause on the Continent. Yet for all this, his letter is colored by feelings of reluctance that are only half articulated. Robert's rich prospect of relative leisure, travel, and study engages Sidney so much that he goes on for several pages, jotting down ideas about history, poetry, the Latin language, geometry, and other subjects. If he is content to be immersed in politics once again, he seems to betray another, equally powerful allegiance in the excitement and vigor with which he talks about his brother's studies. Thinking of the "delight" he had himself discovered in "the mathematicals" prompts him to the sudden valediction which falls so casually from his pen: "I write this to you as one, that for myself have given over the delights in the world, but wish to you as much, if not more, than to myself." Those delights concerned the pleasures of study, but they seem also to have been associated with Wilton in Sidney's mind, and they made his recent return from there to London seem a particularly decisive and symbolic step. At Wilton, there had been time for reading, for reflection, for friends, and for poetry. The *Arcadia* ("My toyful books") had been begun and nearly finished during the leisurely months spent in his sister's company.[2] By October, however, literature and leisure were set aside. Sidney journeyed back to court with its "tedious business" of state affairs, and the move seemed to inaugurate a time in which the pleasures of a private, secluded existence were to be exchanged, once and for all, for the very different regimen of the public world. Undoubtedly he saw the episode too simply. His life in fact changed less sharply than he expected, for England continued to sit idly by, watching her neighbors' fires. His farewell to the world's delights proved to be premature, and its self-conscious finality revealed more than anything else his powerful desire to give dramatic shape to his life. In the years after 1580, he still found time to study, reflect, and write, although he was probably correct in sensing that conditions would never again be so idyllic as they had been at Wilton in 1578–1580. The court and then the Netherlands swallowed up more and more of his time, and there was indeed a sense in which he had lost the Arcadian world of Wilton forever.

To test the depth of unexpressed regret that lies beneath the surface of Sidney's letter to Robert one need only turn to his correspondence with Hubert Languet, the humanist diplomat who was both a friend and a mentor to Sidney throughout the 1570's. Sidney must have written to Languet sometime early in October, telling him of his return to London, for a letter from Languet—dated October 22— begins:

> Your letter was on many accounts most delightful to me, but especially because I learn from it that you have come forth from that hiding place of yours into open day. (Pears, 187)

From Languet's point of view, the move was a happy conclusion to an episode that had worried and deeply concerned him. His protégé had for some time been suggesting the merits and appeals of a retired life, and more than once had seemed uncomfortably close to throwing over the public career for which he had been so carefully trained. It may be worth reviewing the history of Sidney's apparent vacillations, since his biographers have generally made less of the subject than it deserves, and since it bears directly upon the discussion of the *Arcadia* that follows in the next chapter.[3]

Certainly there were political factors, and even financial problems, which helped to keep Sidney at the Countess of Pembroke's for so long a time.[4] But one of Languet's last letters sheds light on another aspect of the situation—one which the young courtier might not willingly have exposed either to his father or to his uncle Leicester:

> You used sometimes to say that you were by nature entirely averse to the excitement and the fascinations of a court, and that when you returned home, nothing would delight you more than to pass your life with your friends in dignified ease, if ever such a lot should be granted to you. I was indeed afraid you were speaking seriously, when I thought of your modesty, and how free from all ambition you were; but I judged that though that was then your resolution, you would change your mind as you grew older, and even if you should persevere in it, your country would never permit itself to be cheated of the benefit of your character, which it had a right to claim as its own. (Pears, 184)

The passage occurs in a long letter which Languet wrote on September 24, 1580, when Sidney was still at Wilton, and it is the culmination of a series of letters in which the older man grows increasingly concerned, and the younger man rather more bold, about the problems of retirement and duty. As early as 1574, when he was receiving Languet's weekly reports on the political tensions of Europe, Sidney declared that

> in your letters I fancy I see a picture of the age in which we live: an age that resembles a bow too long bent, it must be unstrung or it will break.   (Pears, 36)

Sidney, of course, had moments when he preferred to think of the bow as an instrument of action, but his impulse frequently took him in the opposite direction—in the direction of relaxing tensions and withdrawing from action. It is he, for example, who usually provided the leaven of wit in the Languet correspondence, pressing often to keep the letters informal and unsolemn: "I do not like the excessive politeness of that expression 'you would not have troubled me about the book, if you had not believed it to be in print.' . . . And therefore use not such elegant speech any more, unless we are to have a new quarrel" (Pears, 72). After one particularly lengthy bout of rather strained humor, Sidney feels momentarily obliged to pull up short:

> But my dear Languet, what are we doing? Jesting in times like these? . . . But here we have the true enjoyment, or rather the true fruit of friendship, namely, that the recollection of a dear friend is not only a great relief under all sorrow, but that it doth in the midst of most grave affairs, force a man to descend to a certain relaxation of his mind. And this refreshing of the mind consists, more than any thing else, in that seemly play of humour which is so natural, and so ingrafted, so to speak, in the characters of some of the wisest men, that neither Socrates nor our own More could lose their jest even in the hour of death. So let us even be merry.   (Pears, 65)

Sidney is serious about "times like these," but he also finds it quite easy to slip into a justification of wit as a necessary refreshing of the mind. Wit and friendship, he suggests, are forms of relaxation, valuable allies of a mind committed to the strenuous life of public affairs. In other moods and circumstances, however, they might also threaten that life, and after Sidney returned from his Continental tour in the spring of 1575, he clearly gave himself over more fully than Languet liked to the genial pleasures of court and country. In the letters of 1575 and thereafter, Languet sends periodic warnings to the effect that the "court is by no means a frugal oeconomist of time" (Pears, 95); that it offers "so many temptations to waste time" (Pears, 97); and that it may interfere with Sidney's cultivation of a good Latin prose style—"if you cast away the study altogether, I shall be compelled to charge you with doing it through indolence and love of ease" (Pears, 97). Yet these admonitions are only uttered by the way, and Languet begins to be seriously concerned only when his pupil offers to argue the case for consciously indulged idleness and relaxation, as he does in a letter of March 1578:

> And the use of the pen, as you may perceive, has plainly fallen from me; and my mind itself, if it was ever active in any thing, is now beginning, by reason of my indolent ease, imperceptibly to lose its strength, and to relax without any reluctance. For to what purpose should our thoughts be directed to various kinds of knowledge, unless room be afforded for putting it into practice, so that public advantage may be the result, which in a corrupt age we cannot hope for? Who would learn music except for the sake of giving pleasure? or architecture except with a view to building? But the mind itself, you will say, that particle of the divine mind, is cultivated in this manner. This indeed, if we allow it to be the case, is a very great advantage: but let us see whether we are not giving a beautiful but false appearance to our splendid errors. For while the mind is thus, as it were, drawn out of itself, it cannot turn its powers inward for thorough self-examination; to which employment no labour that men can undertake, is any way to be compared. Do you not see that I am cleverly playing the stoic? yea and I shall be a cynic too, unless you reclaim me.
>
> (Pears, 143)

Sidney's inactivity in 1578 was of course partly enforced, and he often found it oppressive.[5] But in the passage just quoted, he is clearly yielding to "indolent ease," and he willingly allows his mind to "lose its strength." What other road is open to the man of action in "a corrupt age," when there is no field for the performance of heroic, virtuous deeds? Sidney anticipates Languet's reply: one should continue to study "various kinds of knowledge" because they cultivate the mind, keeping it alert, active, and ready for use when occasion demands. Throughout the letters, Languet has often urged that Sidney study essentially what is important to his career and estate in life—he will, for example, have little time for "literary leisure" (Pears, 25). Sidney now challenges his friend on the point. Why study Latin (useful for diplomats) when there is little hope of being employed as an ambassador, or architecture, unless one has some prospect of being able to build, or music, unless one can practice it and so give pleasure to others? As Sidney continues, his tone alters revealingly. He argues more and more in a spirit of serious banter, and rather plays with ideas as they come to him. Leisure, he suggests, allows one time for self-examination, for reflection, and is this not a higher vocation than any other which one might follow? The indolence and inactivity of mind he mentioned moments earlier, however, scarcely suggest that he is engaged in very strenuous meditation or vigorous self-scrutiny, and he is quick to catch himself in this regard. By the end of the passage, he all but admits that he has mainly been looking for ways of rationalizing his idleness: "Do you not see that I am cleverly playing the stoic?" And he ends by daring the older man to "reclaim" him.

It has seemed important to pay close attention to this particular letter, partly because the interpretation offered here differs radically from that in recent studies,[6] and partly because the passage as a whole expresses beautifully the quality and complexity of Sidney's mind, especially his habit of using serious issues as the substance of witty dialogue. He is supple in the face of Languet's sturdy point of view. His wit is partly defensive, but it is also too firmly under control to suggest any fatal weaknesses; and if his apology for leisure and indulged relaxation has an air of rationalization about it, the rationalization is of a serious sort, rooted in experiences which seem to declare their own validity and value to him. Beneath the easy manner of the prose, one can sense throughout the pull of rival claims upon Sidney and feel, too, how effortlessly he manages to convert stress into a mode of courtly debate that hovers somewhere between a proper and a sophistic use of rhetoric.

Unfortunately, scarcely any of Sidney's last letters to Languet have been preserved, but we can guess at some of their substance from Languet's replies. In October 1578, the older man wrote:

> I am especially sorry to hear you say that you are weary of the
> life to which I have no doubt God has called you, and desire to fly
> from the light of your court and betake yourself to the privacy of
> secluded places to escape the tempest of affairs by which statesmen
> are generally harrassed; ... (Pears, 155)

Finally, in September 1580, Languet wrote the lengthy and strong
remonstrance, part of which was quoted earlier. He himself refused
to condemn Sidney, but he wrote that other friends on the Continent

> are astonished that you find pleasure in your long retirement; and
> though they readily believe that it is made most delightful to you by
> the society of your dearest friends, still they think you ought very
> carefully to reflect whether it is consistent with your character to
> remain so long concealed. They fear that those who do not so well
> know your constancy may suspect that you are tired of that toilsome
> path which leads to virtue, which you formerly pursued with so
> much earnestness. They are fearful too, that the sweetness of your
> lengthened retirements may somewhat relax the vigorous energy
> with which you used to rise to noble undertakings, and a love of ease,
> which you once despised, creep by degrees over your spirit.
> (Pears, 182–83)

Leicester was also pressing Sidney to return to court, for political
reasons, and Languet's letter undoubtedly acted as an additional
spur.[7] A number of factors had drawn Sidney initially to Wilton—
the Anjou affair, his lack of a post at court, his relative impecunious-
ness, and his inclination to "escape the tempest of affairs by which
statesmen are generally harrassed." When he finally returned to
London and Leicester House, he must certainly have felt glad to be
busy once again; but he was also quite sure that he had "given over
the delights in the world" for the "tedious business" of state.

If part of the Languet correspondence seems to reveal Sidney as a
complex and divided personality, an equal portion sustains the
traditional view of him as the ideal courtier, the man who declares
in the *Apologie for Poetrie* that "the ending end of all earthly learning" is virtuous action. He studies geometry because "it is of the

greatest service in the art of war" (Pears, 28). Of Aristotle's work, he considers the *Politics* "the most worth reading" (Pears, 28). He cultivates his Latin prose, grows acquainted with the Protestant princes of Europe, and generally accepts the role which his family and friends had determined for him. That role was only too carefully defined. Languet's very first letter to Sidney warns him to be careful in his Continental travels:

> You remember how often and how solemnly you have promised me to be cautious. . . . To offend *me* is of little consequence, but reflect how grievously you would be sinning against your excellent Father, who has placed all his hopes in you, and who . . . expects to see the full harvest of all those virtues, which your character promises so largely to produce.   (Pears, 2)

Again and again, throughout the letters, Sidney is called upon to remember his destiny:

> you will always find good men who will receive you with hearty kindness, if only you are true to yourself, and do not permit yourself to be transformed into another person.   (Pears, 6)

> My very dear Sidney, I am anxious for your safety, because I consider your birth, your disposition, your thirst for goodness, the progress you have already made—and I know what your country has a right to hope of you, . . .   (Pears, 42)

> I had no doubt, if God granted you long life, your country would find no small assistance in dangers from your virtue; especially since I observed, in addition to those mental endowments, splendour of birth, majesty of person, the expectation of great wealth, the authority and influence of your relations in your country, and all those other things which are commonly called gifts of fortune.
>   (Pears, 183–84)

Languet's tone modulates between eulogy and admonishment. He acts, not only as friend and counselor, but also as conscience. There are, as he warns Sidney, evils upon every side, threatening "the full harvest of all those virtues, which your character promises so largely to produce." When Sidney writes excitedly, for example, about Frobisher's expedition to the New World, Languet answers with a surprisingly fierce sermon: "Beware I entreat you, and do not let the cursed hunger after gold which the Poet speaks of, creep over that spirit of yours, into which nothing has hitherto been admitted but the love of goodness" (Pears, 126). Later, after Languet's visit to England in the winter of 1578–79, he finds renewed cause for concern:

> to speak plainly, the habits of your court seemed to me somewhat less manly than I could have wished, and most of your noblemen appeared to me to seek for a reputation more by a kind of affected courtesy than by those virtues which are wholesome to the state, and which are most becoming to generous spirits and men of high birth. I was sorry therefore, and so were other friends of yours, to see you wasting the flower of your life on such things, and I feared lest that noble nature of yours should be dulled, and lest from habit you should be brought to take pleasure in pursuits which only enervate the mind. (Pears, 167)

The court, with all of its "temptations to vice" (Pears, 155), fosters affectation and dulls the mind, although Sidney himself obviously enjoyed the practice of that "courtesy" which so predictably distressed his older friend. Sidney was able to reconcile Castiglione and Calvin in a way that Languet would not have understood, while the social ritual of Elizabeth's court must often have seemed frivolous to the pupil of Melanchthon. Moreover, if young noblemen were not idle and affected, they were apt to be proud and foolishly adventurous. When Languet was not worried about Sidney's tendency to withdraw from public affairs altogether, or to be corrupted by the court, he was afraid of his possible involvement in some rash scheme calculated to win honor and glory. When Sidney thought of rushing off to the Belgian wars, Languet dealt severely with him:

> But you, out of mere love of fame and honour, and to have an opportunity of displaying your courage, determined to regard as your enemies those who appeared to be doing the wrong in this war. It is not your business, nor any private person's, to pass a judgment on a question of this kind; . . . You and your fellows, I mean men of noble birth, consider that nothing brings you more honour than wholesale slaughter; . . . (Pears, 154)

Against Sidney's chivalric impulses, Languet set the ideal of elevated, responsible civil service: "if your desire of fame and glory
makes your present inactivity irksome to you, place before you the
example of the old Chandoses and Talbots" (Pears, 127).[8] To put
one's personal will at the disposal of the state and to follow the letter
of the law sternly and selflessly were the prerequisites for Christian
service to a prince: "Cato the elder wrote to his son on his going to
Spain, and charged him not to use his sword until he had taken the
oath to the commander of the army, . . . But this age of ours has lost
all honourable discipline, and laughs at such things" (Pears, 154–
55). Indeed, Languet was not really at ease until the summer of
1578, when Sidney was given more specific duties at court:

> now that you are no longer your own master, and that your new
> honours have so tied you to your country that you must henceforth
> consult its advantage rather than your own inclination, I am to a
> certain extent relieved of the anxiety which troubled me.
>
> (Pears, 150)

Languet's relief did not, of course, last very long. The more
Sidney was denied employment at court, the more he was prone to
restlessness. He vacillated between the extremes of indulged idleness
and impetuous action, and Languet worked conscientiously at the
task of keeping his pupil and friend steadily on course. Under such
circumstances, it is not surprising that the two correspondents tended
occasionally to view each other in terms of the more generalized
roles which age and experience seemed to assign them. In one letter,
Sidney chides Languet (quite unjustifiably) for not writing and tells
him good-humoredly to

> observe what Aristotle says of old men in his Rhetoric; namely,
> that they are cold in love, and that we are deceiving our own
> spirits in cultivating [their] friendship, as if they were nothing else
> but the smoke of youthful ardour.   (Pears, 121)

Languet, conversely, attributed Sidney's fluctuations either to
"youthful ardour" or to youthful idleness. He valued high spirits
and courage, but was continually on his guard against their dangers.
When Sidney seemed ready to fight under Leicester's command in
Belgium, Languet wrote:

I would not even if I could, weaken or blunt the edge of your spirit, still I must advise you now and then to reflect that young men who rush into danger incautiously almost always meet an inglorious end, and deprive themselves of the power of serving their country; . . . Let not therefore an excessive desire of fame hurry you out of your course; and be sure you do not give the glorious name of courage to a fault which only seems to have something in common with it.

(Pears, 137)

"Young men" needed to be kept in hand. Languet confided in a later letter that "I was fearful before, that the ardour of youth might suggest to you some rash project, and your destiny snatch you from your country" (Pears, 150). And at the time of the Frobisher expedition, he had warned:

Whenever, therefore, any feeling new to yourself shall agitate your mind, do not hastily indulge it, . . . reflect carefully what it is that tempts you, for if you set out on any course hastily, you will be compelled to wheel about, when you find you are going wrong, or, . . . will refuse through false shame to confess you have gone wrong, and therefore go on with your purpose.   (Pears, 126–27)

The predicament which Languet frames in the final clauses of this passage is particularly interesting, and ought to recall similar ones in Sidney's verse and prose—a verse and prose concerned very much with the youthful ardors of impetuous young men. Indeed, as will be seen, the entire substance of the Languet correspondence is pertinent to Sidney's writing as a whole. For the moment, however, it seems worth while stressing once again the fact that the friendship between Sidney and Languet was perhaps both richer and more complex than biographers and critics have generally allowed. Especially, it was a friendship of sympathetic and concordant personalities whose significant differences were less personal than generic. A distinct variety of Reformation humanism brought the two men together and provided them with a durable bond of common concerns and interests. But Languet, by temperament and training, represented a serious, even severe, tradition of Continental Protestantism: a pupil of Melanchthon, a doctor of the University of Padua, and an able and experienced diplomat, he was a man whom the bitter history of his time had brought to near despair. He saw in Sidney, not only a friend, but a hope for the age, and he concentrated his efforts on making the nephew of Leicester into a manly, learned, dutiful Christian courtier. The sober blend of gnosis and praxis which he himself epitomized was the heritage determined upon for the young Englishman, and his letters return again and again to speak of "that toilsome path which leads to virtue." In his creed, there is no time for retirement and idleness that sap the energies of mind and spirit, and little patience with young noblemen who neglect all discipline or flaunt the commands of princes. There is mainly worried concern for the ardor of youth, with its willfulness and rashness.

Sidney, on his side, was generally a willing disciple, but he was sometimes an erratic one. The letters of 1578, in particular, show how suddenly his inclinations could change, propelling him in quite contrary directions in the shortest space of time. In January and February, he is prepared and eager for the Belgian wars, but when the Leicester project collapses, he begins to show signs of frustration. By March, he writes his witty but serious defense of withdrawal and reflection, and by midsummer, he seems to have left the court altogether. The situation was such that Languet, in the single long letter of October 22, 1578, could reproach Sidney both for rushing into battle against the will of his sovereign and also for trying to "escape the tempest of affairs" by haunting "the privacy of secluded places." If Languet had had Sidney's temperament, he might have found ample material for comedy in such swift reversals and might have chided the younger man for his delightful inconsistencies. The plot of Sidney's life throughout 1578–1580 bristles with potential ironies, but they remain absolutely beyond the reach of the grave Burgundian. Languet's tone is consistently pedagogical, and he rarely indulges in that "seemly play of humour" which Sidney praised so much in More and Socrates, and loved so much himself.

The inconsistent may be comic, but it may also be the sign of an interesting and appealingly complex personality. This was certainly the case with Sidney. He was attracted to and was obviously full of respect for Languet's ideal of dutiful public service, and when he wrote to his brother Robert, he often slipped naturally into the role of sage counselor and monitor.[9] But he was also drawn variously by the high drama of chivalric exploits, by the graces of Italianate courtesy,

and by the pleasures of a life of "dignified ease"—and these were all
out of Languet's range. Together, they suggest the great degree to
which Sidney's response to life was romantic, aesthetic, poetic. The
frustrations of unemployment at court might help to drive him to the
country, but he clearly found the country more delightful in and for
itself than suited Languet's taste. He "used sometimes to say" that
he was "by nature entirely averse to the excitement and the fascinations of a court." "Entirely averse" is not by any means an
equivocal way of putting the matter, and it suggests at the very least
how strongly Sidney valued that kind of leisurely existence in which
the pleasures of living are their own reward.[10]

Whatever his inclinations may have been, however, it is also true
that Sidney's letters never carry the argument for leisure or retirement very far. When he broaches such matters, he is inevitably on
the defensive, and he finds it necessary either to invoke More and
Socrates (as precedents for jesting in grave times) or to play self-
consciously the roles of Stoic and Cynic, ending with a witty plea to
be reclaimed. Roleplaying and wit become in fact convenient ways
of side-stepping important issues—or, perhaps one should say, of
momentarily reconciling conflicting feelings without really solving
the conflict. It is difficult to do anything but pardon a charming and
self-confessed truant, and Sidney's way of presenting his dilemmas
tends to compel such pardon. He was a rather more indulgent judge
of himself than was Languet, largely because his vision of the good
life was in some ways fuller and more inclusive. When Sidney finally
returned to Leicester House in October 1580, Languet's cheer was
unqualified, but Sidney himself recorded with some regret that he
had given over the delights of the world. Languet always stressed
"that toilsome path which leads to virtue," but Sidney preferred to
suggest in the *Apologie for Poetrie* that there was "so sweet a prospect
into the way, as will entice any man to enter it." Sidney's heroes,
similarly, prefer sweet prospects, and Arcadia provides the first of
them.

CHAPTER II

The Letters and the Old Arcadia

❧❧❧

I F LANGUET SAW Sidney's vacillations between court and country as cause for considerable anxiety and serious moral commentary, there is good evidence to suggest that Sidney was capable of viewing them with detachment and good humor. The debate with Languet on the question of pastoral retirement occupied mainly those letters between March 1578 and October 1580, and this—so far as can be determined—was precisely the time when Sidney was composing the original *Arcadia* at Wilton. A great many of the problems discussed in the letters recur in the *Old Arcadia*, and the parallels are close enough to define much more than an accidental or vaguely peripheral relationship between the two. Languet, for example, often mentioned Sidney's tendency to melancholy and complained (in a passage already quoted):

> I am especially sorry to hear you say that you are weary of the life to which I have no doubt God has called you, and desire to fly from the light of your court and betake yourself to the privacy of secluded places to escape the tempest of affairs by which statesmen are generally harrassed; . . . (Pears, 155)

Sidney, meanwhile, was praising in fiction the life of leisure and poetry enjoyed by his Arcadians:

> the peace wherein they did so notably florish (and specially the sweete enjoyng of theyre peace to so pleasant uses) drew dyvers straungers aswell of greate, as meane howses; Especially suche, whome inwarde Melancholyes, made weary of the Worldes eyes, to come and live amonge them, . . . (F, IV. 52)

The opening pages of the *Old Arcadia* center, of course, on a series of sudden withdrawals from the public world of affairs: Basilius retires in an effort to avoid the doom predicted by the oracle, and he is soon followed by Pyrocles and Musidorus, who are drawn by love to leave off their active pursuit of fame and honor. Pyrocles is the first of the princes to defect, and in his long debate with Musidorus (F, IV. 10–23), one hears continual echoes of the Sidney-Languet letters. Musidorus takes up a narrowly orthodox point of view. He has noticed

> a Relenting truely and slaking of ye mayne Carryer yow had so notably begun and allmoste performed. And yt in suche sorte as I can not fynde sufficyent reasons in my greate love towardes yow howe to allowe yt: For, . . . whereas yow are wonte in all the places yow came, to give youre self vehemently to knowledg of those thinges wch mighte better youre mynde, to seeke the familiarity of excellent men in Learning and Souldyery, and lastly to putt all these thinges in practize, bothe by continuall wyse proceedinges and worthy enterpryses as occasions fell for them. Yow, now, leave all these thinges undone, yow let youre mynde falle a sleepe, . . . and lastly . . . yow subject youre self to solitarynes, the slye Enimy yt moste dothe seperate a man from well doyng. (F, IV. 10–11)

This is a version of Languet's general point of view: the stress is on training the mind and guarding it from sleep, on useful knowledge, on "Learning," "Souldyery," and "well doyng." The passage, with its tone of reproof and its staunch allegiance to a simple creed of duty from which there must be no slacking, is essentially a translation into fictional terms of Languet's various (if sometimes oblique) reproaches:

> [Your friends] fear that those who do not so well know your constancy may suspect that you are tired of that toilsome path which leads to virtue, which you formerly pursued with so much earnestness. They are fearful too, that the sweetness of your lengthened retirements may somewhat relax the vigorous energy with which you used to rise to noble undertakings, . . .   (Pears, 183)

If Musidorus is well armed with the standard proofs for a life of heroic action, Pyrocles conceals the fact that he is in love with

Philoclea and offers a series of arguments to justify his recent conduct. He is largely on the defensive, and "his blusshing Cheekes did
witnesse with him, hee rather coulde not help, then did not knowe
his faulte" (F, IV. 11). Nonetheless, despite his feeling of guilt, he
rises to a strong rebuttal:

> I fynde not my self wholly to bee Condempned, bycause I doo not
> with a Continuall vehemency followe those knowlledges wch yow
> calle ye betteringes of my mynde. For, bothe the mynde yt self
> must, (like other thinges) some tymes bee unbent, or else yt will bee
> eyther weykened or broken, and these knowlledges, as they are of
> good use, so are they not all the mynde may stretche yt self unto:
> who knowes whether I feede my myndes with higher thoughtes?,
> truely, as I knowe not all the particularityes, so yet, see I the boundes
> of all these knoulledges, but the workinges of the mynde I fynde
> muche more infinite then can bee ledd unto by ye eye, or imagined
> by any that distract theyre thoughtes wthowte them selves, and in
> such Contemplacyons, or as I thincke more excellent I enjoye my
> solitarynes, and my solitarynes perchaunce ys the Nurse of these
> Contemplacyons. . . . Condempne not therefore my mynde some
> tyme, to enjoy yt self, nor blame not, the taking of suche tymes as
> serve moste fitt for yt.   (F, IV. 11–12)

Pyrocles here expands on the abortive defense of relaxation and reflection Sidney makes in the letters. He borrows (and alters slightly)
the image of the bow (Pears, 36: "it must be unstrung or it will
break").[1] He questions the value of useful knowledge and points out
the limitations of those who "distract theyre thoughtes wthowte
them selves" (Pears, 143: "For to what purpose should our thoughts
be directed to various kinds of knowledge, . . . For while the mind is
thus, as it were, drawn out of itself, it cannot turn its powers inward
for thorough self-examination"). Like Sidney's in the letters, Pyrocles' arguments savor of rationalization. His use of the conditional
("who knowes whether") and his pervasive tentativeness ("per-
chaunce") tend to undermine the boldness of his defense, and the
reader of course knows that love, rather than mere contemplation,
is the main cause of the prince's waywardness. When he embarks a
moment later on an extended and hyperbolic praise of Arcadia's
landscape, he seems to be mainly the victim of delightful, comic

infatuation. Musidorus notes his friend's "affected praysing of the place," and is certain that "Contemplacyon ys but a gloryous tytle to Idlenes" (F, IV. 13). He wonders how "so excellent a mynde coulde have beene thus blemisshed" and calls Pyrocles to think

> how fitt yt will bee for yow in this youre tender youthe, (borne so greate a Prince, and of so rare not onely expectation, but proof) desyered of youre oulde Father & wanted of youre native Contry, . . . to direct youre thoughtes from the way of goodnes, to loose, nay, to abuse youre tyme? (F, IV. 16)

Musidorus has all the heavy artillery on his side. He can invoke Pyrocles' father, his native country, and the great "expectation" which his character and training seemed to assure. Again, Languet stands behind Musidorus: "To offend *me* is of little consequence, but reflect how grievously you would be sinning against your excellent Father, who . . . expects to see the full harvest of all those virtues" (Pears, 2); "Consider well, I entreat you, how far it is honourable to you to lurk where you are, whilst your country is imploring the aid and support of her sons" (Pears, 185). Pyrocles, like Sidney in 1578–1580, is a truant from the noble school of heroic virtues in which he had been bred, and both youths find it extraordinarily difficult to deal with adversaries who are well fortified with so great a supply of certified good doctrine. Each feels his own delinquency, and the tactics of each suggest that "hee rather coulde not help, then did not knowe his faulte."

Yet, as I suggested earlier, the rationalizations of Sidney have a considerable substance of felt experience behind them, and those of Pyrocles are hardly less well grounded. If love of Philoclea is Pyrocles' main motive for lingering in Arcadia, that same love has opened his spirit to a realm of feelings altogether inaccessible to Musidorus. After Musidorus has "informed him self fully of the strengthe and Riches of ye Contry, of the nature of the people, and of the manner of theyre Lawes," he is ready to leave Arcadia (F, IV. 10). But Pyrocles has discovered quite different objects to intrigue him:

> And Lorde, deare Cossyn (sayde hee) dothe not the pleasantnes of this place, carry in yt self sufficyent Rewarde, for any tyme lost in yt or for any suche daunger that mighte ensewe? . . . And see yow not

> the rest of all these beutyfull flowers, eche of whiche woulde requyer
> a mans witt to knowe, and his lyfe to express? . . . Dothe not the
> Ayer breath health whiche the Byrdes, (bothe delightfull bothe to
> the eare and eye) do dayly solempnize with the sweete consent of
> theyre voyces?   (F, IV. 12)

Pyrocles has suddenly discovered the beauties and delights of an
ideal pastoral world, where there are no deeds to be done because
there is no strife. He now finds even the commonest objects to be
inexhaustibly rich, and is sure that each of the flowers "woulde re-
quyer a mans witt to knowe, and his lyfe to express." The landscape
is simply its own reward, and Pyrocles is content to be moved to
contemplation and wonder by it. He no longer responds to life
purely in terms of Musidorus' heroic code but now reacts in a way
that can only be called poetic, as Sidney would have understood and
used the word. Moved by the beauty of the world about him, he is
carried away by the most fundamental of all poetic impulses—those
of praise and celebration, the lyric counterparts of wonder and contemplation. His style quickens under the impetus of newly aroused
feeling:

> Ys not every Eccho here a perfect Musick? and these fressh and
> delightfull brookes, how slowly they slyde away, as, lothe to leave
> the Company of so many thinges united in perfection, and with how
> sweete a Murmer they lament theyre fore[ced] departure: Cer-
> teynly, certeynly Cossyn yt must needes bee, that some Goddess this
> Dezert belonges unto, who ys the sowle of this soile, for, neyther ys
> any lesse then a Goddess worthy to bee shryned in suche a heape of
> pleasures, nor any less then a Goddess coulde have made yt so per-
> fect a Moddell of the heavenly dwellinges: . . .   (F, IV. 12–13)

The particular kinds of rhetorical heightening which this passage
reveals are precisely those Sidney associated most intimately with
lyric poetry: the energetic apostrophes, the personifications, the
images of a harmonious and animated landscape, the creation of a
lively speaking voice, and an effective rendering of the speaker's im-
passioned response to a vision of beauty and perfection. In the
Apologie for Poetrie, for example, Sidney declared that David's Psalms
were "a divine Poem":[2]

For what els is the awaking his musicall instruments; the often and free changing of persons; his notable *Prosopopeias*, when he maketh you as it were, see God comming in his Maiestie;[3] his telling of the Beastes ioyfulnes, and hills leaping, but a heavenlie poesie, wherein almost hee sheweth himselfe a passionate lover of that unspeakable and everlasting beautie to be seene by the eyes of the minde, onely cleered by fayth?   (*Apologie*, 6–7)

Pyrocles has become just such a passionate poet-lover. The sight of Philoclea has opened his eyes to the world's delights in all their apparent freshness and purity and allowed him to recognize them as images of a spiritual perfection "to be seene by the eyes of the minde." It is worth noting that the old shepherd Dorcas, in *The Lady of May*, describes a similar vision in similar terms:

> O sweete hony milken Lommes, and is there any so flintie a hart, that can find about him to speake against them, that have the charge of such good soules as you be, among whom there is no envy, and all obedience, where it is lawfull for a man to be good if he list, and hath no outward cause to withdraw him from it, where the eye may be busied in considering the works of nature, and the hart quietly rejoyced in the honest using them.[4]   (F, II. 335)

To discover the beauties of the Arcadian or any other pastoral land-scape is to glimpse the possibility of an ideal life, free from envy, "where it is lawfull for a man to be good if he list." Contemplation of nature rejoices the heart, and that joy rises naturally into a poetry of praise whose external signs are the apostrophes and personifica-tions noted in Pyrocles' speech and in Sidney's description of the Psalms. Meanwhile, Rombus, the pedantic schoolmaster in *The Lady of May*, can only notice that Dorcas has used a "certaine rhe-toricall invasion into the point, as if in deed he had conference with his Lams," and he goes on to criticize the shepherd for his faulty use of the syllogism and the enthymeme (F, II. 336). But Rombus is quickly brushed aside, and even the testy Rixus admits to Dorcas that "Your life indeede hath some goodnesse."

It would be a mistake to place Pyrocles in too solemn a context. As suggested, he is on the defensive, and we are asked to see him with considerable irony throughout his opening scene with

2+

Musidorus. But it is equally important to notice the way in which he has discovered a world of feeling and a style of poetry (in Sidney's terms) that set him off from Musidorus. Sidney had set himself off from Languet in similar ways, although not quite so boldly; and if he failed to expand on the beauties of landscape or the infinite joys of contemplation when speaking to Languet, he was clearly less shy about them in the *Arcadia* and the *Apologie*. Many of Sidney's letters are lost, of course, but we can judge from Languet's replies that they too must have been concerned, at least partly, with the pleasures (and problems) of retirement. They may well have contained passages more in the spirit of Pyrocles or Dorcas; or perhaps, since Sidney must have known his audience would be nearly as unsympathetic as Musidorus, he restrained his strongest impulses in that direction. Languet's tone did not necessarily encourage confidences of such a kind. It was he, after all, who had written that Sidney's Continental friends were

> astonished that you find pleasure in your long retirement; and though they readily believe that it is made most delightful to you by the society of your dearest friends, still they think you ought very carefully to reflect whether it is consistent with your character to remain so long concealed.   (Pears, 182–83)

CHAPTER III

Love in Arcadia

᭥᭜᭥

I

Viewing the *Old Arcadia* in the light of Sidney's letters suggests—as has been seen—important ways in which Pyrocles acts as an unofficial apologist for Sidney himself, not only by virtue of his explicit praise of contemplation and retirement, but more generally because he is the spokesman for a poetic view of experience. He sees in the golden world of Arcadia a vision of perfect harmony and beauty; and it is just such visions, with their "hart-ravishing knowledge" (*Apologie*, 5), that Sidney's ideal poets are capable of responding to and creating. Pyrocles' style, moreover, is infused with the kinds of energy which Sidney praised in his discussion of the Psalms. The young prince becomes, in other words, an unwitting apologist for poetry, and the fact suggests how closely the defense of pastoral retirement and ease, the defense of contemplation or reflection, and the defense of poetry were linked in Sidney's mind. This is a subject which will demand more careful discussion in a later chapter. For the moment, it is more pertinent to notice the way in which Pyrocles and Sidney take up the defense of love.

Love is of course never mentioned in the Languet correspondence. Apart from one or two good-natured exchanges concerning marriage (Pears, 133, 144, and 148), the letters never allude to the subject of romance. Yet several of the more general ideas and attitudes they reveal are extremely relevant to the *Old Arcadia*'s treatment of love themes. The latent conflict between impetuous youth and restraining age, between indulged pleasure and the rigorous demands of duty, between a sophisticated, complex view of experience and a more astringent, moral one—each of these bears directly upon the *Old Arcadia* and helps to illuminate its pastoral, heroic, and romantic materials.

One should first notice that, although love lies at the heart of the original *Arcadia*, there is surprisingly little theoretical or philosophical discussion of it. Moreover, those who attack love are frequently more vigorous and discursive than those who rise in its defense—a fact which marks one of the greatest differences of emphasis between the early and late versions of Sidney's romance. There are, of course, some important passages suggesting the ennobling or elevating nature of desire,[1] but these are significantly qualified by the action of the book as a whole. For example, Sidney's heroes undoubtedly aspire to a chaste, virtuous love capable of purifying them and of drawing them to the performance of admirable deeds. Yet they fall prey to sudden, wholly sensual desire, and (except in one or two minor episodes) they are never offered an opportunity to display their courage and resolution in love's behalf—nearly all the chivalric material is a later addition. The main emphasis of the book falls, rather, on the delighted, but also puzzled, initial response to love on the part of characters who have never before felt its power, and who are prevented—partly by temperament, and partly by circumstance —from giving ideal, entirely noble expression to their feelings. Although the princes learn the arts of amorous persuasion very quickly, they are seen generally as *ingénus*. They are embarrassed by love's onset, tentative in their arguments for its defense, and yet instinctively sure of its goodness. They suggest hesitantly that it may well be possible to reconcile the claims of love and those of duty, even as Sidney had once suggested to Languet that certain relaxations of the mind might be a positive help to men engaged in "most grave affairs" (Pears, 65). The plot of the *Old Arcadia*, however, tends to stress the difficulty of such reconciliations, and the spirit of the book is in this sense very closely related to that of Sidney's letters: both were the product of a period when the young nephew of Leicester felt particularly keenly the conflict between the delights of the world and the rigors of "that toilsome path which leads to virtue." At times, Sidney sensed and affirmed the full richness and potential goodness of the world's delights; at times, he seemed to relish them purely for their own sake; and at times, he entertained the hope that they might indeed be beautifully harmonized with the life of virtue. The literary result was a series of letters and a pastoral romance characterized by the self-conscious, critical, defensive, ironic, and witty tones I have been noticing. If Sidney looked on approvingly while Pyrocles and Musidorus lingered in Arcadia in order to court Philoclea and Pamela, he also proceeded—with typical wit and awareness—to tell a tale which cast them in the role of truants and thus pointed up the possible dangers of their chosen course. In effect, he allowed them to play the parts of Stoic, Cynic, and even Epicure, while at the same time suggesting that perhaps they ought really to be reclaimed. Thus, although the *Old Arcadia* is in many senses an important apology for "delight" as opposed to duty, it also shares with Sidney's letters a quality of irresolution which sets both off from the later, more assertive revised *Arcadia*, with its rationalized defenses of love, and its images of a world in which love and heroic virtue might truly be united.

A few examples may help to pinpoint some of the differences between the two versions of Sidney's romance. The revised *Arcadia* (unlike the original) opens with the sustained, eloquent praise of Urania offered by Strephon and Klaius (F, I. 7–8): "hath not the onely love of her made us . . . raise up our thoughts above the ordinary levell of the worlde, . . . hath not the desire to seeme worthie in her eyes made us when others were sleeping, to sit vewing the course of heavens?" Urania has ennobled the shepherds, raising up their thoughts, throwing "reason upon [their] desires." The entire passage was interpolated into the revision, and there is nothing resembling it in the original. It is true that Pyrocles, in the *Old Arcadia*, also connected love with contemplation, but the whole texture of his speech in the debate with Musidorus forced the reader to view him with considerable irony. Although Sidney left that debate scene essentially unaltered in the revision, he qualified it by adding the Strephon-Klaius passage, and he went on to enter several additional eloquent pleas in love's behalf. He interpolated the entire Argalus-Parthenia episode (F, I. 31–36, *et passim*), as well as Amphialus' explicit challenge to all those who have characterized love as a despoiler of heroic resolution. As Amphialus prepares to fight in order to keep possession of Philoclea, he would

> accuse, and in himselfe condemne all those wits, that durst affirme
> Idlenesse to be the well-spring of Love. O, would he say, al you that
> affect the title of wisdome, by ungratefull scorning the ornaments of
> Nature, am I now piping in a shaddow? or doo slouthfull feathers
> now enwrap me? Is not hate before me, and doubte behinde me?
> . . . The more I stirre about urgent affaires, the more me thinks the
> very stirring breeds a breath to blow the coales of my love: the more
> I exercise my thoughts, the more they encrease the appetite of my
> desires.   (F, I. 375)

For Amphialus, the energies of love give noble purpose to the will,
strengthening it for "urgent affaires." If the imperiousness of his
desire is ominous and even destructive, it nonetheless generates the
chivalric heroism and honor which distinguish him. As in the case of
Strephon and Klaius, a vision of love gives rise to and includes a
vision of life "above the ordinary levell of the worlde." Love and
valor, love and contemplation, love and the life of reason are either
actually or potentially harmonized, and Sidney expanded upon this
glimpsed vision of harmony in a final, important passage which he
also added to the *New Arcadia*. Helen of Corinth, one of his heroines,
is said to have

> made her people by peace, warlike; her courtiers by sports, learned;
> her Ladies by Love, chast. For by continuall martiall exercises with-
> out bloud, she made them perfect in that bloudy art. Her sportes
> were such as caried riches of Knowledge upon the streame of
> Delight: . . . so as it seemed, that court to have bene the mariage
> place of Love and Vertue, & that her selfe was a *Diana* apparelled
> in the garments of *Venus*.   (F, I. 283)

Castiglione, Urbino, and the entire *Book of the Courtier* are in the background here, and the *New Arcadia* altogether is rich in such images
suggesting the possibility of a perfect courtly society which might be
the marriage place of knowledge and delight, virtue and love.

The original *Arcadia*, by contrast, offers very little in this vein. Its
particular spirit is captured more nearly by Pyrocles' tentative,
charming, comic reply to Musidorus' attack on love as "ingendred
betuixt lust and Idlenes":

> this I willingly confess, that yt likes mee muche better, when I fynde
> vertue in a fayre Lodging, then when I am bounde to seeke yt in an

yll favored Creature, . . . Those trublesome effectes yow say [Love]
breedes bee not the faultes of Love, but of him, that loves, as an
unable vessell to beare suche a power, . . . Eeven that heavenly love
yow speake of ys accompanyed in some hartes with hopes, greeffes,
Longinges and Dispayres, and in yt heavenly love synce there are
twoo partes, the one the Love of yt self, the other, the excellency of
the thing loved, I (not able at the first leape, to frame bothe in my
self) doo now like a diligent worckman, make redy the cheef Instrument, and first parte of that great worcke wch ys love yt self: whiche,
when I have a while practized in this sorte, then, yow shall see mee
turne yt to greater matters.   (F, IV. 18–19)

Like Amphialus, Pyrocles suggests that love can ultimately inspire
one to "greater matters," but he lacks the confidence to expand on
the point in debate, and the plot of the *Old Arcadia* offers him no real
opportunity to prove it in action. Rather, he admits that the first
effects of love have been "trublesome," and he acknowledges that he
is not quite "able at the first leape" to subordinate the simple
demands of desire to a concentration on "the excellency of the thing
loved." Love is initially a straightforward matter of feeling and
passion, and he yields to its authority without being at all certain
where it will lead him. Philoclea is indeed virtuous—and therefore
capable of inspiring virtuous conduct—but the young prince is
strongly drawn by that "fayre Lodging" in which her virtue resides.
Unlike Amphialus, he talks much less about the uses of love—the
noble deeds which it might inspire—than about the clear, inescapable fact of it; he has seen Philoclea's picture, and "that beauty
did pearse so through my eyes to my harte, that the Impression
dothe not lye but live there in suche sorte, as the questyon ys not
nowe, whether I shall love or not, but whether Loving I shall live
or dye" (F, IV. 14–15).
    Thus Pyrocles and (shortly afterward) Musidorus commit them-
selves to love, saying a minimum about its high ennobling power
(although praising their ladies in a proper Petrarchan way), impro-
vising upon events as they develop, and hoping for the best. If they
sometimes speak in more lofty tones about turning love to greater
matters, they frequently discover themselves to be more "unable
vessels" than they had suspected. For the most part, they respond to

Philoclea and Pamela very much as Pyrocles had responded to Arcadia's beautiful landscape: they emphasize the potential joy and delight of their new estate and find the pleasures of love to be their own reward. At one point in the second set of eclogues, a group of shepherds declares that "Who *Passion* doth forsake, lives void of joy."[2] Pyrocles echoes the sentiment in his debate with Musidorus:

> the head gives yow direction and the harte gives mee lyfe . . .
>
> (F, IV. 20)

> that beauty did pearse so through my eyes to my harte, that the Impression dothe not lye but live there . . .   (F, IV. 14–15)

And at the end of the book, when the heroes are awaiting trial, Pyrocles says nothing about the noble deeds love might have inspired but declares only that

> no torment nor deathe coulde make mee forgoo the least parte of the inwarde honor, essentiall pleasure and living lyfe I have enjoyed in ye presence of the faultless *Philoclea*.   (F, IV. 345)

Philoclea and Pamela do indeed promote "honor," but it is all "inwarde," and it is linked indissolubly to the essential pleasure and the irradiated sense of living life which Pyrocles and Musidorus feel in the presence of their ladies. Life for the princes has ceased to be primarily a matter of deeds and duties—the strict, rather mechanical regimen that they had known before entering Arcadia. They have tasted delight and experienced the kind of deeply fulfilling joy which is its own reward. One possibility which Sidney's romance holds out, of course, is that such delight and joy will ultimately induce the heroes to live virtuous and noble lives worthy of their loves. But the original *Arcadia* is much less concerned than the revised version to trace or insist upon such a development. Rather, Sidney places a great many obstacles in the path of his characters and does what he can to suggest how difficult it may be to manage the "trublesome effectes" of love or to "turne yt to greater matters."

2

The precise nature of those obstacles, and Sidney's particular way of handling them, are well worth attention. In general, the narrative voice of the *Old Arcadia* is very closely related to that of Sidney's

letters: it is sometimes serious, but very often witty, pliant, playful.
It is essentially the voice of the young man who told Languet how
much he enjoyed that "seemly play of humour" in Socrates and
More, neither of whom could bear to "lose [his] jest even in the
hour of death" (Pears, 65). Such an attitude suggests, at the very
least, an ability to look upon even the most critical and threatening
situations with an eye for their latent or actual ironies, incongruities,
absurdities. It also suggests—in conjunction with passages from other
letters—that Sidney would be apt to regard the lapses and minor
misdemeanors of his heroes with something less than solemnity. On
the whole, such intimations are amply confirmed by the text of the
original *Arcadia*. When Pyrocles disguises himself as an Amazon,
for example, and changes his name to Cleophila, the narrator views
him with affectionate indulgence:

> For, I my self feele suche Compassion of his passyon, that, I fynde
> even parte of his feare, leste his name shoulde bee uttered before
> fitt tyme were for yt: whiche yow faire Ladyes, that vouchesave to
> reade this (I doubte not) will accoumpte excusable. (F, IV. 24)

Sidney here imitates the tender manner of romances, alters it with
his characteristically muted ironies, and appeals to an audience of
sophisticated courtly ladies who can be counted on to share his
"Compassion" for Pyrocles and all other servants of love. His sympathy for the young prince's need to disguise himself is readily
"excusable." Love, moreover, is seen very much as a world unto
itself, and those who have never known its delights and despairs are
delicately excluded from the intimate conversation which the narrator
carries on with his readers:

> But so wonderfull and in effect incredible, was the passion wch
> rayned aswell in *Ginecia*, as *Basilius* and all for the pore *Cleophila*
> dedicated, an other way: That yt seemes to my self I use not wordes
> enowe to make yow see, how they coulde in one moment bee so over-
> taken. But, yow worthy Ladyes, that have at any tyme feelingly
> knowne what yt meanes, will easily beleeve the possibility of yt, let
> the ignorant sorte of people give credit unto them that have passed
> the Dolefull passage, and duely fynde, that quickly ys the infection
> gotten, whiche in longe tyme ys hardly cured: ... (F, IV. 45)

2*

The ignorant people—like Musidorus in his opening debate with Pyrocles—are outside the garden and have no way of knowing the "inwarde honor, essentiall pleasure and living lyfe" which love inspires. Although Sidney's language in the passage quoted above also suggests the painful and disruptive aspects of love ("Dolefull . . . infection"), his tone assures us that everything in the *Old Arcadia* will be kept well within the bounds of comedy. Indeed, the perspective maintained upon the characters and events of his tale seems framed as a sympathetic but sophisticated response to the request which Pyrocles makes of Musidorus at the end of their first debate: "continew to loove mee, and looke upon my Imperfections, with more affection then Judgmt" (F, IV. 22–23).

If Sidney views his characters indulgently, however, one ought also to remember the modicum of irony he directs at them, particularly at their postures and attitudes as lovers. Pyrocles and Musidorus become proper servants to their ladies, reverencing them, praising their virtue and beauty, and pleading for some sign of mercy in return. This conduct is all perfectly decorous, perfectly à la mode. The narrator, meanwhile, looks on approvingly, but also critically. He applauds their idealism and devotion, but his admiration is mixed with a kind of witty realism which Sidney may well have learned from Castiglione. As David Kalstone has suggested,[3] much in the *Old Arcadia* reminds us particularly of the Lady Emilia's shrewd, playful response to the Neoplatonic flights of Pietro Bembo:

> When Bembo had hetherto spoken with such vehemencie, . . . hee stood still without once moving, holding his eyes towarde heaven as astonied: when the Ladie Emilia, which together with the rest gave most diligent eare to this talke, tooke him by the plaite of his garment, and plucking him a little said.
>
> Take heede (Maister Peter) that these thoughts make not your soule also to forsake the bodie.[4]

Sidney's heroes, like Bembo, are continually plucked by the garment and brought back to earth, either by the narrator, by events, or by their own unmanageable desires. When Pyrocles praises the exquisite beauties of Arcadia's landscape, for instance, Musidorus mocks his friend's hyperboles: they are like those of poets,

whose liberall pennes can as easily traveyll over mounteynes as
Mole hilles, and so like well disposed men, sett upp every thinge to
the highest Noate, especially, when they putt suche wordes in the
mouthe of one of these Fantasticall mynde infected people, yt
Children and Musicians calle Lovers.   (F, IV. 14)

Musidorus' naiveté and his own fondness for hyperbole are exposed
here, but his criticism is nonetheless echoed by Sidney himself.
When Pyrocles falls in love, the narrator observes: "hee sawe no
grass upon wch hee thoughte *Philoclea* mighte happ to treade, but
that hee envyed ye happynes of yt: And yet, with a contrary folly
wolde sometymes recomend his whole estate unto yt" (F, IV. 9).
Love produces "contrary follies" in nearly all the inhabitants of
Arcadia, and the narrator records them with wry humor. When
Basilius makes love to Gynecia, believing her to be Cleophila, he
praises her charms over those of his wife. Gynecia, meanwhile,
"hearde with what parciality hee did preferr her self to her self";
she "sawe in hym how muche fancy dothe [not] onely darcken
reason, but beguyled sence"; she "founde opinyon Mistris of the
Lovers Judgmt" (F, IV. 257). Pyrocles and Musidorus, of course,
show better judgment in love than Basilius, but Sidney never hesi-
tates to treat them with mild irony, even at the most critical moments of
their tale. When Pyrocles is at last about to be reunited with Philoclea,
he hears her singing in an adjoining room, and is transported with
delight; the narrator interrupts his story at this crucial point and
turns aside to comment generally on the peculiarities of lovers:

> The force of Love to those pore folcke that feele yt ys many wayes
> very straunge, but no way straunger, then that yt dothe so encharme
> the Lovers Judgement, uppon her that holdes the Raynes of his
> mynde, that what soever shee dothe ys ever in his eyes best; And that
> best beeyng by the Continuall motyons of oure chaunging lyfe
> turned by her to any other no thing, that thing ageane becometh
> best. So that *Nature* in eche kynde suffering but one Superlatyve, the
> Lover onely admittes no positive yf shee sitt still, that ys best, . . . yf
> shee walke, no doubt that ys best, . . .   (F, IV. 217)

A literature that is so accomplished in puncturing the amorous
extravagances of its heroes, and so quick to deflate their "Superla-
tyves," is obviously very far removed from the more serious world of

a Bembo or a Petrarch, where praise is never excessive, and inspired celebration is the only possible response to the lady's supreme virtue and beauty. Sidney's ladies are also virtuous and beautiful, but they and their suitors live in a complex realm utterly different from the insulated, private sphere of meditation and spiritual devotion that we find, for example, in the sonnets to Laura. Petrarchan praise and celebration undoubtedly have their serious uses in the *Arcadia*, but Sidney often suggests that they are the product of charming, youthful infatuation. His Petrarch has been modified by his Castiglione, and informed also by Ovid's brand of psychological realism and Terence's urbane comedy:

> Good Gods! What a malady is this! That a man should become so changed through love, that you wouldn't know him to be the same person! Not anyone was there less inclined to folly than he, and no one more discreet or more temperate . . .[5]

I should remark, by way of concluding this section, that the narrator's tendency to undercut Petrarchan gestures of praise is reinforced in the *Old Arcadia* by Sidney's general management of the plot, especially by his willingness to point up the ironies of the love intrigue in which all the main characters are involved. The expectations of his lovers are continually thwarted. Pyrocles' disguise makes it virtually impossible for Philoclea to recognize him as a suitor, but it immediately elicits the highly unwelcome overtures of Gynecia and Basilius. Basilius, expecting to find Cleophila in the cave, discovers only his wife. More important, the stoutest vows of the princes and princesses are consistently and wittily undermined. Musidorus, after the opening debate with Pyrocles,

> woulde often say to him self. O sweete *Pyrocles* how arte thow bewitched? where ys thy vertue? where ys the use of thy reason? Howe muche am I inferior unto thee in all the powers of thy mynde? And yet knowe I, that all the heavens, can not bring mee to suche a thraldome. Scarsely (thinck I) hee had spoken these wordes, but that the *Duchess* . . . came oute with her twoo Daughters: Where the beames of ye Princess *Pamelas* beauty, had no sooner stricken into his eyes, but, that hee was wounded with more sodeyn vyolence of Love then ever Pyrocles was.   (F, IV. 36–37)

Similarly, Philoclea had, "a fewe dayes before *Cleophilas* comyng" (F, IV. 104), vowed eternal chastity to the gods (OA 18). But no sooner has she engraved her vow in marble than she is forced to recant (OA 19). Finally, both Pyrocles and Musidorus break their promise of chastity, and Musidorus' fall comes directly after his most resounding declarations of good faith. Pamela has urged Musidorus to "govern youre Love towardes mee, as I may still remayne worthy to bee Loved" (F, IV. 185). Musidorus replies: "youre Contentment ys derer to mee then myne owne. And therefore Doubt not of his mynde, whose thoughtes are so thralled unto yow, as yow are to bende or slack them as yt shall seeme best unto yow" (F, IV. 186). Moments later, the lovers stop to refresh themselves, and Musidorus is prevented from ravishing the sleeping Pamela only by the sudden intrusion of a group of rebel Arcadians (F, IV. 190).

The plot of the *Arcadia* points up, then, a series of ironies—of swift reversals in which noble oaths are juxtaposed with rather less noble actions. Yet Sidney's attitude on such occasions remains generally sympathetic, indulgent, worldly-wise. Musidorus' original fall into love is treated as a piece of gentle comedy, and Philoclea's recantation is charming and delicate. Moreover, the two "seduction" scenes are narrated with obvious sophistication and delight. Pyrocles, like Chaucer's Troilus, faints at the crucial moment, and is revived only by Philoclea's embraces (F, IV. 222–23). Sidney, meanwhile, discourses on the psychology of lovers (F, IV. 217) and finally closes the scene just as the lovers reach Philoclea's bed. Pyrocles has been recalling a song of Philisides, and the narrator cautions:

> But doo not thincke (Fayre Ladyes) his thoughtes had suche Leysure as to ronne over so longe a Ditty: The onely generall fancy of yt came into his mynde fixed uppon the sence of the sweet Subject. Where using the benefitt of the Tyme, and fortifying hym self, with the Confessing her late faulte, . . . turning the passed greeffes and unkyndenes, to the excess of all kynde Joyes . . . beginning nowe to envy *Argus* thowsand eyes *Brierius* hundred handes, feighting ageanst a Weyke resistance whiche did stryve to bee overcome; Hee gives mee occasyon to leave hym in so happy a plighte, least my Penn mighte seeme to grudge, at the due Blisse of these pore Lovers, whose Loyalty had but smalle respite of theyre fyery Agonyes.
>
> (F, IV. 226–27)

There is perhaps the slightest touch of coarseness in the analogies here ("*Argus* thowsand eyes *Brierius* hundred handes") and in the description of unrestrained desire ("using . . . fortifying . . .feighting"), but all such dissonances are ultimately resolved by Sidney's defense of his "pore Lovers," whose loyalty and genuine love are more than enough to redeem their minor lapses. Musidorus' attempt on Pamela (F, IV. 189–90), though treated differently and more strictly, is also ultimately excused. The *Arcadia's* heroes fall, but only back to earth.

3

For all the sympathy he extends to the main characters of the *Old Arcadia*, Sidney complicates matters somewhat more than the preceding discussion is apt to suggest. Even as narrator, he occasionally takes the part of judge rather than advocate. The capture of Musidorus is said to be a "just punishment of his broken promyse" (F, IV. 190), and the Fourth Book opens on an apocalyptic note:

> The Everlasting Justice (using oure selves to bee the punisshers of oure faultes, and making oure owne actions the beginninge of oure Chastisement, that oure shame may bee the more manifest, and oure Repentance followe the sooner,) tooke *Dametas* at this present (by whose folly the others wysdome mighte receyve the greater overthrowe) to bee the instrument of reveyling the secrettst Connyng: So evill a grounde dothe evell stande uppon, and so manifest yt ys, that no thing Remaynes strongly, but that whiche hathe the good foundacyon of goodnes.   (F, IV. 247)

The precise tone here is difficult to determine. Using Dametas as the instrument of Everlasting Justice injects enough wit into the passage to make it read like a parody of high moral judgments and providential plots. But the very last clauses are too serious and insistent to bear out such a reading. Sidney altered the passage, of course, in his revision, omitting everything that might be construed as an indictment of his heroes.[6] His original impulse, however, is a revealing one, and it shows how easily he could adopt a tone and a view of experience much closer to Languet's. If he generally asks us to see Pyrocles and Musidorus as noble, idealistic, and pardonably human in their minor faults, he also frequently reminds us of the debilitating and destructive effects of unrestrained desire. The courtiers of the *Arcadia* are ultimately called upon to account for their deeds, and the narrator's tendency to pardon them is qualified and complicated by an inclination to judge them harshly. This conflict is dramatized in a series of dialogues which are never fully resolved. Different points of view meet in opposition, and the final effect is sometimes serious, sometimes comic. Within a context that generally vindicates his courtier-heroes, Sidney cultivates a conscious ambiguity, frequently shifting our perspective, and suggesting the limitations of both sides, in the *Arcadia*'s numerous debates.

The form of the pastoral eclogue lent itself particularly well to such purposes, and at least two of the eclogues are worth special notice. Both debate the problem of love's values and dangers, and they do so in a way that relates to the Sidney-Languet letters: "youthful ardour" and rashness confront the often tedious wisdom of old age; young truants argue with stern moralists in a set of dialogues which articulate some of the main tensions discovered in Sidney's correspondence.

The first of these eclogues, a debate between Geron and Philisides, is an important comic poem, and it owes something both to Sannazaro and to a quite different tradition of moral eclogues—that represented (among others) by Mantuan, Turberville, and Googe. Sannazaro seems to have been the immediate source (see Ringler, 388). The poem that closes the Eighth Prose of his *Arcadia* presents the love complaint of the learned shepherd Clonico ("dottissimo e nella musica esperto").[7] Unrequited love has driven Clonico to thoughts of suicide, and he elaborates self-consciously on the sorrows which his lady will presumably feel after his death (lines 88–108). The verse is melodic, melancholic, full of rich sentiment. Throughout the poem, Sannazaro uses only the *sdrucciola* form of *terza rima*—trisyllabic falling rhymes associated particularly with the verse of formal satire. The general effect is elegiac and monotonous. Eugenio, the other member of the dialogue, takes up the role of counselor. He speaks of the foolishness of love and indulges in occasional wit, but his tone is mainly reflective and philosophic: "This mortal life resembles a day which, as it approaches its end, is colored by disgrace at sunset. When old age comes, bringing to a close the misspent years that have flown by so swiftly, shame and grief grow in the heart" (lines 37–42). Clonico, interestingly enough, agrees with his friend, and is very willing to be done with love: "Eugenio, if I could ever free my soul, or loosen the evil and terrible bonds, . . . there would be no wood or rich field without my song" (lines 13–18). The problem is to find an effective remedy for love, and in the final stanzas of the poem, Eugenio urges Clonico to turn to the delights of Apollo and Pan: plant the earth, nurture the trees, hunt the wolf, and lay snares for birds. The eclogue comes quietly to a close with Eugenio's lyric celebration of the harmonious, restorative powers of nature.

Sidney's modifications of Sannazaro are, as usual, more interesting than his borrowings. In Sannazaro, Clonico is "un uomo maturo,"[8] well past the age when youth serves as an excuse for passion, and Eugenio is apparently his contemporary. Sidney makes his lover (Philisides) a young courtier, and his counselor (Geron) an old shepherd. Sannazaro's entire poem was pitched in an elegant minor key—lyric, reflective music, enhanced by the languor of the *terza sdrucciola*. Sidney avoids the *sdrucciola* altogether (although he imitated Sannazaro's use of it in OA 7 and OA 28) and makes explosive drama out of the harmonies of the Italian. Far from agreeing with Geron (as Clonico did with Eugenio), Philisides counters with a burst of anger and sarcasm:

> O gods, how long this old foole hath annoi'd
> My wearied eares! O gods yet graunt me this,
> That soone the world of his false tong be void.
> O noble age who place their only blisse
> In being heard untill the hearer dye
> Uttring a serpent's minde with serpent's hisse.
> Then who will heare a well autoris'd lye,
> (And pacience hath) let him goe learne of him
> What swarmes of vertues did in his youth flye . . .
>
> (OA 9, 66–74)

Philisides is, of course, Sidney's own comic self-portrait (*Phili-sides*), and it is drawn with obvious, engaging irony. Sidney plays the role of rash, impetuous youth, and he does it with self-conscious wit, exaggerating his pose as confirmed lover, and enjoying the chance to mock the garrulousness and moral orthodoxy of his antagonist. He is clearly the hero of the piece—animated, attractive, and properly faithful to the fair Mira, "Whose wit the starres, whose fortune fortune thralls" (OA 9). But if Philisides is in many ways related to Pyrocles and the Sidney of the letters, he is a less serious advocate than they. His arguments are all *ad hominem*. Since he knows his love will never be requited (see OA 73), he has given himself over to be "Ruine's relique, care's web, and sorrowe's foode" (OA 9). He never suggests, as does Pyrocles, that he will be able to turn love to greater matters. Far from ennobling him, desire has left him melancholy and frustrated, with a "minde drownd in annoyes" (Philisides' own phrase, OA 9).

In such circumstances, Philisides' perseverance in love seems culpable, and Geron's remonstrances have considerable point. Unlike Sannazaro's Eugenio, Geron spends little time in lyric meditation. He is full of urgent imperatives, and brings the Elizabethan language of Virtue and Reason to bear on poor Philisides:

> Then vertue try, if she can worke in thee
> That which we see in many time hath wrought,
> And weakest harts to constant temper brought.
>
> . . . .
>
> Alas what falls are falne unto thy minde?
>
> . . . .
>
> If that thy face were hid, or I were blinde,
> I yet should know a young man speaketh now,
> Such wandring reasons in thy speech I finde.
> He is a beast, that beaste's use will allowe
> For proofe of man, who sprong of heav'nly fire
> Hath strongest soule, when most his raynes do bowe.
>
> (OA 9, 13–15, 32, and 96–101)

We will find nothing like this in Sannazaro's *Arcadia*, where shepherds may talk about the foolishness of love, but never with so consistent and rigid an ethical vocabulary. The prototype for Geron is to be found, rather, in poems like Mantuan's second and third eclogues, or Googe's sixth. There, wise old shepherds like Felix and

Fortunatus chide and advise young lovers, urging them to control
"the Rage of fonde Desyre."⁹ The lovers are sometimes seen sympathetically, but they are apt to end badly: Amyntas, for example,
commits suicide, and there is no disagreement about the moral of his
tale. Fortunatus warns:

> fixe thou fast in minde
> That man in womans pleasures and
>   delights is not assinde
> To wast away his youthfull Prime.
>   for why the foolish toy
> And wicked lust of wanton Loue
>   doth tender age annoy.¹⁰

His friend Faustus agrees: "Seest how this vile Affection fonde / our
inwarde eyes of mynd / Shutts up . . ."¹¹ The moralists may be dull,
but events substantiate their point of view. Googe even goes so far
as to bring back from hell the ghost of young Dametas (another
suicide for love) to warn all other lovers: "Why had I Reason delt
to me? / and coulde not Reason vse. / Why gaue I Brydle to my
wyll? / when I myght well refuse."¹²

If Sidney has borrowed the language and ethics of the Tudor
eclogues, however, he has obviously put them to more sophisticated
uses. Geron is made so comically shrill and stiff that his reliance on
reason is judged to be as inadequate as Philisides' stubborn commitment to passion. Moreover, when the old shepherd tries to close the
eclogue with an imitation of Eugenio's lovely pastoral passage, he is
interrupted by Philisides' sharp reply. It is Histor, a bystander, who
is finally permitted to conclude the debate with a wry summary:

> Thus may you see, howe youthe estemeth aige
> And never hathe therof arightelye deemde
> Whyle hote desyres do Raigne in fancie's rage
> Till aige it self do make it self esteemde.
>
> (OA 9, 138–41)

Both characters are thus judged, held firmly in witty antithesis by
Sidney's special handling of the pastoral-eclogue form. The impetuousness of youth and the self-congratulatory rigidity of age are

weighed against one another, and the comic quality of the poem works mainly to suggest the limitations of each. There is clearly no resolution, only an implicit plea for a little more reason and restraint on one side, and a little more tolerance and vitality on the other.

This same conflict is repeated in a more serious and powerful poem involving Boulon (described as a "wise shepherd") and Plangus (a young courtier). Plangus is presented sympathetically as a heroic figure, passionate in his love for Erona, and angry at the heavens for having allowed her to be imprisoned. His rage and grief combine to create a moving, persuasive poetry of despair. Men are merely

> Balles to the starres, and thralles to Fortune's raigne;
>> Turnd from themselves, infected with their cage,
>> Where death is feard, and life is held with paine.
> Like players plast to fill a filthy stage,
>> Where chaunge of thoughts one foole to other shewes,
>> And all but jests, save onely sorrowe's rage.
>
> (OA 30, 17–22)

The gods are indicted ("those high powers, which idly sit above"), and as Plangus moves from indignation to blasphemy, Boulon cautions him to accept the will of Providence with patience (lines 65–82). At this point, Boulon sounds like the tedious shepherds of Googe and Turberville. He is full of crabbed commonplaces: "O man, take heed, how thou the Gods do move / To causefull wrath, . . ." But after the extraordinarily moving passage in which Plangus recalls his parting from Erona (lines 116–24), the old shepherd responds differently:

> Thy wailing words do much my spirits move,
>> They uttred are in such a feeling fashion,
>> That sorrowe's worke against my will I prove.
> Me-thinkes I am partaker of thy passion,
>> And in thy case do glasse mine owne debilitie:
>
> . . . .
>
> Yet Reason saith, Reason should have abilitie,
>> To hold these worldly things in such proportion,
>> As let them come or go with even facilitie.

>   But our Desire's tyrannicall extortion
>   Doth force us there to set our chiefe delightfulnes, . . .

(OA 30, 125-29 and 131-35)

Boulon's sympathetic response here is very unlike Geron's self-congratulatory piety. It suggests that a common "debilitie" binds all men together; it asks us to see Plangus (and the other heroes of the *Arcadia*) in a much wider perspective—as men driven tragically by noble but unmanageable desires:

>   Woe to poore man: ech outward thing annoyes him
>   In divers kinds; yet as he were not filled,
>   He heapes in inward griefe, that most destroyes him.
>   Thus is our thought with paine for thistles tilled:
>   Thus be our noblest parts dryed up with sorrow:
>   Thus is our mind with too much minding spilled.
>
>   .   .   .   .
>
>   Betwixt the good and shade of good divided,
>   We pittie deeme that which but weakenes is:
>   So are we from our high creation slided.

(OA 30, 170-75 and 179-81)

Boulon's reduction of Plangus' grief to mere weakness is ultimately inadequate, but it derives from his deep responsiveness to that "high creation" from which man has fallen. The blend of compassion and strict judgment in his voice, and his arresting vision of man "Betwixt the good and shade of good divided," force us to see the lovers of Arcadia from a new vantage point. If Plangus achieves a form of poetic vindication by virtue of his constancy and noble sorrow, Boulon compels us to view him more soberly, *sub specie aeternitatis*. That Sidney wanted us to take such a view seriously, and that he associated it explicitly with Languet, seem clearly borne out by one of the poems assigned to Philisides in the third set of eclogues. Three stanzas near the beginning of the poem are the most relevant:

>   The songe I sange old Languet had me taught,
>   Languet, the shepheard best swift *Ister* knewe,
>   For clerkly reed, and hating what is naught,
>   For faithfull hart, cleane hands, and mouth as true:

With his sweet skill my skillesse youth he drewe,
   To have a feeling tast of him that sitts
   Beyond the heaven, far more beyond your witts.

He said, the Musique best thilke powers pleasd
Was jumpe concorde betweene our wit and will:
Where highest notes to godlines are raisd,
And lowest sinke not downe to jote of ill: . . .

He liked me, but pitied lustfull youth:
His good strong staffe my slippry yeares upbore:
He still hop'd well, because I loved truth; . . .
        (OA 66, 22–32 and 36–38)

Languet is presented here as an old and wise shepherd, aware of the
faults of "lustfull youth," urging "concorde betweene our wit and
will," and calling Philisides to the sober, godly life expounded in the
letters to Sidney.[13] As in the dialogues between Philisides and Geron,
and Plangus and Boulon, the tension between "skillesse youth" and
restraining age is maintained here, though with a different effect.
Philisides now acknowledges his own faults and submits equably to
Languet's virtue and wisdom. The older man, though firm, is sympathetic, acting as guide and support. He has none of Geron's shrillness
or Boulon's aroused sternness. As much as possible, his tone is designed to promote conciliation rather than conflict: "He still hop'd
well, because I loved truth." At such moments, the *Arcadia* comes
very close indeed to reflecting the strong bonds of affection and
interest which formed the basis of the Sidney-Languet friendship,
despite the differences between the two men.

4

I have so far suggested that the *Old Arcadia* can be legitimately, if
only partially, viewed as presenting a series of variations on the
themes announced in the Sidney-Languet correspondence. Taken
together, the book's several dialogues reflect Sidney's continual
probing of issues and problems which had always concerned him but
which were particularly on his mind in 1578–1580. They offer, not
solutions, but simply alternative ways of presenting or considering dilemmas. Sidney is able to parody his own impetuousness in

Philisides, or to dramatize youthful ardor and love sympathetically in Plangus; he can undercut the vows of Pyrocles and Musidorus, while praising them for their fidelity and noble feelings; he laughs at Geron's moralizing, makes us respond much more positively to Boulon's, and finally allows Languet to make us realize how weak is "lustfull youth" in the sight of "him that sitts / Beyond the heaven." The trial scene which concludes the *Arcadia* presents a similar complexity. Pyrocles and Musidorus are there arraigned for having broken Arcadia's laws. The crime of abducting the princesses is punishable by death, but although the princes are clearly at fault, a great many circumstances work to mitigate their guilt. They are young, they are attractive, they have previously saved the kingdom by putting down a dangerous rebellion, and they have rescued the princesses from Cecropia's wild beasts. Basilius had been wrong in the first place to sequester Philoclea and Pamela, and in normal circumstances, Pyrocles and Musidorus would have been ideal suitors for the sisters. The most sensible solution would seem to be to ignore the crime of abduction (particularly since it has had in itself no serious consequences) and to let the heroes marry their ladies. The supposed murder of Basilius, however, places all events in a serious perspective and makes the strictest possible conduct of justice seem necessary. Euarchus, the judge, is a grave and sober man with a scrupulous, unyielding regard for the law. He had journeyed to Arcadia "to see whether by his authority hee might drawe *Basilius* . . . to returne ageane to employ his oulde yeares in doyng good, the onely happy action of mans lyfe" (F, IV. 332). He was himself famous for

> ye greatnes of his mynde. In somuche that those thinges wch often tymes the best sorte thinck rewardes of Vertue, hee helde them not at so hye a pryce, but esteemed them Servauntes to well dooyng: The Reward of vertue beeyng in yt self, on wch his Inward love was so fixed, that never was yt dissolved into other desyers, but keeping his thoughtes true to them selves, was neither beguyled with the paynted glasse of pleasure, nor dazeled with ye false lighte of Ambition. This made the Lyne of his actions streighte, and allwayes like yt self, no worldly thing beeynge able to shake the Constancy of yt; . . .   (F, IV. 331)

Euarchus embodies in serious form the doctrine of "well dooyng" which Musidorus had articulated in his first debate with Pyrocles and which Languet had continually urged upon Sidney.[14] Virtuous action is the heart of his creed, and his love for such virtue was "so fixed, that never was yt dissolved into other desyers." The young princes, of course, had been deflected from their life of heroic deeds precisely because of such other desires, and Euarchus now makes their conduct seem trivial and foolish. Sidney had confronted Phili-sides with Languet in OA 66, and he now forces Pyrocles and Musi-dorus to encounter Euarchus, a man who is obviously cast in the same mold. Both confrontations have the effect of placing the *Arcadia*'s various heroes in a new perspective. They are no longer measured by the scale of a Geron or even a Boulon, but by men who "made the Lyne of [their] actions streighte, and allwayes like yt self, no worldly thing beeynge able to shake the Constancy of yt."

In the face of such constancy, Pyrocles and Musidorus argue for their own pardon. By and large, they plead very much as Pyrocles did at the very beginning of the book, asking that their judge "looke upon [their] Imperfections, with more affection then Judgmt." Their only fault was love, "a passion farr more easily reprehended then refrayned" (F, IV. 365). Pyrocles asks that Euarchus "bee mooved rather with pitty at a Just Cause of teares"; nor is he, even at so critical a moment, shy of wit and irony:

> in fyne I offered force to her (Love offered more force to mee) lett her Beuty bee compared to my yeares, and suche effectes will be made no myrackles. (F, IV. 367)

Musidorus agrees, and is certain that others "will deeme yt a veniall trespass to seeke the satisfaction of honorable desyers" (F, IV. 375). In short, the impetuousness of youthful desires, the power and poten-tial nobility of love, and the essential virtue of the princes and their ladies are weighed against the clear, unequivocal demands of justice and the law. At first, the "never chaunging Justice" (F, IV. 379) seems to triumph; the princes are condemned to death and are counseled:

> Yf that unbrydeled Desyer wch ys intituled Love mighte purge suche a sicknes as this, surely wee shoulde have many Loving ex-cuses of hatefull myscheefes: Nay, rather no myscheef shoulde bee

committed that shoulde not bee vailed under the name of Love. . . .
But love may have no suche priviledge. That sweete and heavenly
uniting of the myndes, wch properly ys called Love, hathe no other
knott but vertue: And therefore, yf yt bee a Right Love, yt can
never slyde into any action yt ys not vertuous.   (F, IV. 378–79)

Euarchus demands a moral strictness and consistency of conduct
similar to that which Languet had asked of the young Sidney, and
these demands are here translated into legal imperatives. Moments
later, however, Menalcas enters and reveals the true identity of
Pyrocles and Musidorus (who have to this point remained disguised): they are in fact the long-lost son and nephew of Euarchus
himself. The stage is thus set for a typical romance finale—a comic,
happy reunion of parents and children, to be followed by the happy
marriage of princes and princesses. But in spite of the new revelation,
and in spite of his private feelings, Euarchus persists in his initial
judgment: "never, never let sacred Rightfullnes falle, yt ys Immortall and Immortall oughte to bee preserved: yf Rightly I have
judged, then rightly I have judged myne owne Children" (F, IV.
383). Justice, which previously seemed both necessary and admirable,
now begins to triumph only at the expense of joy and life itself.
Euarchus' constancy verges on a ridiculous adherence to law for the
sake of law rather like Geron's unthinking devotion to reason. "And
take heede O Father," says Pyrocles, "least, seeking too precyse a
Course of Justice, yow bee not thoughte moste unjust" (F, IV. 386).
As in the pastoral eclogues, the tables of the trial scene are turned in
such a way as to expose the limitations of moral rigor and old age as
well as those of ardent youth. The dilemma is solved, moreover, in
precisely the way that so many of Sidney's dilemmas are solved: wit
intervenes, and Basilius is revived from his supposed death.[15] In the
delightful confusion which follows, the trial collapses, the princes are
pardoned, and Basilius makes a public confession of his own truancy
in love. None of the issues raised is finally settled, and the *Old
Arcadia* ends with an equivocal apology for noble youth: a suggestion
that its energies are admirable, and its delights honorable, combined
with an admission of its waywardness and its potentially dangerous
imperfections. That such concerns were indeed on Sidney's mind as
he wrote the *Arcadia*, and that he in fact thought of the book itself as

yet another example of pardonable, charming truancy, seem amply borne out by the Dedication to the Countess of Pembroke. All of Sidney's wit, irony, *sprezzatura*, and love of role playing come together there, to demonstrate how deftly he could turn his own concerns to comic uses:

> Here now have you (most deare, and most worthy to be most deare Lady) this idle worke of mine: . . . Now, it is done onelie for you, onely to you: if you keepe it to your selfe, or to such friendes, who will weigh errors in the ballaunce of good will, I hope, for the fathers sake, it will be pardoned, perchance made much of, though in it selfe it have deformities. For indeede, for severer eyes it is not, being but a trifle, and that triflinglie handled. . . . In summe, a young head, not so well stayed as I would it were, (and shall be when God will) having many many fancies begotten in it, if it had not ben in some way delivered, would have growen a monster, . . . Read it then at your idle tymes, and the follyes your good judgement wil finde in it, blame not, but laugh at. And so, . . . you will continue to love the writer, who doth excedinglie love you; . . . (F, I. 3-4)

Like Pyrocles, Sidney wittily asks the Countess of Pembroke: "continew to loove mee, and looke upon my Imperfections, with more affection then Judgmt"; but he does so in such a way as to suggest that those imperfections are themselves attractive, and altogether pardonable.[16]

CHAPTER IV

The Apologie for Poetrie

IF THE *Arcadia* is approached from the Sidney-Languet letters, the book takes on a new kind of relevance, and its treatment of pastoral and heroic themes betrays an emphasis which we might not otherwise expect. Studied in the light of Sannazaro or Spenser, the work may seem to be primarily a critique of traditional pastoral values. That critical quality is, of course, an integral part of the *Arcadia*, but the correspondence inevitably places the book in a slightly different perspective. It reveals itself then as a fictional extension of Sidney's letters in defense of relaxation, reflection, and a life of dignified ease. With all its tentativeness and complexity, it ends as a witty and youthful plea entered, against imposing adversaries, on behalf of the delights of the world. "Prepare yourself to attack me," Sidney had written to Languet, after confessing that his mind was learning to "relax without reluctance." "I have now pointed out the field of battle, and I openly declare war against you" (Pears, 143–44). The *Arcadia* continues that war, and Sidney arranges matters in such a way that his heroes emerge from it as slightly battered but essentially unblemished victors.

It was suggested earlier that the defense of leisure, reflection, and love was closely connected in Sidney's mind with the defense of poetry, and it may be helpful to expand upon this point before discussing the *Arcadia*'s verse. The enemies of poetry in the sixteenth century had a great deal in common with the enemies of leisure and love, and their lines of attack were likely to be similar. Musidorus, for example, had declared that love was "ingendred betuixt lust and Idlenes," that it bred only a "base weykenes" fatal to the life of heroic action. In 1579, Stephen Gosson's *Schoole of Abuse* employed precisely the same arguments against poetry and drama:

> I may well liken *Homer* to *Mithecus*, and Poets to Cookes the pleasures
> of the one winnes the body from labor, and conquereth the sense;
> the allurement of the other drawes the mind from vertue, and con-
> foundeth wit.[1]

> Our wreastling at armes, is turned to wallowyng in Ladies laps, our
> courage, to cowardice, our running to ryot, . . .[2]

Predicting the results of meddling with poems or plays was, for
Gosson, as easy as declining nouns: one was led from "Pyping to
playing, from play to pleasure, from pleasure to slouth, from slouth
to sleepe, from sleepe to sinne."[3] It was Gosson, almost certainly,
who provoked the *Apologie for Poetrie*, and Sidney may have begun
that project as early as 1580, before completing the *Arcadia*.[4] That he
had in mind an audience like Gosson or Musidorus before his conversion, and that he expected any apology for poetry to involve an
apology for love, seem clear from the nature of his essay. After discussing two possible objections to poetry, he declares that "the
principall, if not the onely abuse I can heare alledged" is poetry's
supposed power to harm "mens wit, trayning it to wanton sinfulnes,
and lustfull love":

> They say, the Lirick is larded with passionate Sonnets. The Elegiack
> weepes the want of his mistresse. And that even to the Heroical
> *Cupid* hath ambitiously climed. Alas Love, I would thou couldest as
> well defende thy selfe, as thou canst offende others! I would those,
> on whom thou doost attend, could eyther put thee away, or yeelde
> good reason why they keepe thee! But grant love of beautie to be
> a beastlie fault, (although it be very hard, sith onely man, and no
> beast, hath that gyft to discerne beauty.) Grant, that lovely name of
> Love to deserve all hatefull reproches: (although even some of my
> Maisters the Philosophers, spent a good deale of theyr Lamp-oyle,
> in setting foorth the excellencie of it.) Grant, I say, what soever they
> wil have granted; that not onely love, but lust, but vanitie, but (if
> they list) scurrilitie, possesseth many leaves of the Poets bookes:
> yet thinke I, when this is granted, they will finde theyr sentence
> may, with good manners, put the last words foremost: and not
> say, that Poetrie abuseth mans wit, but that mans wit abuseth
> Poetrie.   (*Apologie*, 40)

This passage is in Sidney's finest ironic manner: the mock helplessness, the intentionally hyperbolic concessions ("a beastlie fault"),
the casual tucking of powerful arguments into parentheses, and the
concluding logical twist. The tone, in all its grace and playful intimacy ("Alas Love, etc."), is quintessential Sidney, although the
strategy may well have been learned from More, Erasmus, or the
studied guilelessness of Socrates. Love is vindicated, poetry acquit-
ted, and the terms in which Sidney manages this feat are strikingly
similar to those employed by Pyrocles in his reply to Musidorus:

> And, pore Love (sayde hee) Dere Cossyn, ys litle beholding unto
> yow, since yow are not contented to spoyle yt of ye honor, of the
> highest power of the mynde, wch notable men have attributed unto
> yt, but yow deject yt, belowe all other passions (in truthe) some
> thinge straungely; . . . Those trublesome effectes yow say yt breedes
> bee not the faultes of Love, but of him, that loves, . . . (F, IV. 19)

Pyrocles' passage lacks all the sophistication of the *Apologie*'s, but its
rationale is the same, and it even offers a touch of similar irony
("pore Love"). The differences between the two are significant, but
the similarities are at least equally important, and they suggest the
considerable degree to which the *Arcadia*, the *Apologie*, and the letters
to Languet may be conceived as parts of a single, central debate.
Other parallels among the three works tend to confirm this impression. Pyrocles' discourse on contemplation, for example, which
borrowed ideas and images from Sidney's letters, is very closely
related to the *Apologie*'s definition of poetic imagination. For Pyrocles, to unbend the mind was not simply to make it idle but to free it
from outward demands and distractions: "the workinges of the
mynde I fynde muche more infinite then can bee ledd unto by ye
eye, or imagined by any that distract theyre thoughtes wthowte
them selves, . . . Egles wee see flye alone, and they are but sheepe
wch allway heard together" (F, IV. 12). It was just this uninhibited,
free-ranging capacity of the mind—the image of eagles flying alone
—which Sidney associated with poetic creativity or invention. He
stressed "that high flying liberty of conceit proper to the Poet"
(*Apologie*, 6) and the free "course of [the poet's] owne invention"
(*Apologie*, 11). All other men have the works of nature as their
principal object: "Onely the Poet, disdayning to be tied to any such

subiection, lifted up with the vigor of his owne invention, dooth
growe in effect another nature, . . . not inclosed within the narrow
warrant of [Nature's] guifts, but freely ranging onely within the
Zodiack of his owne wit" (*Apologie*, 8). The land of Arcadia be-
stows such power and freedom. It makes poets of its inhabitants, and
Musidorus celebrates this quality, using images that are clearly
related to the passage just quoted from the *Apologie*:

> O sweet woods the delight of solitarines!
> O how much I do like your solitarines!
> *Where man's mind hath a freed consideration*
> Of goodnes to receive lovely direction.
> Where senses do behold th'order of heav'nly hoste,
> And wise thoughts do behold what the creator is:
> Contemplation here holdeth his only seate:
> *Bownded with no limitts, borne with a wing of hope*
> *Clymes even unto the starres, Nature is under it.*
>
> (OA 34, 1–9, my italics)

Arcadia, then, is a realm of poetry and imagination as well as of
leisure and love. It was suggested earlier that Pyrocles' hymn to the
Arcadian landscape made him an unwitting apologist for poetry, a
passionate poet-lover whose style revealed the kind of energy which
Sidney had praised in his discussion of the Psalms. In Sidney's terms,
to be a lover was automatically to be a poet (and vice versa), since
the distinguishing capacity of both was the ability to respond to
beauty, and to feel beauty's potential unity with virtue. In this, they
differ strongly from the moral philosophers mentioned in the
Apologie. The latter bear in some particulars a family resemblance to
shepherds like Geron, and they are invariably treated with good-
natured contempt: "me thinketh, I see [them] comming towards me
with a sullen gravity, as though they could not abide vice by day
light; rudely clothed for to witnes outwardly their contempt of outward things" (*Apologie*, 14). They teach "vertue by certaine abstract
considerations," they deal in "thorny argument," and they often
end by losing their followers in a "mistie" way (*Apologie*, 15–16).
The poet and the lover, by contrast, delight in outward things.
Neither will grant "love of beautie to be a beastlie fault," because

"onely man, and no beast, hath that gyft to discerne beauty"
(*Apologie*, 40). Both find a kind of knowledge in beauty—a vision of
perfection and harmony, of virtue given sensuous form—that is
altogether different from the disputative and abstract knowledge of
moral philosophers. One might recall in this context Sidney's
admonition to his brother Robert, in the famous letter of October
1580: "remember, 'gratior est veniens in pulchro corpore virtus'"
(Pears, 202). Pyrocles, of course, echoes the sentiment when he confesses wryly that "yt likes mee muche better, when I fynde vertue in
a fayre Lodging, then when I am bounde to seeke yt in an yll
favored Creature" (F, IV. 18), and after Musidorus has played
abstract philosopher, suggesting that "the Love of heaven makes one
heavenly, the love of vertue vertuous," Pyrocles replies indignantly:

> For, yf wee love vertue, in whome shall wee love yt, but in vertuous
> Creatures, withoute youre meaning bee, I shoulde love this worde
> of *Vertue*, when I see yt written in a Booke: . . .   (F, IV. 19)

Philosophers love words, but poets and lovers are enamored of beautiful images which delight the heart and fire the spirit. Both dwell in
a rich world of feeling and imagination that is all but closed to
Gosson and Geron—even to Boulon and Languet. And whatever
difficulties and dangers lie within that world, Sidney has no doubts
concerning the final value of encountering them.

It is in just this matter of dangers and difficulties, however, that
the *Apologie* reveals an emphasis much closer to that of the revised
Arcadia than to that either of the original or of Sidney's letters to
Languet. In the latter two works, beauty and delight very often
conflict with virtue: the letters offer a life of relaxation and dignified
ease as a possible alternative to the life of noble action, and the
heroes of the *Old Arcadia* barely escape paying the death penalty for
their dalliance in the land of love and ease. Such complications are
mainly swept aside in the *Apologie*, for obvious rhetorical reasons.
Sidney admits in passing that poetry (like love)

> may not onely be abused, but that beeing abused, by the reason of
> his sweete charming force, it can doe more hurt then any other
> Armie of words: . . .   (*Apologie*, 41)

But we hear little more on the subject. Rather, we are told that beauty and delight are the main allies of the mind, drawing it to love and imitate "notable images" or examples of virtue (*Apologie*, 12). Nor is there any doubt that "the ending end of all earthly learning" is virtuous action (*Apologie*, 14). Relaxation, reflection, or the exercise of poetic imagination are never presented as real threats, and are certainly never allowed to become possible ends in themselves; they are seen only as aids to a life of noble deeds. Sidney makes a point of answering critics like Gosson who charge that

> before Poets beganne to be in price, our Nation hath set their harts delight upon action, and not upon imagination: rather doing things worthy to bee written, then writing things fitte to be done.
>
> (*Apologie*, 41–42)

> before Poets did soften us, we were full of courage, given to martiall exercises; the pillers of manlyke liberty, and not lulled a sleepe in shady idlenes with Poets pastimes.[5]   (*Apologie*, 37)

Sidney responds by stating that "Poetrie is the companion of the Campes" (*Apologie*, 42), and that "right poets" have always written tales designed to move men to an emulation of heroic actions.[5] In short, he simplifies matters—partly because the nature of persuasive rhetoric promotes such simplifications, and partly because Sidney was undoubtedly allured by the vision of a life which could indeed harmonize contemplation and action, love and chivalric exploit, poetic and practical knowledge, leisure and vigor. The *Apologie*, however, suggests that accommodations between the delights of beauty and the demands of virtue are easier to arrange than either the *Old Arcadia* or the letters would seem to imply. In this, it is like the revised *Arcadia*, with its vision of an ideal society whose "sportes were such as caried riches of Knowledge upon the streame of Delight: . . . So as it seemed, that court to have bene the mariage place of Love and Vertue, & that [its queen] was a *Diana* apparelled in the garments of *Venus*" (F, I. 283).

Sidney's critics and biographers have frequently accepted the declarations and resounding generalizations of the *Apologie* as a kind of blueprint of his life and work. Yet the *Apologie*, for all its grace and ease of manner, is something of a manifesto: a public, carefully marshalled, consistent (in spite of its inconsistencies) rhetorical argument. It does indeed articulate genuine aspirations which are echoed time and time again throughout Sidney's writings. But it also banishes all the conflicting feelings and inclinations, the alternative impulses, and the doubts which the letters to Languet, the verse, and the *Arcadia* itself reveal. It banishes, that is, much of what makes Sidney an absorbing personality and a beguiling poet. The *Apologie* is eloquent in its definition of certain ideals which undoubtedly motivated the prominent young nephew of Leicester; but other works suggest his hesitations and misgivings, and point in rather different directions. Taken together, Sidney's various writings resemble the dialogues of the *Arcadia*: they qualify, correct, and debate with one another, turning over and over again the same issues and tensions, never resolving them, yet always placing them in fresh perspectives. The wit and vivacity of these encounters, and the seriousness of the conflict which underlies their irresolution, are perhaps the greatest source of their richness and continuing interest to us.

CHAPTER V

Ornament and Rhetoric

❦

THE POETRY OF the *Arcadia* has received very little critical comment, and most of that has been adverse. Hazlitt's judgment has
formed the basis of nearly all later opinions—a fact which, in itself,
ought to make us wary. He declared that the "Sonnets, inlaid in the
Arcadia, are jejune, far-fetched and frigid."[1] As for the book as a
whole:

> It is not romantic, but scholastic; not poetry, but casuistry; not
> nature, but art, and the worst sort of art, which thinks it can do
> better than nature. . . . Out of five hundred folio pages, there are
> hardly, I conceive, half a dozen sentences expressed simply and
> directly, with the sincere desire to convey the image implied, and
> without a systematic interpolation of the wit, learning, ingenuity,
> wisdom and everlasting impertinence of the writer, . . . Every page
> is 'with centric and eccentric scribbled o'er;' his Muse is tattooed
> and tricked out like an Indian goddess.[2]

It was Hazlitt who first found the *Arcadia* deficient in simplicity,
directness, and sincerity, and who began to turn the *Apologie*'s
criticism of other writers against Sidney himself. Sidney had in his
own essay complained of "far-fetched" words and phrases, and particularly of writers who, "like those Indians, . . . thrust Iewels
through their nose and lippes, because they will be sure to be fine"
(*Apologie*, 58). Hazlitt suggested that these complaints were equally
applicable to the *Arcadia*, and later critics have tended to follow suit.
Theodore Spencer, in a very appreciative essay, stressed the "conventional" quality of the *Arcadia*'s verse and contrasted it with the
personal and sincere poetry of *Astrophel*.[3] William Empson rescued

the double sestina,[4] but John Crowe Ransom, in a friendly rejoinder, suggested that the "materials of this poem are so shopworn that our interest in it might amount to almost a literary affectation, if immediate interest were not fortified by a more speculative admiration for the technical excellences."[5] Kenneth Muir found that the "chief importance" of the *Arcadia* poems "lies in the fact that they are mostly poetic exercises."[6] Robert Montgomery's recent book has stressed the poetry's overdecorative, ornate qualities. Sidney was concerned with "manner" rather than "matter,"[7] and revealed in the *Arcadia* a "tendency to hunt verbal ornament at the expense of other goals."[8] Later, dissatisfied with his own work, he adopted a plainer and more dramatic idiom for *Astrophel*. This view has lately been given tacit support by William Ringler, who stresses Sidney's interest in rhetoric, but adds: "In the *Old Arcadia* the rhetoric is sometimes obtrusive, in the best of the *Astrophil and Stella* sonnets it is less obvious because more completely functional."[9] The implication is that obvious or obtrusive rhetoric is to be avoided as "unfunctional" and that Sidney, realizing this, managed to correct himself in *Astrophel*. Thus, the *Arcadia*'s verse has been almost universally disparaged;[10] and insofar as Sidney's poetic development has been discussed at all, it has been described mainly in terms of rapid growth and sharp changes: the mannered, overdecorative style of the early work superseded by the substantial, mature mode of *Astrophel*. Two points are ultimately at stake: whether the *Arcadia* is indeed excessively and, as it were, meaninglessly ornate; and whether Sidney, at a later time, repudiated that ornateness in favor of a quite different conception of poetic style.

What this and the following three chapters will suggest is that the *Arcadia*'s poetry is much more diverse than has been generally noticed, and that this diversity in itself forces us to be more attentive to the motives that tend to govern Sidney's changes of style from poem to poem within the work as a whole. Much of the verse is—for very good reasons—in an undeniably artificial, rhetorical mode. But several of the pastoral eclogues, as will be shown in Chapter Seven, are in a thoroughly "plain" dramatic style intimately connected with that of *Astrophel*. Indeed, the *Astrophel* manner announces itself very clearly in the pages of the *Old Arcadia*, and once this fact is acknowledged, it becomes necessary to reconsider established theories concerning Sidney's development. Most important, it is essential to find fresh ways of approaching the *Arcadia*'s ornamental verse by attempting to account for its special quality without suggesting that it is simply the result of an early preference for decorative writing on Sidney's part. The rhetoric is indeed obtrusive, but it is worth while asking again why Sidney chose to have it so. That it *was* a choice is proved beyond question by the mere presence of radically different styles in the *Arcadia*. Nor should this realization come as a great surprise. Sidney was much too good a poet to do things mechanically, and nothing we know of either his life or his work gives us reason to suppose that he was ever satisfied with the purely conventional, or that he blindly overvalued manner at the expense of matter. It would be odd if his first important poetic venture prompted us to think differently of him.

Renaissance ideas of decorum can offer some help in formulating an initial approach to the *Arcadia*'s rhetorical style. Kenneth Myrick demonstrated some years ago, for example, that the *Arcadia*'s prose was fashioned to fit the specific requirements of the book's genre. He objected personally to Sidney's "gorgeous phraseology," but he saw nonetheless that it was designed to suit the needs of pastoral-heroic romance.[11] That the *Arcadia*'s verse observes a similar decorum has been sometimes suggested, but the implications of the fact have never been sufficiently stressed or developed. Compare, for instance, the very different styles of the princess Philoclea and the shepherd Geron:

> O stealing time the subject of delaie,
> (Delay, the racke of unrefrain'd desire)
> What strange dessein hast thou my hopes to staie,
> My hopes which do but to mine owne aspire?
>
> Mine owne? ô word on whose sweete sound doth pray
> My greedy soule, with gripe of inward fire: . . .
> > (Philoclea, OA 53, 1–6)

> In faith, good *Histor*, long is your delay,
> From holy marriage, sweet and surest meane

Our foolish lustes in honest rules to stay.

.   .   .   .

Beleeve me man, there is no greater blisse,
Then is the quiet joy of loving wife;
Which who so wants, halfe of himselfe doth misse.

(Geron, OA 67, 1–3 and 7–9)

Philoclea's lines are in an elevated, self-consciously rhetorical style: parallel apostrophes ("O stealing time," "ô word"), intentionally obtrusive anadiplosis,[12] carefully balanced alliteration, and correct diction give the passage an air of calculated artificiality and formality. Geron, meanwhile, speaks just as a shepherd ought to. His verse is awkward, but it is obviously informal and conversational, with its parenthetical asides ("In faith," "Beleeve me man") and its complete lack of rhetorical heightening. Sidney could write "plain" poetry when he wanted, but he had clearly decided to separate his courtly personages from his shepherds, in order to suggest the greater sophistication, the grace and wit, the more refined feelings and nobler passions of his princes and princesses. Their style is a high style, and the rhetorical figures they employ are designed to "function" in several important ways. Apostrophe, for instance, was considered to be a particularly "efficacious" device in nearly all the Elizabethan rhetoric books: it expressed strong feeling, and was regarded as a powerful weapon in stirring the emotions of an audience. Most of Philoclea's figures, however, function aesthetically rather than "persuasively": in the symmetry they create, in the firm syntactical order and delicate patterns of sound which they articulate, they embody a great deal of what the Elizabethans understood by the word "courtly." They refine passion, translating it into the harmonious forms of artful, polished speech. They express all the grace, the self-consciousness, and the vision of rational self-control converted into aesthetic terms which Castiglione had defined as the essence of the courtly mode. Sidney's high style, in other words, is the outward sign of a particular style of life—a life in which social, moral, and aesthetic values are fused, very much as they were in the sports and activities of Helen of Corinth's ideal court (F, I. 283). Ornament is integral to that life: not as something superfluously added, but as a part of its very texture. The Elizabethan rhetoricians were entirely clear on this point. Puttenham insisted that rhetorical figures were "a certaine liuelie or good grace set vpon wordes, speaches and sentences *to some purpose* and not in vaine, *giuing them ornament or efficacie*" (my italics).[13] "Ornament" was a perfectly legitimate "purpose," and it bestowed necessary grace upon poetry. It made poems into beautiful, artfully wrought objects—and I have noticed in previous chapters how much Sidney valued such beauty. Girolamo Fracastoro, among others, would seem to agree with Puttenham's statement:

> ought we to think splendid garments extraneous because poor ones are sufficient? Do you not see that just as perfection and ornament are a real part of the things which nature produces, so they are the things which art produces? What perfection and beauty are, only the great artists know. And if you take them away from the subject, assuredly you have somehow taken away life itself.[14]

For Sidney, too, the ornament of "splendid garments" gave an altogether necessary beauty and perfection to the subject at hand. It aided in the creation of that golden world which he expected poetry to fashion for us. His Arcadia, of course, is not all golden, nor are his heroes and heroines quite perfect; but the princes and princesses live in the rarefied atmosphere of pastoral and chivalric romance where virtue and beauty are always striving to be united, and where speech is appropriately distinguished by the "good grace" which formal rhetoric brings to it.

Granted all this, however, it remains true that the *Arcadia*'s courtly style is of a very special kind. It is not simply polished, self-conscious speech, but has in fact an unusually artificial air, an elaborate formality which can only be understood in relation to the spirit of the *Arcadia* as a whole. Most comments on the book's verse tend to imply that it should be viewed in the same light and judged by the same standards as *Astrophel*, that it should be approached, in other words, as if it were the intimate, rather private verse of a courtier, written *in propria persona*. Judged by such standards, it is bound to seem stiff and inadequate. But Sidney was not simply trying to write verse like *Astrophel*'s and doing a bad job of it. He was

framing a style that would relate plausibly to the fictional world he
had created in the *Arcadia*'s prose—a romance world that was in
many ways very remote indeed from the real world. In such circumstances, the mannered style he created for his courtly characters
is the perfect medium for his purposes. It manages to convey their
sophistication and refined idealism; it is capable of extraordinarily
powerful and yet highly formal expressions of emotion; and it can
suggest, equally, the youthful, naive, exaggerated feelings and gestures of romantic young lovers. One can appreciate these capacities
of the style most fully, perhaps, by examining a few passages of the
Arcadia's prose, and by proceeding afterward to a consideration of
the poetry's relationship to that prose. The passage in which Musidorus is narrating his adventures to Pamela provides an excellent
point of departure:

> To tell yow what pityfull myshappes fell to the younge Prince of
> *Macedon* ... I shoulde too muche fill youre eares with strange
> horrors: Neyther will I stay upon those Laboursome adventures nor
> loathsome mysadventures to whiche and throughe wch his fortune
> and corage conducted hym, my speeche hasteth ytself to come to ye
> full poynte of all *Musidorus* infortunes. ... *Arcadia, Arcadia* was the
> place prepared to bee stage of his endles overthrowe *Arcadia,* was,
> (alas well might I say yt ys) the Charmed Circle where all his spirites
> shoulde for ever bee enchaunted. ... Here here did hee see the
> *Arcadian* Dukes eldest Daughter, in whome hee forthe with placed
> so all his hopes of joy and joyfull partes of his harte that, hee lefte in
> hym self no thinge but a mase of Longing and a Dongeon of sorrowe.
>   (F, IV. 100)

The rhetoric of this prose—with its heightened apostrophes, repetitions, and other forms of verbal play—is clearly similar to that of
the *Arcadia*'s poetry, although it is used here in a special way. The
particular charm of the passage derives from the way in which its
language distances us from Musidorus. It invites us to watch him
with amusement, mild irony, and affectionate regard. His narration
is simultaneously a self-conscious performance, a calculated persuasion to love, and an exaggerated expression of youthful feeling.
If the prince's grief is in one sense real, the style nonetheless keeps us

outside the action, very much as Sidney's own narrative descriptions often do. Here is Pyrocles celebrating Arcadia:

> Certeynly, certeynly Cossyn yt must needes bee, that some Goddess this Dezert belonges unto, who ys the sowle of this soile, for, neyther ys any lesse then a Goddess worthy to bee shryned in suche a heape of pleasures, nor any less then a Goddess coulde have made yt so perfect a Moddell of the heavenly dwellinges: And so hee ended with a deepe sighe, rufully casting his eye uppon *Musidorus*, as more desyerus of pitty, then pleading. (F, IV. 12–13)

Exaggerated rhetoric is here linked directly to exaggerated gesture. The description of Pyrocles' sighs and rueful looks makes comedy of his love, and the elevated strain of his speech is inseparable from the quality of his behavior as a whole. Reading the poetry in context serves to underline its affinities to such prose and to stress the extent to which it participates in the book's delicate, artificial, witty spirit. For instance, when Pamela and Musidorus are fleeing Arcadia, they rest momentarily in a lovely forest:

> *Pamela* had muche more pleasure to walke under those Trees, making in theyre Barckes prity knottes wch tyed together the names of *Musidorus* and *Pamela*, sometymes intermixedly chaungyng them to *Pamedorus* and *Musimela*, with xxti other Flowers of her traveling fancyes wch had bounde them selves to a greater Restraynt, then they coulde withoute muche payne well endure: And to one Tree more beholding to her then the Rest, shee entrusted the Treasure of her thoughtes in these verses.

> *Doo not Disdayne O streighte uprAysed Pyne?*
> *That, wounding thee, my Thoughtes in thee I grave,*
> *Synce that my thoughtes as Streighte as streightnes thyne,*
> *No smaller wounde, (Alas) furr deeper have?*

> *Deeper engraved whiche salve nor Tyme can save,*
> *Given to my harte by my fore wounded eyen . . .*
> (F, IV. 186–87)

Pamela is seen as charming and naive, making love knots and indulging fancies in a scene that is suffused with the particular blend of grace, delicacy, and irony which Sidney manages so well. Her song, which seems so stiff when it is read in isolation, rises very naturally from the context created for it. A poetry of "sincere personal feeling," full of tension and drama, in a plain or conversational idiom, is precisely what the situation will *not* bear. Rather, we expect the passion of Sidney's *ingénus* to be filtered and refined, to express itself in forms of speech and gesture which combine beauty, control, and youthful charm. The narrator's manner of introducing the lyrics, moreover, tends to heighten this expectation. The poems are carefully prepared for—presented as if they were set performances rather than spontaneous outbursts, arias rather than recitative. In Book One, after Pyrocles disguises himself as the Amazon Cleophila, he (she) walks

> up and downe in that solitary place, with many intricate determinacions, at last, wearyed bothe in mynde & body satt her downe: And beginning to tune her voyce, wth many sobbes and teares, sange this songe, wch shee had made, synce her first determinacyon, thus to chaunge her estate.

> *Transformde in shewe, but more transformde in mynde,*
> *I cease to stryve, with duble Conquest foylde; . . .*

> I might enterteyne yow, (faire Ladyes) a greate while, yf I shoulde make as many interruptions in the repeating, as shee did in the singing: For no verse did pass oute of her mouthe, but that yt was wayted on wth suche abundance of sighes, . . . that thoughe the wordes were fewe, yet the tyme was long shee employed in uttering them, Allthoughe her pawses chose so fitt tymes, that they rather strengthened a sweeter passyon then hindered the harmony.
>
> (F, IV. 25–26)

Pyrocles' song is a witty exercise in self-scrutiny, formally delivered, and wittily commented upon by the narrator. Sidney keeps the reader at a comfortable distance from the entire action, and he turns aside immediately after the lyric to chat with his audience of fair ladies. All of Pyrocles' sobs and tears are treated as material for light comedy and ironically tender romance. The pauses created by his sighs come happily just where caesuras are proper, so that "they rather strengthened . . . then hindered the harmony." Everything is done, in other words, to disengage the reader, to keep him outside the scene, to "enterteyne" him. Again, a personal and dramatic poetry, demanding quite another kind of response and involvement, would be most disruptive and inappropriate in such contexts.

Thus, if one takes the decorum of the *Arcadia* into account, as well as the texture of its prose and the quality of its atmosphere, it is possible to discover several important ways in which the book's ornamental poetry seems altogether "functional" and necessary. This poetry reveals, not a triumph of manner over matter, but a style of life and speech whose manner is indissolubly part of its matter as expressive of a whole range of courtly and romantic values, feelings, and ideals. Theodore Spencer seems to have had this idea in mind when he urged, in 1945, that

> Sidney's poetry deserves close attention, not only because of its historical importance, but also because it is a striking example, one of the most striking in existence, of the relationship between form and content, convention and passion, experiment and accomplishment.[15]

Spencer did not, unfortunately, explore very far the special "relationship between form and content" which he noticed, but the preceding pages have tried to suggest some of the ways in which a consideration of the *Arcadia*'s ornate style might bear out his claim. The details of individual lyrics, moreover, are equally striking in this respect, and the remainder of this chapter is devoted to a more thorough analysis of how Sidney's formal rhetoric works from line to line, or figure to figure. As much as possible, the poetry is related to the *Arcadia*'s prose in an effort to suggest both the thematic and the stylistic connections between the two.

Perhaps none of the *Arcadia*'s lyrics so obviously tests our responses to the book's poetry as the sonnet which Philoclea sings when she believes Pyrocles has ceased to love her. She relates that "shee had lately with some arte Curyously written" the verses (F, IV. 216), and she accompanies herself on a lute in performing them:

$$\overset{1}{\text{Vertue,}} \overset{2}{\text{beawtie,}} \text{and} \overset{3}{\text{speach,}} \text{did} \overset{1}{\text{strike,}} \overset{2}{\text{wound,}} \overset{3}{\text{charme,}}$$

$$\overset{1}{\text{My harte,}} \overset{2}{\text{eyes,}} \overset{3}{\text{eares,}} \text{with} \overset{1}{\text{wonder,}} \overset{2}{\text{love,}} \overset{3}{\text{delight:}}$$

3*

    1   2   3   1   2   3
First, second, last, did binde, enforce, and arme,
    1   2   3   1   2   3
His workes, showes, suites, with wit, grace, and vow's might.

     1   2   3   1   2   3
Thus honour, liking, trust, much, farre, and deepe,
    1   2   3   1   2   3
Held, pearst, possest, my judgement, sence, and will,
    1   2   3   1   2   3
Till wrong, contempt, deceipt, did growe, steale, creepe,
    1   2   3   1   2   3
Bandes, favour, faith, to breake, defile, and kill.

     1   2   3   1   2   3
Then greefe, unkindnes, proofe, tooke, kindled, tought,
    1   2   3 1   2   3
Well grounded, noble, due, spite, rage, disdaine,
    1 2   3   1   2   3
But ah, alas! (In vayne) my minde, sight, thought,
    1   2   3   1   2   3
Doth him, his face, his words, leave, shunne, refraine,
      1   2   3   1   2   3
For no thing, time, nor place, can loose, quench, ease,
      1   2   3   1   2   3
Mine owne, embraced, sought, knot, fire, desease.

                           (OA 60)

The poem is of just that kind which might easily be dismissed as frivolous or overornamental. We miss the point, however, unless we see Philoclea's sonnet as a self-conscious tour de force, a witty lyric in which Sidney has neatly adjusted a fashionable rhetorical form—"correlative" verse—to suit his own purposes. The wit of the poem, moreover, has been well prepared for. Throughout the scene, we have watched Philoclea's grief with relatively detached amusement for we know that Pyrocles has not betrayed her, that he is, in fact, on his way to join her, and is listening to her sing. The episode is treated in a light comic manner, and Sidney interrupts the narrative several times (once immediately following the song) to comment ironically on his young lovers. The situation and the prevailing tone demand poetry that will not disturb the fine texture of the scene, and Philoclea's "Curyously written" sonnet fulfills this requirement admirably. It is not so much a lyrical expression of personal grief as a miniature narrative that relates the various actions which have created her present plight: the impulse of her original love, reversed by her strong declaration of disdain, followed finally by a wry confession of the fact that nothing can "loose, quench, ease, / Mine owne, embraced, sought, knot, fire, desease." The poem, in other words, provides another example of Sidney's ironic plotting: it juxtaposes two contrary currents of feeling, only to have its reversals come to rest in the witty paradox of the closing lines. Like so much else in the *Arcadia*, it suggests the susceptibility of Sidney's characters to love, the contradictory feelings which love arouses in them, and the air of sophisticated resignation with which they yield to those feelings.

What is particularly interesting in the sonnet is the unusual relationship between form and content, manner and matter, which it reveals. The poem acts out in highly schematic terms the progress of Philoclea's love. It is constructed of two-line "blocks," each of which is a discrete, self-contained unit narrating a separate stage of the total movement. The focus, therefore, is not really on Philoclea herself, but on the particular phases of the poem's action as they follow one another in strict succession. Even within each two-line unit, there is a clear concentration on such schematic plotting. The basic structure, repeated again and again, is a subject-verb-object pattern which aims at imitating the action it describes:

$$\overset{1}{\text{Vertue,}} \overset{2}{\text{beawtie,}} \text{and } \overset{3}{\text{speach,}} \overset{1}{\text{did strike,}} \overset{2}{\text{wound,}} \overset{3}{\text{charme,}}$$
$$\overset{1}{\text{My harte,}} \overset{2}{\text{eyes,}} \overset{3}{\text{eares,}} \ldots$$

$$\overset{1}{\text{Thus honour,}} \overset{2}{\text{liking,}} \overset{3}{\text{trust,}} \overset{1}{\text{much,}} \overset{2}{\text{farre,}} \text{and } \overset{3}{\text{deepe,}}$$
$$\overset{1}{\text{Held,}} \overset{2}{\text{pearst,}} \overset{3}{\text{possest,}} \overset{1}{\text{my judgement,}} \overset{2}{\text{sence,}} \text{and } \overset{3}{\text{will,}} \ldots$$

The verse traces out the line of each action as it develops, rendering its essential structure in skeletal form. The poetry is in this sense fundamentally mimetic: its meanings reside to a large extent in the shapes or patterns created on the page by syntax and rhetoric. The result is a type of verbal iconography: its pleasures derive mainly from an appreciation of the wit and skill with which Sidney manages its complexities. Everything is given external, diagrammatic form, and the speaker, meanwhile, has no real shaping or controlling force in the poem. Philoclea is only the locus where the various forces of virtue, honor, wrong, grief, and disdain come together and vie with one another. She narrates the action, but her speech obviously tells us little about the precise quality of her feelings, or about her personality or character. It is essentially toneless, and lacks completely the more subtle modulations of emotion and response which the freer syntax and diction of conversational language might give. This omission, too, is part of Sidney's intention, and seems a witty consequence of another important aspect of the poem—its vision of the extraordinary power of love, grief, anger, and indeed all human passions. Philoclea is rendered helpless by the tides of conflicting feelings which sweep over her, and that helplessness is neatly expressed by the total subordination of her own voice to the mimetic patterns just examined. To intensify the effect, Sidney has adopted an unusually complicated form of correlative verse in which every major grammatical element of a given sentence is trebled. Since nearly all the sentences have an identical, simplified structure, and since there are as few connectives as possible, the result is a taut, constricted, forceful poem with staccato rhythms and an impelling forward movement. The dense phrasing makes for spondaic meters, and Sidney has purposely loaded the verse with sharp monosyllables:

> Thus hónour, líking, trúst, múch, fárre, and déepe,
> Héld, péarst, possést, my júdgement, sénce, and wíll,
> Till wróng, contémpt, decéipt, did grówe, stéale, créepe,
> Bándes, fávour, fáith, to bréake, defíle, and kíll.

The words grow increasingly strong as the stanza progresses and reach a violent climax in the last line. Sidney's sound effects also come into play to buttress the general impression of power and force: plosives (p), dentals (d, t), backstops (g, k), and fricatives (f) crowd the verse and help to suggest the full turbulence and rigor of the conflict in which Philoclea is involved.

Much of the *Arcadia*'s poetry is written in the mode of "Vertue, beawtie, and speach," and nearly all of it reveals a similar kind of witty congruity between matter and manner. It is certainly exhibitionist verse, but its very artificiality is an important element in the spirit of the book as a whole. And though it often (but not always) treats its themes in a self-consciously witty way, those themes are by no means peripheral or trivial. The violence of love, or of the passions generally, which Philoclea experiences is absolutely central to the *Arcadia*, and Sidney announces the fact in the opening book of his romance: "For yt seemed that Love had purposed, to make in those solitary woodes, a perfect Demonstration of his unresistable force, to shewe that no Dezart place can avoyde his Darte hee must flie from him self that will shonne his evill" (F, IV. 45). The theme has a special relevance, since most of the characters yield to love reluctantly and regard it as a threat to the equable, virtuous life they have previously led. It disrupts the heroic quest of Pyrocles and Musidorus, forces Philoclea to break her vow of chastity, and drives Basilius and Gynecia to near adultery. Musidorus is "wounded with more sodeyn vyolence of Love then ever *Pyrocles* was" (F, IV. 36–37), and Gynecia is a witness to "the Tryumphe of Love, who coulde in one moment overthrowe the harte of a wyse Lady, so, yt neyther Honor longe meynteyned, nor Love of husband and Children coulde withstand yt" (F, IV. 44). Philoclea, meanwhile, is as troubled and tossed in prose as she is in poetry:

> O mee unfortunate wretche (saide shee) what poysonous heates bee these that thus possess mee, how hathe the sighte of this Straunge guest invaded my sowle? Alas what entrance founde this desyer, or what strength had yt, thus to conquer mee? ... O yee starres judge rightly of mee: And yf I have willingly made my self a pray to fancy, or yf by any idle lustes I framed my hart fitt for suche an Impression, then let this plaigue daily increase in mee, till my name bee made odyous in womankynde. But, yf extreme and unresistable vyolence have oppressed mee, who will ever doo any of yow sacrifice O, yee starres, yf yee doo not succour mee? (F, IV. 105–106)

Philoclea uses energetic prose to give vivid expression to her state of mind. Her lyrics maintain a similar heightened quality of feeling, but they employ quite different means of suggesting her powerlessness in the face of passion. Here, for example, is a companion piece to the poem just examined:

The love which is imprinted in my soule
With beautie's seale, and vertue faire disguis'de,
With inward cries putts up a bitter role
Of huge complaintes, that now it is despis'de.

Thus thus the more I love, the wronge the more
Monstrous appeares, long trueth receaved late,
Wrong sturres remorsed greefe, griefe's deadly sore
Unkindnes breedes, unkindnes fostreth hate.

But ah the more I hate, the more I thinke
Whome I doe hate, the more I thinke on him,
The more his matchlesse giftes do deepely sinck
Into my breste, and loves renewed swimme.
What medicin then, can such desease remove
Where love draws hate, and hate engendreth love?

(OA 61)

This sonnet, like the previous one, is less concerned to express the subtle shades and precise qualities of Philoclea's feelings than to plot the way in which those feelings develop and interact. After the expository opening, the second quatrain traces the growth of love into an awareness of "wrong," and from there, the progress is steady to grief, unkindness, and finally hate. This action, moreover, seems entirely autonomous. There is no sense of Philoclea's controlling and directing her feelings; on the contrary, the feelings have an inflexible logic of their own, and seem to operate purely according to their own laws. The rhetoric enforces this impression. Sidney has used anadiplosis in the last two lines of the second quatrain, and the figure has the effect of binding the clauses tightly to one another in a chainlike sequence. Each clause gives rise to the next, and seems to determine it (italics mine here and below):

Wrong sturres remorsed *greefe, griefe*'s deadly sore
Unkindnes breedes, *unkindnes* fostreth *hate.*

But ah the more I *hate,* . . .

The lines thus act out the inevitable course of Philoclea's progress from love to hate, and the third quatrain proceeds to reverse the movement. There, Sidney capitalizes on a device he introduced in lines five and six:

> Thus thus *the more* I love, the wronge *the more*
> Monstrous appeares, . . .

> But ah *the more* I hate, *the more* I thinke
> Whome I doe hate, *the more* I thinke on him,
> *The more* his matchlesse giftes . . .

The continual repetition of "the more" links clauses and makes them seem self-operating; this impression is strengthened particularly by the logical implications of the construction: "the more" one thing happens, "the more"—necessarily and automatically— another thing happens. The very process of hating forces Philoclea to concentrate on Pyrocles, and that in turn brings to mind his "matchelesse giftes," and so on. Hate leads back to love, and the couplet sums up neatly the poem's double action:

> What medicin then, can such desease remove
> Where *love* draws *hate*, and *hate* engendreth *love*?

The chiasmus of the last line, with its reversal of the main nouns, acts out in little the whole process of mutual drawing or engendering which the sonnet's rhetoric has attempted to imitate. And Philoclea —as before—is powerless to control the forceful operation of those feelings which tyrannize over her.

Such strict rhetorical patterning is confined mainly to the *Arcadia*'s verse, but it is worth noting that Sidney often used the devices just mentioned in his prose, as well as elsewhere in the poetry, in order to achieve similar effects:

> *The more* I stirre about urgent affaires, *the more* me thinks the very stirring breeds a breath to blow the coales of my love: *the more* I exercise my thoughts, *the more* they encrease the appetite of my desires.   (F, I. 375)

> But even this arguyng with him self, came to a further thoughte, and *the more* hee argued, *the more* his thoughte increased. (F, IV, 9)

> *suspition* bred the mind of *crueltie*, and the effectes of *crueltie* stirred a new cause of *suspition*.   (F, I. 197)

> Wyth two strange fires of equall heate possest,
> The one of Love, the other Jealousie,
> Both still do worke, in neither finde I rest:
> For both, alas, their strengthes together tie:
> The one aloft doth holde the other hie.
>   *Love* wakes the *jealous eye* least thence it moves:
>   The *jealous eye, the more* it lookes, it *loves.*
>   (Gynecia, OA 22, 1–7)

This moved *Pyrocles* to falle into *questions* of [*Philoclea*], . . . As the moste noble harte ys moste subject unto yt, from *questyons* grewe to *pitty*, and when with *pitty* once his harte was made kinder according to the aptnes of the humor, yt receyved streight a crewell impression of that wonderfull passion, wch . . . ys called *Love.*   (F, IV. 9)

The couplet from Gynecia's lyric (OA 22) is closely related to Philoclea's sonnet in its deft use of chiasmus to suggest the interaction of love and jealousy, and the subdued anadiplosis in the final example gives a nice articulation to Pyrocles' movement through a series of inevitable stages—from questions, to pity, to love. In all such passages, Sidney is concerned with finding a rhetoric to express —sometimes delicately, sometimes wittily, sometimes energetically— the "unresistable force" of human passions. That rhetoric is undoubtedly formal and ornate, but the very stiffness and shape of its patterns are often the key to its meanings or "matter." I need not multiply examples, but at least two other lyrics are worth examining:

> Beautie hath force to catche the humane sight.
> Sight doth bewitch, the fancie evill awaked.
> Fancie we feele, encludes all passion's mighte,
> Passion rebelde, oft reason's strength hath shaked.
>
> No wondre then, though sighte my sighte did tainte,
> And though thereby my fancie was infected,
> Though (yoked so) my minde with sicknes fainte,
> Had reason's weight for passion's ease rejected.
>
> But now the fitt is past: and time hath giv'ne
> Leasure to weigh what due deserte requireth.

All thoughts so spronge, are from their dwelling driv'n,
And wisdome to his wonted seate aspireth.
    Crying in me: eye hopes deceitefull prove.
    Thinges rightelie prizde, love is the bande of love.
                  (Cleophila, OA 57)

Transformd in shew, but more transformd in minde,
I cease to strive, with double conquest foild:
For (woe is me) my powers all I finde
With outward force and inward treason spoild.

For from without came to mine eyes the blowe,
Whereto mine inward thoughts did faintly yeeld;
Both these conspird poore Reason's overthrowe;
False in my selfe, thus have I lost the field.

Thus are my eyes still Captive to one sight:
Thus all my thoughts are slaves to one thought still:
Thus Reason to his servants yeelds his right;
Thus is my power transformed to your will.
    What marvaile then I take a woman's hew,
    Since what I see, thinke, know is all but you?
                  (Cleophila, OA 2)

The first of these poems is organized differently from those already mentioned. Both of Philoclea's sonnets traced a coil-recoil action, with one part of the poem simply reversing the movement of the previous part. But Cleophila's sonnet plays two rather different kinds of movement against one another, in order to suggest the effect of a sudden release from love's power. The first two quatrains use a familiar set of devices to notate the process of falling in love. Anadiplosis binds the sequence of events together, linking beauty to sight, sight to fancy, fancy to passion, and passion to reason. Once the sequence has begun, it proceeds automatically, shaking "reason's strength." In the face of such power, Cleophila finds it is "No wondre" she yielded to passion, and the second quatrain repeats the main terms of the first in precisely the same order. Each of the first eight lines is end-stopped, each is tightly organized rhetorically and acoustically, and each has a strong fourth-syllable caesura. Masculine rhymes alternate with feminine, and there are no deviations from absolutely strict iambics except for the initial reversals in lines one to four—"Béautie," "Síght doth," "Fáncie," "Pássion"—all of which strengthen the impression of rigor and force in the opening quatrains.

The sestet alters everything, suddenly breaking the chainlike action of the octave, and setting a quite different kind of poetry in motion. "But now the fitt is past"—the initial clause, with its clipped monosyllables and abrupt close at the colon, cuts sharply into the poem's established rhythms and signals Cleophila's assumption of control over the passions which have ruled her. The lines begin to breathe. The ninth has the poem's first sixth-syllable caesura, as well as its first enjambment (combined with the striking inversion of "Leasure"). The rhymes are subtly changed from the octave's strong words with dominant backstops and dentals ("mighte," "shaked," "tainte," "infected," "rejected") to the softened end-consonants of the sestet ("giv'ne," "requireth," "prove"). A new kind of fluidity and more relaxed rhythms suggest release from the tight bonds of the octave, and this release is particularly evident in the last three lines:

> And wísdome to his wónted séate aspíreth.
> Crýing in mé: eȳe hòpes deceítefull próve.
> Thìnges rȋghtelie prízde, lŏve is the bánde of lóve.

If the lines are not to be nonsense, they demand to be read more or less as I have scanned them—with italics, so to speak, on "eye," "righte-," and "love." In this way, the passage takes on some of the qualities of conversational speech. Not only does the sestet alter the rhetoric of the octave, but Cleophila's voice asserts itself in such a way as to complicate the pattern of rigid iambics previously established. Freedom from the bonds of passion gives rise to a more dramatic kind of poetry in which the inflections of a speaking voice make themselves clearly felt; and the effect is reinforced by the participle "Crying," which initiates a bold movement across the last quatrain into the couplet. One should notice, however, that the diction is not colloquial, and that the language of the sestet generally remains highly patterned (especially in its balanced alliterations and tautly controlled syntax). Even the metrical variations are carefully restricted. In other words, Sidney has not so much juxtaposed "rhetorical" patterned verse with freer "conversational" poetry as he has created two different sorts of rhetorical patterning: one suggests the constraint and tyrannical power of love, the other a release from that constraint.

The second sonnet (OA 2) works in a related but slightly different way. After the introductory first quatrain, it tells a similar story of defeat at the hands of love: the eyes receive a blow, "inward thoughts" yield to it, and reason is finally overthrown. Here again is a miniature narrative in which the "I" of the poem surrenders to powers which have a dominant rhetoric of their own. Unlike the other lyrics I have examined, however, this one is entirely one-directional: it uses tight logic and a correlative scheme to suggest the irreversible quality of passion's conquest. The sequence of eyes-thought-reason is repeated in the third quatrian, where each line is controlled by a strong "Thus"; and the couplet acts both as a logical "conclusion" to the whole and as the collector of the main correlative terms:

> What marvaile then I take a woman's hew,
> Since what I see, thinke, know is all but you?

See, think, and know are parallel to eyes, thought, and reason; and Cleophila-Pyrocles ends the poem with a witty proof: since love is inescapable, and since a beautiful woman has transformed him inwardly, is not his disguise as a beautiful Amazon a natural expression of this transformation? Thus the main structures of meaning in the sonnet all work to buttress one another in the last lines: the rhetorical scheme collects itself, the logic reaches final conclusion, and both of these elements have a self-contained, inevitable quality which suggests the prisonlike, enclosed world of love.

Not all of the *Arcadia*'s verse lends itself to this kind of analysis, but a great many of the poems do indeed seem to have been conceived in ways like those I have just discussed. David Kalstone has recently shown how the rhetoric of two other sonnets (OA 14 and OA 21) works to suggest "the unbreakable circle of desire,"[16] and several other examples could be adduced. In all of them, Sidney has played with elaborate rhetorical, logical, and syntactical patterns, trying to elicit from them a range of meanings implicit in their very shape or structure. Scaliger had described correlative verse as that in which "verba ipsa modo regunt: ubi inter se respondent" ("the words themselves govern the measure and, in effect, respond to one another").[17] Hoskins noted that, in anadiplosis, the last word of one sentence "*begetts* the next Clause" (my italics).[18] Sidney grasped and capitalized upon the inherent qualities of both devices, and he used them to create a self-governing, self-begetting poetry which related closely to his theme of love's "unresistable force." The result was verse which emphasizes, not the assertive tones and complex shades of feeling of individual, dramatic voices, but the autonomous, inevitable movement of omnipotent desire.

The evidence of the poems themselves is the best argument for adopting such an approach to Sidney's rhetoric, but Elizabethan commentators offer helpful suggestions by way of corroboration. Puttenham, Fraunce, Hoskins, and others rarely talk extensively (or incisively) about the use of specific figures, but occasionally they say something revealing. They never doubt that all schemes and devices—even the most elaborate ones—are intended to be functional, and that their function is to convey "meaning." Hoskins is certain that "in speech there is noe repeticion wthout importance,"[19] and Puttenham, in the course of discussing some bad verse, mentions what kinds of importance one might legitimately expect:

> *To loue him and loue him, as sinners should doo.*

> These repetitions be not figuratiue but phantastical, for a figure is ever vsed to a purpose, either of beautie or of efficacie: and these last recited be to no purpose, for neither can ye say that it vrges affection, nor that it beautifieth or enforceth the sence, nor hath any other subtilitie in it, and therefore is a very foolish impertinency of speech, and not a figure.[20]

Figures can be employed to persuade (for "efficacie"), but also to beautify or "enforce" the sence and achieve certain kinds of "subtilitie." These last uses, as Puttenham explicates them, turn out to be very similar in their action to those noticed in Sidney. In prosonomasia, for example,

> Ye haue a figure by which ye play with a couple of words or names much resembling, and because the one seemes to answere / th'other by manner of illusion, and doth, as it were, nick him, I call him the *Nicknamer.* . . . As, *Tiberius* the Emperor, because he was a great drinker of wine, they called him by way of derision to his owne name, *Caldius Biberius Mero,* insteade of *Claudius Tiberius Nero:* . . . But euery name geuen in iest or by way of a surname, if it do not resemble the true, is not by this figure, . . . Now when such resemblance happens betweene words of another nature, and not vpon mens names, yet doeth the Poet or maker finde prety sport to play with them in his verse, specially the Comicall Poet and the Epigrammatist. Sir *Philip Sidney* in a dittie plaide very pretily with these two words, *Loue* and *liue,* thus.

> *And all my life I will confesse,*
> *The lesse I loue, I liue the lesse.*[21]

It is hard to take all of Puttenham's prattle very solemnly, but the point he makes nonetheless does tell us something about the kinds of "subtilitie" which Elizabethans looked for in their rhetoric. Sidney's play on love-live works because his lines suggest the close dependency of one upon the other: they tend to equate "living" with "loving," and this identity between the two actions is highlighted by the near identity of sounds in the two words. The success of the figure depends, in other words, on the metaphoric relationship it suggests between formal elements—in this case, sounds—and "content" or meaning. This is true of a great many so-called auricular figures. Quintilian made a similar point in his own discussion of paronomasia. He gave the example, "Non *emissus* ex urbe, sed *immissus* in urbem esse videatur" ("He would seem not so much to have been sent out from, but to have been launched against, the city").[22] Such sentences "distinguish the exact meaning of things" and are "better still and more emphatic when our pleasure is derived both from the figurative form and the excellence of the sense."[23] In effect, figurative form reinforces sense, very much as it does in

Sidney's lines. Puttenham, to offer one more instance, defined antimetavole as taking

> a couple of words to play with in a verse, and by making them to chaunge and shift one into others place they do very pretily exchange and shift the sence, as thus.

> *We dwell not here to build us boures,*
> *And halles for pleasure and good cheare:*
> *But halles we build for us and ours,*
> *To dwell in them whilest we are here.*[24]

Puttenham points out that the reversed order of words in his lyric underlines and imitates the reversed meanings, and the technique is not very different in principle from Sidney's various kinds of reversals:

> What medicin then, can such desease remove
> Where love draws hate, and hate engendreth love?

> Love wakes the jealous eye least thence it moves:
> The jealous eye, the more it lookes, it loves.

That such lines are light, courtly, and witty no one would deny. But that their rhetoric is consequently unfunctional or awkwardly obtrusive does not at all follow. The very obtrusiveness of figures like anadiplosis and chiasmus is, as has been seen, essential to Sidney's whole conception of the *Arcadia*'s high style. Exploiting the inherent or potential meanings latent in their patterns gives rise to the various kinds of effects which Puttenham mentioned as a major "purpose" of formal rhetoric. Certainly it never occurred to the Elizabethans themselves that Sidney's rhetoric was in any sense overdecorative. The pages of Puttenham, Hoskins, Fraunce, and others are crowded with examples from the *Arcadia*—examples intended to show the proper uses of schemes and devices for the purpose of achieving grace, beauty, efficacy, and "subtilitie."

CHAPTER VI

Style as Convention

❦

I

Once the *Arcadia*'s artificial, rhetorical manner has been accepted
as a mature style with clearly defined and perfectly legitimate aims
of its own, one is in a better position to generalize more broadly
about its technical means, particularly about its prosody. Recent
study has done much to define Sidney's crucial role in the development of English metrics, but there has been essentially no discussion
of the uses to which Sidney actually put his meters, little mention of
the motives which prompted his experiments, and no comment on
the interesting relationship between meter and rhyme as Sidney conceived of them. This chapter will concentrate primarily on the
Arcadia's prosody, relating it generally to the qualities and purposes
of the book's ornate style. That style, as already suggested, is
characterized by its rigorous exclusion of colloquial diction or conversational speech, its relative lack of tonal complexity, its unconcern
with any significant expression of individual character or personality, and its reliance on a highly developed repertoire of rhetorical
devices. Such a style might well be called "conventional": not as
Theodore Spencer used the term to describe the *Arcadia*'s poetry
—the sense in which the pastoral is said to be a convention—
but as one might use it to characterize the stylized movements of
classical theatre or ballet, where a cultivated artificiality of gesture
and expression is a primary vehicle of meaning. Sidney, as is suggested in the preceding chapter, uses his rhetorical schemes very
much as fixed structures or patterns—gestures—which work both to
convey quite precise meanings and to create a more general manner,

a courtly bearing and atmosphere, for his characters and their tale. The prosody of the *Arcadia*, like the rhetoric to which it is so closely related, is equally an integral part of the book's meaning and manner. It is carefully tailored to suit particular needs, and the following pages attempt to suggest what those needs were, and how Sidney tried to meet them.

Before dealing directly with problems of meter and rhyme, it is important to remember that not all of the *Arcadia*'s ornate verse relies on the particular schemes and figures described in the last chapter. Some of the poems are much less concerned to trace witty verbal patterns than to capture—although in a very special way—the moods and emotions of various characters. In the three sestinas (OA 70, OA 71, and OA 76), the corona *dizaine* (OA 72), and some of the *terza rima* (OA 30 and OA 75), Sidney was clearly writing an energetic, moving poetry capable of communicating the over-whelming grief of Plangus, the anguish of Strephon and Klaius, and the hopelessness of all Arcadians as they lament the death of Basilius. It is extraordinarily effective verse, rich in its orchestration of feelings, and in its ability to build power slowly through ordered and carefully altered repetitions. It uses rhetorical schemes, not mimetically or "iconographically," but for the purposes of incantation:

> *Strephon.*   But ah her flight hath my dead reliques spent,
> Her flight from me, from me, though dead to me,
> Yet living still in her, while her beames lent
> Such vitall sparke, that her mine eyes might see.
> But now those living lights absented be,
> Full dead before, I now to dust should fall,
> But that eternall paines my soule have hent,
> And keepe it still within this body thrall:
> That thus I must, while in this death I dwell,
> In earthly fetters feele a lasting hell.

> *Klaius.*   In earthly fetters feele a lasting hell
> Alas I doo; from which to finde release,
> I would the earth, I would the heavens sell.
> But vaine it is to thinke those paines should cease,
> Where life is death, and death cannot breed peace.

O faire, ô onely faire, from thee, alas,
These foule, most foule, disastres to me fell;
Since thou from me (ô me) ô Sunne didst passe.
Therefore esteeming all good blessings toyes,
I joy in griefe, and doo detest all joyes.

(OA 72, 81–100)

This is a superbly musical poetry of incantation, rather different from the shorter lyrics examined in the last chapter. The reader is no longer attending to logical or rhetorical "structures" so much as he is caught up in a music where the words seem scarcely to matter. Quite apart from anything else, the lines reveal how tightly Sidney has interwoven rhetorical and prosodic elements: the modulated rise and fall of the rhythms, the carefully placed run-on lines, the perfectly regular iambics, the dense alliteration and assonance, the apostrophes and exclamations, the corona device linking stanzas, the repeated rhymes carried from one stanza to the next—all combine to create a hypnotic poetry of grief. Heavy and retarded, yet fluid and continuous in its movement, it is fully expressive of that mood of elegiac weariness which pervades so much of the *Arcadia*'s closing books. Yet despite the difference between such verse—with its impetus of powerful human feeling—and that of the *Arcadia*'s shorter lyrics, there is obviously a fundamental similarity between the two. The expressive techniques Sidney developed in the stanzas quoted above are clearly as stylized and "conventional," as remote from the ordinary world of speech and gesture, as are the anadiplosis, chiasmus, and elaborate correlative schemes of the sonnets. The apostrophes and exclamations, for example, are never merely spontaneous cries. Under Sidney's hand, they are shaped and patterned into ritual form—polished, dignified, and controlled:

O faire, ô onely faire, from thee, alas,
These foule, most foule, disastres to me fell;
Since thou from me (ô me) ô Sunne didst passe.
Therefore esteeming all good blessings toyes, . . .

The method is operatic, and the lines recall countless similar ones throughout the *Arcadia*:

But yet, alas! O but yet alas!

No, no: Despaire my dayly lesson saith, . . .

And shall (ô me) all this in ashes rest?

As oh! my selfe, . . .

Thus, thus, alas, I had my losse in chase . . .

But, but alas, like a man condemn'd . . .

Justice, justice, is now (alas) oppressed: . . .

Not only are particular gestures and exclamations given stylized and conventional form, but the larger movements of several elegiac poems are equally patterned. All three of the *Arcadia*'s sestinas, for instance, have a similar structure. They begin in a mood of low-keyed, ritualistic invocation:

> Since wayling is a bud of causefull sorowe,
> Since sorow is the follower of evill fortune,
> Since no evill fortune equalls publique damage: . . .
> (OA 70, 1–3)

> Yee Gote-heard Gods, that love the grassie mountaines,
> Yee Nimphes which haunt the springs in pleasant vallies,
> Ye Satyrs joyde with free and quiet forrests, . . .
> (OA 71, 1–3)

> Farewell ô Sunn, *Arcadia's* clearest light:
> Farewell ô pearl, the poore man's plenteous treasure:
> Farewell ô golden staffe, the weake man's might: . . .
> (OA 76, 1–3)

As each poem progresses, the rigid line-by-line syntax of its opening stanzas is abandoned for something more expansive: lines are en-jambed, and the syntax is suspended to two, three, or more lines in a given stanza. Meanwhile, the curve of feeling in all three sestinas rises gradually toward a powerful climax. Insistent repetitions, a highly constricted syntax, and sharp exclamations suddenly transform the tone and movement of the verse:

> O nature doting olde, ô blinded nature,
> How hast thou torne thy selfe! sought thine owne damage!
>
> . . . .
>
> O that we had, to make our woes more publique,
> Seas in our eyes, and brasen tongues by nature,
> A yelling voice, and heartes compos'd of sorow,
> Breath made of flames, wits knowing nought but damage,
> Our sports murdering our selves, our musiques wailing,
> Our studies fixt upon the falles of fortune.
>
> (OA 70, 19–20 and 25–30)

> I wish to fire the trees of all these forrests;
> I give the Sunne a last farewell each evening;
> I curse the fidling finders out of Musicke:
> With envie I doo hate the loftie mountaines;
> And with despite despise the humble vallies:
> I doo detest night, evening, day, and morning.
>
> (OA 71, 49–54)

> No, no, for ever gone is all our pleasure;
> For ever wandring from all good direction;
> For ever blinded of our clearest light;
> For ever lamed of our suerest might;
> For ever banish'd from well plac'd affection;
> For ever robbed of our royall treasure.
>
> (OA 76, 25–30)

After the climax, emotion quickly subsides, and each of the poems ends on a more subdued note, returning generally to the somber tones with which it had begun. The codas which conclude the sestinas rehearse the rhyme words in their original order, and Sidney has reinforced this closing effect in two of the poems (OA 70 and

OA 76) by having the final lines echo the opening ones. Like the corona *dizaine* (OA 72), they end by taking us back to their beginnings.

Sidney, then, has in a group of related poems created a strikingly similar shape or pattern of lamentation. Both the particular gestures and larger movements of feeling of such verse are sufficiently stylized to be termed "conventional." The speakers vary, and even the occasions, but the techniques for expressing emotion, and the curve which emotions follow, remain extraordinarily similar from poem to poem. As in any set of conventions, human feelings are here given precise, objective forms—are embodied, really, in the strict rhetorical and syntactical patterns which define the *Arcadia*'s ornate style.

Such an account of Sidney's general technique provides the necessary context for approaching the *Arcadia*'s prosody. Equally indispensable are Sidney's own remarks, which occur near the end of the *Apologie*:

> Now, of versifying there are two sorts, the one Auncient, the other Moderne: the Auncient marked the quantitie of each silable, and according to that, framed his verse: the Moderne, observing onely number (with some regarde of the accent), the chiefe life of it standeth in that lyke sounding of the words, which wee call Ryme. Whether of these be the most excellent, would beare many speeches. The Auncient (no doubt) more fit for Musick, both words and tune observing quantity, and more fit lively to expresse divers passions, by the low and lofty sounde of the well-weyed silable. The latter likewise, with hys Ryme, striketh a certaine musick to the eare: and in fine, sith it dooth delight, though by another way, it obtaines the same purpose: there beeing in eyther sweetnes, and wanting in neither maiestie. . . .
>
> Nowe, for the ryme, though wee doe not observe quantity, yet wee observe the accent very precisely; which other languages, eyther cannot doe, or will not doe so absolutely. That *Caesura*, or breathing place in the middest of the verse, neither Italian nor Spanish have, the French and we never almost fayle of. Lastly, even the very ryme it selfe the Italian cannot put in the last silable, by the French named the Masculine ryme, but still in the next to the last, which the French call the Female; or the next before that, which

the Italian terme *Sdrucciola*. The example of the former, is *Buono*, *Suono*, of the *Sdrucciola*, *Femina*, *Semina*. The French, of the other side, hath both the Male, as *Bon*, *Son*, and the Female, as *Plaise*, *Taise*. But the *Sdrucciola* hee hath not: where the English hath all three, as *Due*, *True*, *Father*, *Rather*, *Motion*, *Potion*; . . .   (*Apologie*, 60–61)

Several points are important here. First, Sidney is interested in the technical means by which poetry can "expresse divers passions," and he is fully aware of the important role which prosody plays in this respect. At the beginning of the opening paragraph, he finds classical meters, with their play of "low" and "lofty" sounds, to have a greater expressive range than English ones. By the end of the paragraph, however, he has decided that rhyme is able to create similar effects in English verse, striking "a certaine musick to the eare," full of either "sweetnes" or "maiestie." Moreover, Sidney clearly understands the role that accent plays in shaping the internal structure of English verse lines, and his way of putting the matter suggests that he expects to capitalize on the "precision" of control possible in this regard. Finally, he finds English uniquely suited to all three major forms of rhyme—the masculine, feminine, and *sdrucciola*—a fact that must have been of great importance to a poet who was so obviously interested in the musical and expressive powers of prosody. Taken together, these remarks have considerable bearing on all of Sidney's poetry, but particularly on that of the *Arcadia*. There, Sidney uses all three kinds of rhyme, sometimes in a single poem, and his main concern is to discover ways in which they can be made to "expresse divers passions." He does so, and with a formal precision that is altogether conventional, in the specific sense in which I have been using that term. In the eclogues, especially, he treats rhyme very much as an aspect of rhetoric: shifts of key or mood are effected by an alteration of rhyme scheme, just as they are by a change from one kind of syntax to another, or from invocation to apostrophe or exclamation. Rhyme, in other words, becomes another important, functional element in the *Arcadia*'s special style, and is always worth careful attention. This is not, one should perhaps say, the usual view of Sidney's rhymes. Theodore Spencer saw them mainly as another example of Sidney's willingness to "experiment," although he added that "sometimes, if only briefly, the modulation from one kind to another produces an extra rhythmical vibration which is musically effective."[1] William Empson and David Kalstone have illuminated Sidney's technique by suggesting how the use of the *sdrucciola* in the double sestina helps to create that poem's mood of despair, but neither of them has explored Sidney's rhymes much beyond that.[2] William Ringler has seen the feminine rhymes mainly as a "regularly recurring structural element," and occasionally as "an ornamental variation."[3] In addition, he interprets the singing match between Lalus and Dorus (OA 7), where there is a great deal of rhyme-changing, as a virtuoso competition between the shepherd Lalus and the disguised courtier Dorus.[4] Lalus, underestimating his antagonist, begins with the *sdrucciola*, but is unable to sustain the form; he soon descends to feminine rhymes, and finally, wearied, to the simple masculine. Dorus' responses, meanwhile, are so skillfully and easily managed that poor Lalus is continually forced to fly in sheer desperation to increasingly simple forms.

The poem is undoubtedly competitive and exhibitionist in spirit, and Mr. Ringler's view of it is clearly legitimate, although sometimes difficult to sustain in its details. It is Dorus the skillful courtier, not Lalus the shepherd, who first gives up the complex *sdrucciola* for feminine rhyme (at line 71); and his reasons for doing so seem to have at least as much to do with the poem's subject matter as with his possible lack of prowess. From the beginning of the eclogue, the verse has been decorus and ceremonial. The singers offer formal celebration and praise to their ladies, and the rhymes are suitably elaborate. Sidney employs only the *sdrucciola* throughout the first seventy lines, although by line twenty-five he has already established an important distinction between Lalus' and Dorus' use of the form. Lalus' rhymes are more colloquial, and are frequently split between two words; Dorus' rhymes, on the other hand, generally retain an air of courtly elegance—they are almost invariably trisyllabic and Latinate:[5]

> *Lalus.*   A heape of sweetes she is, where nothing spilled is;
> Who though she be no *Bee*, yet full of honie is:
> A *Lillie* field, with plowe of *Rose* which tilled is.
> Milde as a Lambe, more daintie then a Conie is: . . .

Dorus.   Such *Kala* is: but ah, my fancies raysed be
        In one, whose name to name were high presumption,
        Since vertues all, to make her title, pleased be.
        O happie Gods, which by inward assumption
        Enjoy her soule, in bodie's faire possession,
        And keep it joynde, fearing your seate's consumption.
        How oft with raine of teares skies make confession, . . .

              (OA 7, 28–31 and 37–43)

The rhymes, then, help to maintain the *Arcadia*'s fundamental distinction between the verse of shepherds and that of courtiers. Yet despite differences in the two passages above, they have an important quality in common: both speakers offer only rather generalized praise of their ladies. Lalus' metaphors, though sensuous and homely, are given in simple, catalogue form; and Dorus' lines are highly abstract, formal, ritualistic. Pamela is never named, and she remains remote and unapproachable. We feel this distance particularly strongly just before the sudden change to feminine rhymes— a change that is accompanied by a very different vision of love:

Dorus. Her eyes so maistering me, that such objection
        Seemde but to spoyle the foode of thoughts long famished.
        Her peereles height my minde to high erection
        Drawes up; and if, hope fayling, ende live's *pleasure*,
        Of fayrer death how can I make election?

Lalus.   Once my well-waiting eyes espied my *treasure*,
        With sleeves turnde up, loose haire, and brestes enlarged,
        Her father's corne (moving her faire limmes) measure.
        'O' cried I, 'of so meane worke be discharged:'

   .   .   .   .

        These bolde words she did heare, this fruite I reaped,
        That she, whose looke alone might make me blessed,
        Did smile on me, and then away she leaped.

          (OA 7, 68–76 and 82–84, my italics)

Dorus' unobtrusive shift from the *sdrucciola* to feminine rhyme prepares for the much more intimate and personal tones to come. The sudden scene of Kala with "loose haire," and the obvious involvement of Lalus, alter our perspective, and the change of rhyme

m odifies the rhythm of the lines in such a way as to harmonize with
that alteration. We feel immediately the quick "drop" from the
elevated Petrarchan mode of Sidney's courtier-prince to the warmer,
more relaxed pastoral vision of the shepherd. Similar tonal considerations determine a later shift to masculine rhyme, and when the
speakers begin to sum up, Lalus introduces so-called medial rhyme.
As he does so, he envisions the future of pastoral plentitude and bliss
he expects to share with Kala:

> Constant and *kind*: my sheep your foode shall *breed*,
> Their wooll your *weede*, I will you Musique *yeeld*
> In flowrie *fielde*; and as the day *begins*
> With twenty *ginnes* we will the small birds *take*,
> And pastimes *make*, as Nature things hath *made*.
> But when in *shade* we meet of mirtle bowes,
> Then Love allowes, our pleasures to enrich,
> The thought of which doth passe all worldly pelfe.
>> (OA 7, 123–30, my italics)

One main purpose of the passage is to establish a rhythm of easy
flow and measured pause that is suggestive of Arcadia's pastoral
harmonies, and Sidney's pattern of rhymes—rather than the particular meanings of rhyme words—is an extremely important factor
in creating that rhythm. The second line runs over and stops at the
medial rhyme of the third ("fielde"); then that line too is enjambed,
but carries through to the very end of the fourth. The next has a
medial pause, and is also end-stopped. A very delicate and carefully
modulated rhythm is regulated, now to retard the flow, now to give
a sense of freedom by having the rhyme word skipped over. "Weede,"
"fielde," and "make" restrain the movement of the lines; "ginnes"
and "shade" are by-passed, and the effect is to make us aware of a
sudden release from bonds. Taken as a whole, the passage articu-
lates beautifully the rhythms of freedom and control underlying
Arcadia's life of pastoral love and pastime.

Dorus' rhymes are used altogether differently. By contrast, he
expects little but pain and grief from love:

> My foode is teares; my tunes waymenting yeeld:
> Despaire my fielde; the flowers spirits' warrs:

My day newe cares; my ginnes my daily sight,
In which do light small birds of thoughts orethrowne:
My pastimes none: time passeth on my fall:
Nature made all, but me of dolours made:
I finde no shade, but where my Sunne doth burne:
No place to turne; without, within it fryes:
Nor helpe by life or death who living dyes.

(OA 7, 138–46)

Here, the rhythms and syntax are clogged, the phrasing constricted, and everything is under the restraint imposed by sorrow. All the lines are end-stopped, and all but two have strong medial punctuation. The effect is to convey persuasively the pain and despair which Dorus feels, and the heavy stress upon the rhymes makes them emphatic signals of his grief. They are thrown into sharp relief, and the frequent alliteration on the rhyme words ("teares"-"tunes," "fielde"-"flowers") gives them even stronger force. Sidney has created, in other words, a stylized liturgy of lamentation, in which the rhymes play a major part, as a counterpoint to the freer movements of Lalus' verse.

Sidney uses the threefold rhyme system mentioned in the *Apologie* in three other poems, and their procedure is very similar to that of the Lalus-Dorus dialogue. A particularly striking example of tonal change occurs, for example, in the Dicus-Dorus eclogue (OA 28). Dorus is concluding a passage of praise to his lady:

Thus then (I say) my mischiefes have contributed
A greater good by her divine reflection;
My harmes to me, my blisse to her attributed.
Thus she is framde: her eyes are my direction;
Her love my life; her anger my Instruction;
Lastly what so she be, that's my protection.

(OA 28, 67–72)

The *terza sdrucciola* here is the proper form for courtly complaint and ceremonial praise, and the effect is again heightened by the use of formal, Latinate rhyme words. Nearly all the lines have a strong fourth-syllable caesura, and the balanced syntax creates a controlled,

4+

graceful rhythm appropriate to Petrarchan celebration. But Dicus
the shepherd replies:

> Thy safetie sure is wrapped in destruction:
> For that construction thy owne wordes do beare.
> A man to feare a woman's moodie eye,
> Or Reason lie a slave to servile Sense,
> Theere seeke defence where weakenesse is the force:
> Is Late remorse in follie dearely bought.
>
> (OA 28, 73–78)

The abrupt move to decasyllabics with masculine medial rhyme has
the force of a musical change of key. Dicus bluntly breaks in upon
the refinements of Dorus' verse, and the sudden flatness of his monosyllables is precisely right for the satiric and argumentative passage
which follows. Again, the particular meanings of the individual
rhyme words are not especially important. The change of form is
what matters, and it is just this concern for formal characteristics
which gives the rhymes—and so many other elements of the *Arcadia*'s
ornate poetry—their "conventional" nature. The effort, as much as
possible, is to have the forms speak for themselves. Just as certain
rhetorical figures or syntactical patterns are used, so too the rhymes
are manipulated. And like the rhetorical figures, they are frequently
employed en bloc to help build cumulative power or simply to stress
that the same "kind" of verse or the same tone of voice is continuous
in a given passage.

To demonstrate this technique more carefully, it may be helpful
to examine a single poem in some detail. The Boulon-Plangus dialogue (OA 30) is particularly interesting from this point of view,
because of the great variety of its rhyme changes. Both speakers use
masculine rhyme (with one minor deviation) for the first 125 lines
of their exchange. The tone is argumentative, high-pitched, yet
colored by Plangus' mixture of grief and defiance. The rhymes are
suitably strong. Plangus sees men as simply

> Balles to the starres, and thralles to Fortune's raigne;
> Turnd from themselves, infected with their cage,
> Where death is feard, and life is held with paine.

Like players plast to fill a filthy stage,
　　Where chaunge of thoughts one foole to other shewes,
　　And all but jests, save onely sorrowe's rage.
　　　　　　　　　　　　　　　(OA 30, 17–22)

Boulon is at last moved to pity Plangus:

Thy wailing words do much my spirits move,
　　They uttred are in such a feeling fashion,
　　That sorrowe's worke against my will I prove.
Me-thinkes I am partaker of thy passion,
　　And in thy case do glasse mine owne debilitie:
　　Selfe-guiltie folke must prove to feele compassion.
　　　　　　　　　　　　　　　(OA 30, 125–30)

The transition to newly awakened sympathy is marked by a change
to the *terza sdrucciola*, with its weaker, falling rhythms. Both speakers
continue in this form for several lines, but as Plangus begins his
powerful peroration (lines 149–66), he shifts to simpler and (by
comparison) stronger feminine rhymes:

Can I forget, from how much mourning plainfulnes
　　With Diamond in window-glasse she graved,
　　'*Erona* dye, and end this ougly painefulnes'?
Can I forget in how strange phrase she craved
　　That quickly they would her burne, drowne, or smother,
　　As if by death she onely might be saved?
Then let me eke forget one hand from other:
　　Let me forget that *Plangus* I am called:
　　Let me forget I am sonne to my mother, . . .
　　　　　　　　　　　　　　　(OA 30, 155–63)

The feminine rhymes contrast sharply with the weaker group
("disdainfulnes," "Plainfulnes") which precedes them, and they
gain added strength from the fact that they are all dissyllables
("graved," "other," etc.). The passage moves toward an extraordinarily forceful conclusion, and Boulon responds to it with a
formal lament for "poore man." He too uses feminine rhymes, but
he alters them interestingly:

Who still doth seeke against himselfe offences,
    What pardon can availe? or who employes him
    To hurt himselfe, what shields can be defenses?
Woe to poore man: ech outward thing annoyes him
    In divers kinds; yet as he were not filled,
    He heapes in inward griefe, that most destroyes him.
Thus is our thought with paine for thistles tilled:
    Thus be our noblest parts dryed up with sorrow:
    Thus is our mind with too much minding spilled.
                              (OA 30, 167-75)

Unlike Plangus' feminine rhymes, Boulon's are not dissyllables. The new elegiac tone he introduces is accompanied by unusually weakened feminine forms—so weakened that they seem at first glance to be examples of the *sdrucciola*. The rhyme is frequently broken between two words ("employes him," "annoyes him"), and the last stress of each line is diminished by being buried in the interior of a word ("offénces"; contrast "she gráved"). As Boulon continues, however, he becomes sterner. The emphatic repetitions in the last triad quoted signal his change of mood: "Thus is . . . Thus be . . . Thus is." And it is just at this point that Sidney switches to more forceful dissyllabic rhymes: "tilled," "sorrow," "spilled." Few passages show more dramatically how much he was concerned to correlate rhetorical and prosodic elements in his verse, or how much his rhymes are an integrated part of the *Arcadia*'s formal, conventional rhetoric.

At this stage, a synopsis of a large section of the Boulon-Plangus eclogue may help to make the point even more clearly:

RHYME WORDS

Plangus (lines 110-24)

axe	reclaimes	sprent
flames	face	smart
lackes	hart	spent
frames	place	love
grace	part	bent

Boulon (lines 125–42)

move	abilitie	rightfulnes
fashion	proportion	superfluities
prove	facilitie	sightfulnes
passion	extortion	incongruities
debilitie	delightfulnes	lamentations
compassion	portion	congruities

Plangus (lines 143–66)

consolacyons	contained be	smother
fiction	placing her	saved
exclamations	disdainfulnes	other
affliction	unlasing her	called
maintained be	plainfulnes	mother
malediction	graved	thralled
restrained be	painefulnes	senses
displacing her	craved	unappalled

Boulon (lines 167–76)

offences	annoyes him	tilled
employes him	filled	sorrow
defenses	destroyes him	spilled
		morrow

The first group of rhyme words (Plangus: lines 110–24) are all (but one) monosyllables, and they accompany an equally strict rhetorical pattern: nearly every line begins with a strong apostrophe ("O Mars," "O Venus," etc.), and the rhymes are clearly intended to reinforce the exclamatory strain of the rhetoric. Sidney's main purpose throughout the passage is to capture the violence of Plangus' grief and outrage. The next group (Boulon: lines 125–42) are trisyllabic, and at first alternate "ion" and "ie" endings, varying the pattern slightly toward the end. Boulon's tone of sympathy and sorrow accords with these weaker rhymes. Toward the close of the passage, however, he begins to chide Plangus, and the "congruities" rhyme expresses some of the sharpness of his new manner. The third group (Plangus: lines 143–66) introduce weaker forms of the *sdrucciola* ("maintained be") to emphasize Plangus' grief in contrast to the Latinate polysyllables of Boulon's reproof ("incongruities," "congruities"). As Plangus becomes more defiant, he uses strong dissyllables ("graved"). Finally, Boulon laments again with weakened feminine rhymes ("offences") and finishes more stiffly with stronger ones ("tilled"). In the last lines of the poem, he and Histor both return to the mono-syllabic, masculine rhymes with which Plangus had opened the eclogue.

Quite apart from anything else, such a synopsis suggests how stylized Sidney's treatment of rhyme tends to be, and it stresses the importance of the "kind" of rhyme, used en bloc, as opposed to the individual rhyme words. Shifts in rhyme are frequently integrated with major rhetorical shifts, and both work together to produce the strange, impersonal, moving poetry which Sidney designed for so much of the *Arcadia*. Discovering and articulating the rationale for any particular rhetorical device, or rhyme change, is always a difficult and often a baffling venture. But one can perhaps account for enough of Sidney's practice to know that he was rarely arbitrary or merely decorative in such matters. Certainly there is his own testimony to suggest that the *Arcadia* rhymes were intended to "strike a certaine musick to the eare." Capable of both "sweetnes" and "maiestie," they were fashioned to do for English rhythms what quantity achieved for classical verse: "lively to expresse divers passions." One could scarcely demand a more functional view of them.

2

To turn from rhyme to meter is to raise rather more complicated problems. Fortunately, Mr. John Thompson has recently clarified a great deal in the study of Elizabethan metrics, and his main con-clusions seem generally unimpeachable.[6] His argument is far too dependent upon a close analysis of prosodic details to permit very easy summary, but a brief résumé of some relevant points is essential. Primarily, Thompson sees the main intention of mid-Tudor prosody as a "regularizing" one. Gascoigne first recognized the fact that English poetry aspired, so to speak, to an iambic pattern which the language could approximate or embody in its alternation of slack and stress syllables. Before Gascoigne, English prosody was an un-conscious art. Iambic lines were in fact written, but neither poets nor theorists fully realized (or at least ever articulated) the role that stress played as a determinant of meter. Gascoigne made the important distinction between the metrical norm and the actual language of a given line of verse, and he pinpointed the means by which language might approximate that norm. He himself failed to appreciate the more interesting implications of this discovery. Having defined the basis of English prosody, he proceeded to recommend a perfectly regular iambic line as a model, warning fellow poets to take care "to place every worde in his natural *Emphasis* or sound." Both the demand for regularity and for natural emphasis are clear in the following passage from the "Certayne notes":

> my meaning is, that all the wordes in your verse be so placed as the first sillable may sound short or be depressed, the second long or elevate, the third shorte, the fourth long, the fifth shorte, &c. For example of my meaning in this point marke these two verses:

> I understand your meanyng by your eye.
> Yoùr mèanìng Í ùndérstànd bý yòur éye.

> In these two verses there seemeth no difference at all, since the one hath the very selfe same woordes that the other hath, and yet the latter verse is neyther true nor pleasant, & the first may passe the musters. The fault of the latter verse is that this worde *understand* is therein so placed as the grave accent falleth upŏ *der*, ... which is contrarie to the naturall or usual pronuciation: ... [7]

Natural accent and perfect regularity of meter are thus the goals. An important addition, I should note, is that Gascoigne considers monosyllables to be "indifferent": that is, they are either long (stressed) or short (slack) depending purely upon what the meter demands.

Gascoigne's application of his own formula was competent but hardly imaginative. A stanza from "The arraig[n]ment of a Lover" may be taken as fairly typical:

> At Beautyes barre as I dyd stande,
> When false suspect accused mee,
> *George* (quod the Judge) holde up thy hande,
> Thou art arraignde of Flatterye:
> Tell therefore howe thou wylt bee tryde?
> Whose judgement here wylt thou abyde? [8]

According to Gascoigne's own scheme, there are no metrical irregularities in these lines. He has taken care to place his monosyllables so that they fit tamely into the iambic pattern:

> as Í dyd stánde, . . .

> hówe thou wýlt bee trýde?

> judgement hére wylt thóu abyde?

The only line in which we feel potential tension between the iambic norm and a "natural" reading of the words is the third:

> Geórge (quod the Júdge) hólde ùp thy hánde, . . .

We might well be tempted to scan the line in this way, following the emphases which conversation would force upon it. But according to Thompson (and Gascoigne himself), we ought to resist the temptation. Since monosyllables are "indifferent," they must simply conform to the requirements of the meter. We should read with absolute regularity, so that "the first sillable may sound short or be depressed, the second long or elevate, the third shorte, the fourth long, the fifth shorte, &c."

The final effect of Gascoigne's stanza is curious. For though his diction and phrasing are closer to ordinary speech than much of Sidney's in the *Arcadia*, his verse is obviously far more monotonous and lifeless. There are any number of reasons for this, but one surely is the fact that the discrepancy in Gascoigne between the rigid formality of the regular meter and the relative informality and naturalness of the language is simply too great. "Conversational" speech measured out by a dull metrical rule finally achieves neither the flexibility of actual speech nor the accomplished artificiality of verse which intentionally avoids the familiar. Sidney, by contrast, experimented with a number of effects in the *Arcadia* and found several suggestive ways of putting Gascoigne's regular meters to work:

> Transformd in shew, but more transformd in minde,
> I cease to strive, with double conquest foild: . . .
>
> (OA 2, 1–2)

My true love hath my hart, and I have his,
By just exchange, one for the other giv'ne.

(OA 45, 1–2)

Loved I am, and yet complaine of Love:
As loving not, accus'd, in Love I die.

(OA 20, 1–2)

O hand, which toucht her hand when we did part;
  O lippes, that kist that hand with my teares sprent;
  O toonge, then dumbe, not daring tell my smart; . . .

(OA 30, 119–21)

Yee Gote-heard Gods, that love the grassie mountaines,
Yee Nimphes which haunt the springs in pleasant vallies,
Ye Satyrs joyde with free and quiet forrests, . . .

(OA 71, 1–3)

But ah her flight hath my dead reliques spent,
Her flight from me, from me, though dead to me,
Yet living still in her, while her beames lent
Such vitall sparke, that her mine eyes might see.

(OA 72, 81–84)

The very artificiality of Sidney's medium, in these passages, not only absorbs but also capitalizes upon the strictness of the meters. In the first three examples above, courtly balance and control require the even pace of a regular rhythm. Variety is achieved by the easy play of one half line against another, by the pointed contrasts of "shew" and "minde," or "Loved" and "Love." The entire success of the manner depends upon its distance from the diction and rhythms of ordinary speech. In the fourth example, the gradual build-up of energy and feeling is achieved by steady repetition—by the consistency of rhetorical figure, syntactical structure, and metrical pattern from line to line. In the fifth example, different sorts of repetition are used to create the monotone of elegy, and the regular beat of the meter, with its light fall in the feminine rhymes, obviously plays a major role in this achievement. Finally, in the last passage, another

4*

kind of elegiac weariness is created by the more fluid, yet constantly retarded, rhythms of a poetry that turns its major phrases over and over again in a trancelike way. Sidney has inherited and perfected Gascoigne's system, exploiting its formal characteristics in such a manner as to convert liabilities into advantages.

The illustrations above do not by any means suggest the full range and variety of Sidney's metrical and rhythmical experimentation in the *Arcadia*. They do indicate, however, that he used the iambic pattern as a fixed form very much as he used the formal devices of rhetoric and rhyme. He accepted the structure intact and proceeded to discover whatever expressive potentialities it seemed to possess in itself. As Thompson has remarked:

> In the poems of the *Arcadia*, Sidney brings to perfection the exact, regular correspondence of features of the language to the same features in the metrical pattern. He does this with a thoroughness of organization unknown before in modern English.[9]

The iambic form is filled, and it is put to as many uses as skillfully controlled but perfectly regular meters may be put. For instance, varied line lengths and carefully weighted vowels modify the rhythms in order to produce the restrained but graceful lyricism of Basilius' madrigals:

> Why doost thou haste away
> O *Titan* faire the giver of the daie?
> Is it to carry newes
> To Westerne wightes, what starres in East appeare?
>
> (OA 52, 1–4)

Or varied and frequent pauses alter the phrase lengths and help to establish a mood and tone appropriate for love:

> O Night, the ease of care, the pledge of pleasure,
> Desire's best meane, harvest of hartes affected,
> The seate of peace, the throne which is erected
> Of humane life to be the quiet measure, . . .
>
> (OA 69, 1–4)

The second line here introduces a slight variation—the inversion of the iambic pattern created by the dissyllable "harvest." Thompson has calculated the frequency of such polysyllabic inversions in the *Arcadia*'s verse: they are relatively rare, and are used so strictly that they simply become another "part of [the] ordered system."[10]

The interested reader may seek out the *Arcadia*'s variety for himself. I need here only stress that the meters are used with due regard for their inherent formal characteristics. Like Sidney's rhetorical figures, they retain their own shape and give no sense of being strongly molded by the tones of an emphatic, personal voice. By shifting the caesura, varying the line lengths, or using enjambment, Sidney discovers fresh rhythms in poem after poem of the *Arcadia*. But they are intentionally formal rhythms, and their patterns frequently have a way of seeming like a species of program music:

> *Lalus.*   Constant and kind: my sheep your foode shall breed,
> Their wooll your weede, I will you Musique yeeld
> In flowrie fielde; and as the day begins
> With twenty ginnes we will the small birds take, . . .

> *Dorus.*   My foode is teares; my tunes waymenting yeeld:
> Despaire my fielde; the flowers spirits' warrs:
> My day newe cares; my ginnes my daily sight, . . .
>   (OA 7, 123–26 and 138–40)

The contrast is effective, but clearly schematic. Sidney has constructed an artificial pattern, or established something like a convention, for his opposed visions of blissful and painful love. And once Dorus' pattern of pauses after the medial rhyme word has been set, it is pursued with as much consistency as his previous trisyllabic rhymes or his repetitive invocations.

3

The preceding discussion has been primarily concerned with exploring ways in which Sidney capitalized upon the fact that, in English poetry, "though wee doe not observe quantity, yet wee observe the accent very precisely." This next section suggests that there is another kind of music in the *Arcadia*'s verse—a more complex, irregular music that Sidney was only beginning to understand and

develop. The point is of some historical interest, in addition to whatever light it sheds upon Sidney's own work. For English prosody
changed rapidly in the relatively short time that elapsed between the
writing of the *Arcadia* and the *Astrophel and Stella*, and Sidney himself
seems to have been responsible for the change. John Thompson has
demonstrated the point, but in doing so, he has drawn a firm line
between the *Arcadia*'s absolutely regular meters and the freer system
of *Astrophel*.[11] The former force language into the pattern of the
iambic foot and line; in the latter, the accents and emphases of
natural speech shape the verse in such a way that metrical inversion
becomes an expected part of it. A tension is thus established between speech—the lines read as we might speak them in conversation—and the iambic metrical norm (which, once set, we carry in
our head). In short, we begin to hear in *Astrophel* the kind of counterpoint which is so important to the music of Shakespeare and Donne.

The crucial factor in the creation of such counterpoint is the
handling of monosyllables. In the *Arcadia*, Sidney's phrasing (like
Gascoigne's) is such that the monosyllables are distributed in strict
conformity to the iambic pattern:

> Or dóost thou thínke that héare
> Is léft a Súnne, whose béames thy pláce may úse?
> Yet stáy and wéll perúse, . . .

(OA 52, 5–7)

The significant words are placed so as always to coincide with the
meter's regular accent. There is no tension between the language and
the normative iambic pattern. The lack of tension is so general,
moreover, that it persuades us to regard perfect regularity as
Sidney's intention. If a line seems metrically ambiguous, therefore,
Thompson suggests that we treat it like the others: we should smooth
it over and make it conform to the pervasive pattern. The result may
be slightly awkward, but the system of the *Arcadia* seems to demand it.

Thompson's conclusions are undoubtedly mainly correct, but
they also make it difficult to account for the sharp change from the
Arcadia's practice to that of *Astrophel*. Much of Sidney's experimental
verse is very likely lost, and his earliest efforts in the new meter have
no doubt suffered that fate. Yet it would be odd if we could find no

convincing hint of the later rhythms in all of the *Arcadia*'s (and the *Certain Sonnets*') several thousand lines.[12] In fact, Thompson himself singles out one such hint from the Lalus-Dorus eclogue:

> Seen, and unknowne; heard, but without attention.
>
> [OA 7, line 179]

> It has the ring of speech. Word for word, however, it does fit the metrical pattern, even the exact iambic pattern. Furthermore, even if it is considered to have metrical departures, the departures are of a kind that Sidney establishes so carefully as the only permissible ones that they are a part of his ordered system for the correspondence of language and metrical pattern. Its real departure from the kind of line Sidney writes in the *Arcadia* is the break in the smooth flow of the line caused by the reversal of stress in the third foot together with the pause after *heard* demanded by the powerful likeness to speech.[13]

It is difficult to agree entirely with Thompson's analysis here. What makes the quoted line interesting is the fact that its monosyllables are arranged in such a way that they refuse to fit tamely into the normal iambic pattern, and the effect seems intentional. Thompson suggests that "word for word" the line "does fit the metrical pattern, even the exact iambic pattern." But of course monosyllables always *can* be made to do so if one assumes that they are "indifferent" and that they take whatever value the metrical norm forces upon them. Even the supple lines of *Astrophel*, which Thompson cites to show that "the stresses of the language may depart from the [iambic] pattern in any way,"[14] can be regularized if one so desires:

> And stáid pléasd with the próspect òf the pláce, . . .
> And stáid pleasd wíth the próspect óf the pláce, . . .
>
> (AS 20, 10)

The point about the *Arcadia* line which Thompson quoted is that it works precisely like the lines of *Astrophel*, with one important exception: its monosyllables do indeed create speech rhythms which break up the iambic norm, but those rhythms themselves are more highly patterned than the flexible ones of *Astrophel*. The first and third feet of the line are inverted, the syntax is obtrusively balanced, and the metrical play is thus closely integrated with other kinds of verbal play. In other words, the technique of creating inversion through monosyllables shaped by speech accent is that of *Astrophel*, but the uses of such inversion accord generally with the ornate, patterned mode of the *Arcadia*'s formal style.

If one can accept this proposition, a good number of lines in the *Arcadia* make clearer sense than they might otherwise. And the single line which Thompson mentioned can be related to others like it:

> Blóts to the stóne, sháme to my sélfe I fínde: . . .
>
> (OA 19, 4)

> Lìve lóng, and lóng wítnesse my chósen smárte,
> Which bárde desíres, (bárde by my sélfe) impárte.
>
> (OA 47, 10–11)

> While thát my sóule, shḗ, shé lives ìn afflíction; . . .
>
> (OA 30, 146)

None of these lines is precisely the same as that which Thompson noticed, but all have a sharp medial break, strongly patterned rhetoric and syntax, and strong monosyllables which seem to demand speech accents that conflict with the regular iambic pattern. In the second example, metrical and rhetorical play are very neatly correlated in both lines, and the necessary inversion forced by the dissyllable "witnesse" seems intentionally followed up by that of "barde by." In the last example, commas set off the first "she" very much as they had set off "Seen" and "heard" in Thompson's line. But again, the inversions here have none of the free, supple quality of *Astrophel*'s. They are treated, rather like Sidney's rhymes, as an aspect of the *Arcadia*'s rhetoric.

Perhaps the best way of appraising Sidney's management of such metrics is to examine a single poem in some detail, while trying to bring examples from other poems to bear upon specific points:

> Loved I am, and yet complaine of Love:
> As loving not, accus'd, in Love I die.
> When pittie most I crave, I cruell prove:
> Still seeking Love, love found as much I flie.

Búrnt in my sélfe, I muse at others' fire:
What I call wrong, I doo the same, and more:
Bárd of my wíll, I have beyond desire:
I waile for want, and yet am chokte with store.
 Thís is thỹ wòrke thòu Gód for ever blinde:
Though thousands old, a Boy entit'led still.
Thus children doo the silly birds they finde,
With stroking hurt, and too much cramming kill.
 Yet thús mùch Lóve, O Lóve, I cráve of thée:
Lét me be lóv'd, or èls nŏt lóved bé.

(OA 20)

The iambics here are essentially regular throughout the opening
quatrain, except for the very first foot of the first line. As the sonnet
develops, however, the tone becomes more forceful, and the images
more violent. The reversals at "Burnt" and "Bard" reinforce
Pyrocles' growing indignation, and ask for a vigorous reading.
Sidney often uses strong monosyllables in this position (reinforced
frequently by alliteration or repetition) to achieve similar effects:[15]

Blést be the náme, wherewith my mistres named is: . . .

(OA 28, 55)

Bálles to the stárres, and thrálles to Fortune's raigne;
Túrnd from themsélves, infected with their cage, . . .

Cúrst be gòod háps, and cúrst be they that build . . .

Tórne with her hánds, and those same hands of snow . . .

Búrnt by the Súnne, she first must build her nest.

(OA 30, 17–18, 41, 45, and 103)

Less forceful but related effects are to be found even in some of the
Arcadia's more muted lyrics:

Cáre upon cáre (in steede of doing right)

.   .   .   .

(Tíde to the stáke of dóubt) strànge pássions baite,
While thy known course, observing nature's right,
Stúrres me to thínke what dangers lye in waite.

> For míscheefes gréate, dáye after dáy doth shówe:
> Màke me stìll féare, thy fáire appearing showe.
>
> (OA 56, 7 and 10–14)

> Bítter grìefe tástes me bést, páine is my éase,
> Sícke to the déath, still loving my disease.
>
> (OA 41, 7–8)

Not only is the first foot of several lines inverted here (emphasized, again, by frequent alliteration or repetition): the first example also has an inversion of the third foot, and the second an inversion of the fourth foot. In each of these cases, the inversion follows a strong caesura, and the speech accents which ruffle the iambic pattern are themselves integrated into a larger formal rhetorical structure.

Returning to Pyrocles' sonnet (OA 20), one can see that the whole poem turns on the sudden cry of accusation which opens the sestet: "Thís is thẙ wòrke, thòu Gód . . ." Exposition and narrative burst into drama, and the lines force "This" and "thy" into sharp relief. Both words are given italic stress, so to speak, and the technique is similar to that used in the couplet:

> Yet thus much Love, O Love, I crave of thee:
> Let me be lóv'd, or els nŏt lóved be.

The play of "lov'd" against "not loved" forces the "not" into special prominence and thus alters the regular stress pattern of the meter. The effect is not so much that of conversation as of a momentary introduction of speech emphasis to create rhythmic play analogous to the verbal play which the lines delight in. Sidney used this particular kind of counterpoint several times:

> And wisdome to his wonted seate aspireth.
> Crýing in mé: eyẙ hòpes deceitefull prove.
> Thìnges rẙghtelie prízde, lŏve is the bánde of lóve.
>
> (OA 57, 12–14)

> Párt of my lífe, the loathed part to me,
> Líves to impárt my wearie clay some breath.
> But thàt goŏd pàrt, wherein all comforts be,
> Now dead, doth shew departure is a death.

Yeà wórse then déath, dĕath pàrts both woe and joy,
From jóy Í pàrt still living in annoy.

(CS 20, 9–14)

But this she thinks, oŭr páine hỳe cáuse excuseth,
Where hér who shóuld rŭle pàine, fălse páine abúseth.

(CS 11, 13–14)

All of these passages require a more complex reading than smooth, regular stressing if they are to make any sense at all. Their main intention seems to be to create a form of limited counterpoint which now coincides with, now runs counter to, the pattern of verbal repetitions and oppositions created by the rhetoric.

"Limited" is the important word here. Sidney seems in such lines to be discovering that the music of English verse can be more various than he had perhaps realized. Moreover, if the passages quoted do indeed demand the kinds of reading just suggested, they also reveal precisely the sort of irregularity we might expect: they are controlled by Sidney's rhetorical manner, and seem really to be a natural outgrowth of it. An initial awareness of the possibilities of monosyllabic stress variation might well have been born in such restricted contexts, where the need to make emphatic distinctions between "lov'd" and "not loved," for example, brought the tones of a speaking voice into conflict with the established iambic pattern.[16]

Puttenham may provide an interesting corroboration of this point. According to the chronology worked out by Walker and Willcock, Puttenham's second discussion of meter was written sometime after Stanyhurst's translation of the *Aeneid* (1582), but probably before 1585.[17] There, Puttenham discusses the regular iambics recommended by Gascoigne and makes some revealing remarks in scanning them:

Now furthermore ye are to note, that al your *monosyllables* may receiue the sharp accent, but not so aptly one as another, as in this verse where they serue well to make him *iambicque*, but not *trochaick*.

Gŏd grāunt thĭs pēace mă̆y lōng ĕndūre

Where the sharpe accent falles more tunably vpon [*graunt*] [*peace*] [*long*] [*dure*] then it would by conuersion, as to accent them thus:

Gŏd grăŭnt-thĭs pĕace-mā̆y lŏng-ĕndŭre,

> And yet if ye will aske me the reason, I can not tell it, but that it
> shapes so to myne eare, and as I thinke to euery other mans.[18]

Puttenham, like other sixteenth-century writers before him, knows by
instinct the relative weights of stress among monosyllables in
sequence. He can line them up properly to make passable iambics,
but he is still a step away from realizing that strength of accent in
such circumstances is determined by the relative significance of the
various words in a given phrase or sentence. The accents of his
quoted line cannot be reversed because our conversational habits,
trained by our sense of significance, will not permit them to be.
Gascoigne had earlier stated that monosyllables were utterly "indifferent"; Puttenham has gone further and, while declaring them to
be theoretically indifferent, he realizes that they are not absolutely
so. Yet he has no notion why. He does not quite recognize the importance of speech accent as a determinant of stress among monosyllables, and he shows no clear indication of considering the
different values among monosyllables to be a potential source of
poetic richness. Another passage reveals, however, that he does in
fact respond to certain kinds of metrical variety very similar to those
I have noticed in Sidney:

> many times ye must of necessitie alter the accent of a sillable, and
> put him from his naturall place, and then one sillable, of a word
> *polysillable*, or one word *monosillable*, will abide to be made some-
> times long, sometimes short, as in this *quadreyne* of ours playd in a
> mery moode.

> > *Gèue mé mìne ówne ànd whén Ì dó dèsíre*
> > *Geue others theirs, and nothing that is mine |*
> > *Nòr gíue mè thát, . . .*

Where in your first verse these two words [*giue*] and [*me*] are
accented one high th'other low, in the third verse the same words
are accented contrary, and the reason of this exchange is manifest,
because the maker playes with these two clauses of sundry relations
[*giue me*] and [*giue others*] so as the *monosillable* [*me*] being respectiue
to the word [*others*] and inferring a subtilitie or wittie implication,
ought not to have the same accent, as when he hath no such respect, as in this *distik* of ours.

Prōūe mĕ (*Madame*) ere ye rēprŏue
Meeke minds should ēxcŭse not āccŭse.

In which verse ye see this word [*reprooue,*] the sillable [*prooue*]
alters his sharpe accent into a flat, for naturally it is long . . . & so
is the sillable [*cuse*] in [*excuse*] . . . yet in these verses by reason one of
them doth as it were nicke another, . . . it behoveth to remoue the
sharpe accents from whence they are most naturall, to place them
where the nicke may be more expresly dicouered, . . .[19]

Puttenham's awareness of shifting the accent in certain restricted
contexts in order to "discouer" the "nickes" of rhetorical play suggests that Sidney may very well have had similar intentions in mind
in passages like those noticed earlier. The play of "Proue" and
"reproue," or "excuse" and "accuse," produces a self-conscious
form of italicized stressing which closely resembles Sidney's balance
of "lov'd" and "not loved," or "our paine" and "false paine."
Indeed, Sidney in 1579–1581 and Puttenham in 1582–1585 may be
thought of as being in analogous stages of prosodic awareness:
neither seems to have a full sense of the role speech accent plays or
might play in determining the metrical stress of monosyllables, but
both show an interest in certain kinds of metrical counterpoint
closely associated with rhetorical patterning.[20]

4

Before concluding this chapter, some remarks concerning Sidney's
use of sound-play may be in order. The subject is a complicated one,
but a few observations may help to suggest at least something of his
practice in the *Arcadia*. Generally, the book's sound effects, like so
many other aspects of Sidney's poetic vocabulary, are intentionally
obtrusive and highly patterned. Much of the time, the patterns are
simply one more element in an artificial, ceremonial style:

Muse hold your peace: but thou, my God *Pan*, glorifie
My *Kala's* giftes: who with all good gifts filled is.
Thy pipe, ô *Pan*, shall helpe, though I sing sorilie.

(OA 7, 25–27)

You goodly pines, which still with brave assent
In nature's pride your heads to heav'nwarde heave,
Though you besides such graces earth hath lent,
Of some late grace a greater grace receave, . . .

(OA 49, 1–4)

Occasionally, however, sound works to set a mood:

Locke up, faire liddes, the treasures of my harte:
Preserve those beames, this age's onely lighte:
To her sweete sence, sweete sleepe, some ease imparte,
Her sence too weake to beare her spirit's mighte.

(OA 51, 1–4)

These stately starrs in their now shining faces,
With sinlesse sleepe, and silence, wisdome's mother,
Witnesse his wrong which by they helpe is eased: . . .

(OA 69, 9–11)

In both stanzas, liquids and sibilants are used overtly to invoke the
relaxed and hushed atmosphere of night and love. The lines show
clearly the deliberate formality of Sidney's method: the alliteration
and assonance are extremely heavy, and they act both as legitimate
ornament and as an expressive, evocative element in the verse.
Sidney, moreover, could be dissonant as well as harmonious:

When pittie most I crave, I cruell prove:

.   .   .   .

Burnt in my selfe, I muse at others' fire:
What I call wrong, I doo the same, and more:
Bard of my will, I have beyond desire:
I waile for want, and yet am chokte with store.
This is thy worke, thou God for ever blinde:
Though thousands old, a Boy entit'led still.
Thus children doo the silly birds they finde,
With stroking hurt, and too much cramming kill.

(OA 20, 3 and 5–12)

The forceful, climactic line here is the last one, and every one of its
major sounds has been carefully prepared for. A good deal of energy

is created by the sequence Burnt-Bard-blinde-Boy-birds, but the key phrases are "With stroking hurt" and "too much cramming kill." One can see how much calculation has gone into their preparation:

						*c*rave
					wi*ll*	cruell
*w*ill		Burn*t*			wa*ile*	cho*k*te
*w*aile		wan*t*			st*ill*	wor*k*e
*w*ant	*s*tore	chok*te*	*c*hokte	*c*rave	chi*l*dren	stro*k*ing
*w*orke	*st*ill cho*k*te	ent*it*'led	*c*hildren	*c*ruell	sil*l*y	*c*ramming
WITH	*ST*RO*K*ING	HUR*T* and	*T*OO	MU*C*H	*C*RAMMING	*K*ILL

The violence of the actions and the onomatopoeic suggestiveness of the consonants produce something that is both witty and effective. The sound patterns are intentionally obtrusive, and they take their place in the poetry as a part of its special rhetorical mode. Perhaps more than anything else, they show the full extent to which Sidney has integrated all the elements of his poetic vocabulary to fit the requirements of the *Arcadia*'s ornate, conventional style.

CHAPTER VII

The Drama of Philisides

❦

IT WAS SUGGESTED earlier that the *Arcadia* contains evidence of a dramatic, plain style which is intimately related to that of *Astrophel*: "plain" in its free use of colloquial or conversational diction and syntax, and in a relative absence of ornate rhetoric; "dramatic" in its power to create a strong impression of dialogue—of individual speaking voices or characters engaged in meditation, discussion, or debate. There is a great deal of such poetry in the *Arcadia*, although it is—according to the decorum of the work—largely restricted to the eclogues involving shepherds:

> Downe, downe *Melampus*; what? your fellow bite?
> I set you ore the flock I dearly love,
> Them to defend, not with your selves to fight.
>
> . . . .
>
> What if *Laelaps* a better morsell fyndes
> Then thow earst knew? rather take part with him
> Then jarle: lo, lo, even these how envie blindes.
>
> (OA 10, 1–3 and 7–9)
>
> Kisse her? now mayst thou kisse. I have a fitter match;
> A prettie curre it is; . . .   (OA 29, 39–40)

Despite its awkwardness, this is verse in which the speaking voice has essentially been liberated. The syntax and rhythms are no longer controlled by formal rhetorical patterns. The lines are broken internally, end-stopped, or else freely enjambed, depending purely upon the changing tones and responses of each speaker. The diction is perfectly ordinary and even colloquial, sharp rhetorical questions and exclamations help to energize the lines, and the final impression is that of lively, explosive dialogue. In short, the intentions and the effects of such poetry are fundamentally different from those of the *Arcadia*'s ornate, conventional verse. The fact that both modes exist side by side in the original version of Sidney's pastoral romance obviously has important implications for any discussion of his development—implications which this and the following chapter will attempt to elucidate.

One of the most interesting points concerning the *Arcadia*'s dramatic style is that Sidney reserved its use, not only for his shepherds, but also for his own fictional counterpart, Philisides. Like nearly all of Sidney's heroes, Philisides is a type of the young courtier, reared by noble parents, learned, and trained for a life of virtuous action. He comments of himself: "bycause the myndes Commaundement ys vayne withoute the body bee enhabled to obay yt, my strengthe was exercysed with Horsmanship, weapons, and suche other qualityes, as besydes the practize carryed in them selves some servisable use" (F. IV, 312).[1] As in the case of Pyrocles and Musidorus, love enters suddenly, diverting Philisides' "Course of Tranquility," and breaking the "untrubled Tenor of a well guyded lyfe" (F. IV, 313). He becomes a shepherd, withdraws to Arcadia, and haunts the periphery of Sidney's tale in melancholy isolation. His poetry, however, is anything but somber:

Philisides:	*Echo:*
Faire Rocks, goodly rivers, sweet woods, when	
shall I see peace?	Peace.
Peace? what barrs me my tongue? who	
is it that comes me so ny?	I.
Oh! I do know what guest I have	
mett; it is Echo.	'T is Echo.
Well mett Echo, aproche: then tell	
me thy will too.	I will too.

(OA 31, 1–4)

The Latin meters and the restrictions of the echo format make this a rather special poem, but it shows clearly enough the informal, vigorous, conversational manner that is typical of Philisides. The

dialogue, moreover, becomes increasingly lively as the poem develops: Echo plays the role of a lighthearted cynic discrediting love,
and Philisides is presented as youthful, volatile, and determined:

> What great name may I give to
> so heav'nly a woman?   A woe-man.
> Woe, but seems to me joy, that agrees to
> my thought so.   I thought so.
> Think so, for of my desired blisse it
> is only the course.   Curse.
> Curs'd be thy selfe for cursing that which
> leades me to joies.   Toies.
>
> (OA 31, 37–40)

The argument here recalls some aspects of the debate between
Pyrocles and Musidorus, but the tone is significantly different.
Philisides is no blushing, delicate Pyrocles. He is far more impetuous,
and he relies a great deal on sarcasm and invective. Strong impera-
tives and interrogatives are his nearest tools to hand: "Think so, ... /
Curs'd be thy selfe for cursing that ..." His tone anticipates that of
Astrophel:

> Curst be the night which did your strife resist,
> Curst be the Cochman which did drive so fast, ...
>
> (AS 105, 12–13)

>   your wisdome's golden mine
> Dig deepe with learning's spade, now tell me this,
> Hath this world ought so faire as *Stella* is?
>
> (AS 21, 12–14)

> Why shouldst thou toyle our thornie soile to till?
> Leave sense, and those which sense's objects be:
> Deale thou with powers of thoughts, leave love to will.
>
> (AS 10, 6–8)

Philisides is much less sophisticated and assured than Astrophel, but
it is he who begins to develop that tone of satiric bravado and strong-
minded willfulness which pervades the verse of Sidney's later hero.

We feel this similarity most strongly, perhaps, at the end of the echo poem:

> Tell yet againe me the names of these
>   faire form'd to do ev'lls.   Dev'lls.
> Dev'lls? if in hell such dev'lls do abide,
>   to the hells I do go.   Go.
>
>   (OA 31, 49–50)

> If that be sinne which doth the maners frame,
> . . . .
> If that be sinne which in fixt hearts doth breed
>   A loathing of all loose unchastitie,
>   Then Love is sinne, and let me sinfull be.
>
>   (AS 14, 9 and 12–14)

Even when Philisides' verse is pitched in a rhetorical key closer to that of Pyrocles and Musidorus, one senses his real kinship with Astrophel. He tends to avoid, for example, the courtly niceties which Sidney's other Arcadian heroes feel bound to observe. Pyrocles and Musidorus address very little of their verse directly to Philoclea and Pamela; when they do so, they are properly humble and barely argumentative:

> 'Onely Juell, O only Juell, which only deservest
> That men's harts be thy seate and endlesse fame be thy servant,
> O descende for a while, from this greate height to behold me,
> But nought els do behold (else is nought worth the beholding)
> Save what a worke, by thy selfe is wrought: and since I am altred
> Thus by thy worke, disdaine not that which is by thy selfe done.
> In meane caves oft treasure abides, to an hostry a king comes.
> And so behinde foule clowdes full oft faire starres do ly hidden'.
>
>   (OA 13, 147–154)

Musidorus correctly beseeches Pamela to "descende," and with mild wit he argues that she is obliged to help the lover whose life she has transformed. Philisides, by comparison, is aggressive and full of adolescent fire. He comes armed with a battery of "proofs" which he unleashes:

> O faire, O fairest, are such the triumphs to thy fairnesse?
>   can death beautie become? must I be such a monument?

> Must I be onely the marke, shall prove that Vertue is angrie?
>   shall prove that fiercenes can with a white dove abide?
> Shall to the world appeare that faith and love be rewarded
>   with mortall disdaine, bent to unendly revenge?
> . . . .
> All my'offence was Love: with Love then must I be chastned,
>   and with more, by the lawes that to Revenge doo belong.
> If that love be a fault, more fault in you to be lovely:
>   Love never had me opprest, but what I saw to be lov'd.
> You be the cause that I love: what Reason blameth a shadowe,
>   that with a body't goes? since by a body it is.
>   (OA 74, 31–36 and 41–46)

Even the Latin meters fail to suppress completely the peremptory
tone here. Philisides challenges, demands, and argues with a vehemence which Musidorus and Pyrocles never reveal, and in all these
respects he is much closer to that other strategist, Astrophel. He
plunges forward in a relentless way, occasionally modifying his tone
of fierce insistence with moments of wit and sophistication. Like
Musidorus and Pyrocles, overpowering desire has led him to commit
a "fault"; but his response to such failings is rather different from
theirs:

> O not but such love you say you could have afoorded,
>   as might learne Temp'rance voyde of a rage's events.
> O sweet simplicitie: from whence should Love be so learned?
>   unto *Cupid* that boy shall a Pedante be found?
> Well: but faultie I was: Reason to my Passion yeelded,
>   Passion unto my rage, Rage to a hastie revenge.
> But what's this for a fault, for which such faieth be abolisht,
>   such faith, so staineles, inviolate, violent?
>   (OA 74, 63–70)

Mira's demand for temperance in love is treated lightly as evidence
of her "sweet simplicitie." Since when has Cupid been so pedantic
as to teach lovers perfect self-control? Well, but it was a fault. At
such moments, Philisides comes very close to the witty, self-indulgent
tones noted both in Sidney's letters and in the *Arcadia*'s narrative
asides. The combination of defensiveness, sophisticated self-justifi-

cation, and a charming admission of one's own weakness all look
forward to *Astrophel*:

> Vertue alas, now let me take some rest,
> Thou setst a bate betweene my will and wit,
> If vaine love have my simple soule opprest,
> Leave what thou likest not, deale not thou with it.
>   Thy scepter use in some old *Catoe's* brest;
> Churches or schooles are for thy seate more fit:
> I do confesse, pardon a fault confest,
> My mouth too tender is for thy hard bit.
>
>   (AS 4, 1–8)

Much of Astrophel's energy, like Philisides', is explicitly associated
with his impatience, frustration, and sensuality in love. Both are
rebels against Reason and Virtue, and they duel vigorously with a
series of antagonists who caution temperance or control. If they are
at moments capable of disarming confessions of "fault," they can be
equally brusque and abusive. I have already noticed, in another
context, Philisides' reply to Geron's sage counsel:

> O gods, how long this old foole hath annoi'd
> My wearied eares! O gods yet graunt me this,
> That soone the world of his false tong be void.
> O noble age who place their only blisse
> In being heard untill the hearer dye,
> Uttring a serpent's minde with serpent's hisse.
> Then who will heare a well autoris'd lye,
> (And pacience hath) let him goe learne of him
> What swarmes of vertues did in his youth flye
> Such hartes of brasse, wise heads, and garments trim
> Were in his dayes: which heard, one nothing heares,
> If from his words the falshood he do skim.
> And herein most their folly vaine appeares
> That since they still alledge, *When they were yong*:
> It shews they fetch their wit from youthfull yeares
> Like beast for sacrifice, where save the tong
> And belly nought is left, such sure is he,
> This life-deadman in this old dungeon flong.
>
>   (OA 9, 66–83)

The passage focuses very sharply, not only on Philisides' main qualities of character, but also on the chief characteristics of the *Arcadia*'s plain, dramatic style. The diction is completely informal, and the rhythms freer than anything I have previously examined. There are no dominant rhetorical schemes, and no decorative uses of alliteration. The syntax and vocabulary are always within range of ordinary conversational speech: "this old foole," "swarmes of vertues," "hartes of brasse," "trim," "skim," "fetch," "tong," and "belly." Sentences end abruptly in the middle of lines, many lines are enjambed, and the last two triads are run together—the only instance in the entire *Arcadia* of so free a treatment of *terza rima*. I need hardly point out how different such verse is from that examined in Chapters Five and Six. Its direct connections are not with the mannered lyrics of Pyrocles and Musidorus, or Strephon and Klaius, but with the prose of the shepherd Rixus in *The Lady of May*, and with the poetry of Astrophel. Compare, for example, the following related passages:

> *Rixus.*   O *Midas* why art thou not alive now to lend
> thine eares to this drivle, by the precious
> bones of a hunts-man, he knowes not the
> bleaying of a calfe from the song of a
> nightingale, but if yonder great Gentle-
> woman be as wise as she is faire, *Therion*
> thou shalt have the prize, and thou old
> *Dorcas* with young maister *Espilus* shall
> remaine tame fooles, as you be.
>
> *Dorcas.*   And with cap and knee be it spoken, is it
> your pleasure neighbor *Rixus* to be a wild
> foole?
>
> *Rixus.*   Rather then a sleepish dolt.   (F. II, 334)

> O gods, how long this old foole hath annoi'd
> My wearied eares!
>
> .   .   .   .
>
> And herein most their folly vaine appeares
>
> .   .   .   .
>
> It shews they fetch their wit from youthfull years . . .
>   (OA 9, 66–67, 78, and 80)

Thy scepter use in some old *Catoe's* brest; . . .

(AS 4, 5)

Rich fooles there be, whose base and filthy hart

. . . .

Yet to those fooles heav'n such wit doth impart,

. . . .

But that rich foole, . . .

(AS 24, 1, 5, and 9)

Scarcely any mannerisms are more characteristic of Astrophel than his ironic use of the term "wit" and his satiric use of "fool." Both words appear in conjunction in a number of his sonnets, and it is Philisides (berating Geron) and Rixus (berating the old shepherd Dorcas) who first put them to use. Finally, one should note that the opening line of the *Arcadia* passage just quoted, together with others from the eclogues, provide the first examples in Sidney of Astrophel's later habit of beginning poems abruptly, *in medias res*:

O gods, how long this old foole hath annoi'd
  My wearied eares!   (OA 9, 66–67)

Be your words made (good Sir) of Indian ware,
  That you allow me them by so small rate?

. . . .

  O God, thinke you that satisfies my care?
                  (AS 92, 1–2 and 5)

Alas what falls are falne unto thy minde?
                (OA 9, 32)

Alas, whence came this change of lookes?
                (AS 86, 1)

Downe, downe *Melampus*; what? your fellow bite?
                (OA 10, 1)

Flie, fly, my friends, I have my death wound; fly, . . .
                (AS 20, 1)

Fy man, fy man, what wordes hath thy tonge lent?
(OA 10, 61)

Fy, schoole of Patience, Fy, your lesson is
Far far too long . . .   (AS 56, 1–2)

One source of the dramatic style of *Astrophel*, then, lies in the *Arcadia*'s eclogues, and particularly in the speech of Philisides. The eclogues are largely written in a plain and energetic manner, with all the roughness accorded to them by tradition, and in the young courtier-shepherd one can see some of the aggressiveness, satiric spirit, and eroticism of Astrophel. His poetry is characterized by an expressive colloquial diction, a relatively straightforward syntax, a prosodic freedom, and a minimum of ornate schemes and devices.[2] The combination is an important one: it represents a distinct alternative to the rhetorical, conventional mode analyzed in the previous chapters, and it was obviously to be extremely important in Sidney's later work. It is not, however, precisely the style of *Astrophel and Stella*: it is too plain, and lacks the sense of finish and courtly control which we associate with the polished, witty sonnets of Stella's lover. Philisides is a study for Astrophel, but he is also extraordinarily naive and youthfully impetuous, and these qualities are as much a part of his style as of his character. He and the other shepherds contribute unmistakable, essential elements to the manner of *Astrophel and Stella*, but Sidney was meanwhile developing rather different poetic tones and gestures which were to be equally important for that later work. To discover these, one need only turn to the pages of the *Certain Sonnets*.

CHAPTER VIII

A Courtier's Certain Sonnets

THE *Certain Sonnets* have received no substantial critical attention, although one or two of the lyrics have been regularly included in Elizabethan anthologies. All but the opening two poems appear in a third-state manuscript of the *Old Arcadia*, transcribed probably in 1581. The collection as a whole seems to have been written between 1577 and 1581.[1] It was kept in a loose-leaf notebook, as an apparently personal selection of miscellaneous pieces which Sidney wished to preserve. Two points make them particularly interesting. First, since they were composed while Sidney was also at work on the *Arcadia* verse, they give a clear and important indication of the kind of poetry he was inclined to write informally or privately—outside the strict confines of the pastoral-heroic romance. Second, Sidney seems to have been intrigued by the idea of giving his collection a semblance of dramatic shape or structure. He took the trouble to group the poems according to form and theme in an effort to suggest the growth and final decay of a courtly love affair. Since the lyrics were written over a period of several years, and since their styles sometimes vary according to their forms,[2] the *Certain Sonnets* are obviously not a unified work in the sense that *Astrophel* is. But they possess a kind of order which is too meticulous to be purely accidental. A brief synopsis will be helpful:

CS 1–2.	These are sonnets. The lover yields reluctantly to love, although he declares that, if he is "hardly usde," he will claim the right to rebel. The rebellion in fact takes place in CS 27–32.
CS 3–7.	These are songs, and they develop the themes of the lover's desire and the lady's coldness. CS 3–4 are in identical

stanza forms, and they regret that the lady is "chaste and cruell." The lady is absent in CS 5, and the lover bids desire to be patient in CS 6. The seventh poem manages to accommodate both the lover's frustration and his praise of the lady.

CS 8–11.   These are related sonnets "made when his Ladie had paine in her face." They begin by condemning pain (sickness) for having attacked the lady, but they end on a bitter, satirical note: the poet pities his mistress' suffering, but she is completely indifferent to his.

CS 12–14.   These are translations from the Latin, two of them in Latin meters. They "generalize" the lover's bitterness, dwelling on the mutability of things and on the faithlessness and cruelty of woman.

CS 15–22.   These are sonnets and poems in related lyric (but not song) stanzas. The first compares the lover to a dove as neither free nor bound, and this comparison sets the mood for what follows. Desire has neither waned nor been satisfied, and the result is a state of indecisiveness and suspension. CS 18 and CS 19 show the lover in meditation; CS 20 is "A Farewell," but CS 21 announces the lover's return. CS 22 suggests that "a purest love" must be born of the death of sensual desire.

CS 23–30.   These are songs. Like AS 42 and AS 48, they attempt a Petrarchan resolution of the lover's dilemma: desire is restrained (in response to the suggestion of CS 22), and the lover finds true life in accepting a sacrificial "death" which pays tribute to the lady's virtue (CS 23–26). The balance is a precarious one, however, and CS 27 announces a rebellion, although the lady's weeping brings the lover to submission by the end of the poem. CS 28–29 are translations from Montemayor; CS 28 shows the lover deserted, looking back on lost happiness. CS 30 jubilantly declares that "All love is dead," but it ends again with the lover recanting.

CS 31–32.   These are sonnets, and are clearly intended to complement CS 1–2. They show the lover renouncing desire altogether: "Leave me ô Love" ends both the sequence and the love affair.

The argument for the unity of the *Certain Sonnets* clearly should not be pressed very far.[3] But it seems obvious that Sidney has generally alternated groups of sonnets with groups of songs in the collection, and that each successive group focuses upon a set of related themes or moods. Together, the poems suggest a curve from the narrator's reluctant acceptance of love, through stages of frustration and bitterness, indecisiveness, retraint and "self-sacrifice," to final rebellion. The collection thus probably represents Sidney's first half-random thoughts on the possibility of attempting a lyric sequence, and it indicates—even in its semi-unified state—the general course which his later handling of love themes would take. It reveals, above all, a lover who is a sophisticated strategist, witty in his poetry of compliment and frank in his open avowal of desire. In the very first poem of the sequence, he capitulates to love, but he also moves immediately to strike an advantageous bargain:

> I yeeld, ô Love, unto thy loathed yoke,
> Yet craving law of armes, whose rule doth teach,
> That hardly usde, who ever prison broke,
> In justice quit, of honour made no breach:
> Whereas if I a gratefull gardien have,
> Thou art my Lord, and I thy vowed slave.
>
> (CS 1, 9–14)

This is the voice of a more experienced, self-assured lover than the young courtiers of Arcadia. The speaker of the *Certain Sonnets* never celebrates or implores in the naive, idealistic tones of Pyrocles or Musidorus, and he has far more aplomb than Philisides. His theme is sensual desire, but even in the midst of frustration, he is perfectly capable of appreciating the humor of his predicament:

> I live to pay a mortall fee,
> Dead palsie sicke of all my chiefest parts:
> Like those whom dreames make uglie monsters see,
> And can crie helpe with nought but grones and starts:
> Longing to have, having no wit to wish,
> To starving minds such is God *Cupid's* dish.
>
> (CS 2, 9–14)

5+

Alas she [Philomela] hath no other cause of anguish
But *Thereus'* love, on her by strong hand wrokne,
Wherein she suffring all her spirits' languish,
Full womanlike complaines her will was brokne.
  But I who dayly craving,
  Cannot have to content me,
  Have more cause to lament me,
  Since wanting is more woe then too much having.
(CS 4, 13–20)

Such frank expressions of "craving" recur throughout the sequence. In CS 16a, Dyer writes of a satyr who kissed the fire which Prometheus had brought from heaven, and who never recovered from the burn. The poem is a witty warning to would-be lovers, and Sidney counters in CS 16 with a poem about a satyr who foolishly runs away from a harmless horn:

Even thus might I, for doubts which I conceave
Of mine owne wordes, my owne good hap betray,
And thus might I for feare of may be, leave
The sweete pursute of my desired pray.
  Better like I thy Satyre deerest Dyer,
  Who burnt his lips to kisse faire shining fire.
(CS 16, 9–14)

Finally, in CS 17, the lady "lowers and saith I do not love":

My hand doth not beare witnesse with my hart,
She saith, because I make no wofull laies,
To paint my living death, and endlesse smart:
And so for one that felt god *Cupid's* dart,
She thinks I leade and live too merrie daies.

Are *Poets* then the onely lovers true,
Whose hearts are set on measuring a verse:
Who thinke themselves well blest, if they renew
Some good old dumpe, that *Chaucer's* mistresse knew,
And use but you for matters to rehearse?

> Then good *Apollo* do away thy bowe:
> Take harp and sing in this our versing time:
> And in my braine some sacred humour flowe:
> That all the earth my woes, sighes, teares may know,
> And see you not that I fall now to ryme?
>
> (CS 17, 26–40)

The speaker of the *Certain Sonnets* inhabits a courtly world where ladies expect as a matter of course to be entertained with verses and lovers have sufficient *savoir-faire* to be either nonchalant or, if necessary, obliging. It is an altogether different milieu from Arcadia, where characters are perpetually surprised or embarrassed by love, and where an air of youthful earnestness or delicate shyness prevails in matters of romance. There are, it is true, a handful of lyrics in the *Arcadia* which have something of the spirit of the *Certain Sonnets*: three of Basilius' poems (OA 38, OA 52, and OA 55) and one of Musidorus' (OA 51) possess a similar undertone of erotic wit combined with a certain slickness of argument. But Basilius is a parody of the courtly lover-tactitian, and Musidorus' sonnet is a prelude to his near rape of Pamela. Their lyrics are anomalies in the book as a whole: like those of Philisides, they represent momentary intrusions upon the usually discreet, reverential hymns of praise that we expect from Sidney's young courtiers. What was a minor strain in the verse of the *Arcadia*, however, has become a dominant mode of the *Certain Sonnets*. Urbanity and a form of sophisticated eroticism pervade the sequence, and these are at moments energized by the dramatic vigor and satiric aggressiveness which typify the *Arcadia*'s eclogues.

The four lyrics written "when his Ladie had paine in her face" (CS 8–11) are particularly interesting in this respect. They not only reveal the characteristic tones and qualities of the *Certain Sonnets*, but they also show Sidney treating the sonnet form itself in new and adventurous ways. They open—like so many of Astrophel's sonnets—strongly, abruptly:

> Wo, wo to me, on me returne the smart: . . .

> Thou paine the onely guest of loath'd constraint, . . .

> And have I heard her say, 'ô cruell paine!'
> And doth she know what mould her beautie beares?

This is another manner altogether from that of the *Arcadia*'s sonnets, with their tones of formal complaint and controlled self-analysis. Exclamations and rhetorical questions now animate the verse, and even the less vivid opening of the second example above is striking in its directness of address when compared to the more ritualistic invocations of Philoclea's or Musidorus' lyrics:

> O Stealing time the subject of delaie,
> (Delay, the racke of unrefrain'd desire) . . .
> > (Philoclea, OA 53, 1–2)

> You goodly pines, which still with brave assent
> In nature's pride your heads to heav'nwarde heave, . . .
> > (Musidorus, OA 49, 1–2)

Philoclea's and Musidorus' apostrophes remain simply apostrophes —mere gestures of invocation. But the speaker of the *Certain Sonnets* initiates genuine dialogue: "Thou paine . . ."; "And have I heard her say, . . ." He has a sense of audience, and like the characters of the *Arcadia*'s eclogues, he is free with terms of direct address. Moreover, self-dramatization becomes for him an important method of persuasion; resentment and oblique accusation mixed with compliment are quickly discovered to be a convenient means of provoking response:

> And have I heard her say, 'ô cruell paine!'
> And doth she know what mould her beautie beares?
> Mournes she in truth, and thinks that others faine?
> Feares she to feele, and feeles not others' feares?
> Or doth she thinke all paine the minde forbeares?
> That heavie earth, not fierie sprites may plaine?
> That eyes weepe worse then hart in bloodie teares?
> That sense feeles more then what doth sense containe?
> No, no, she is too wise, she knowes her face
> Hath not such paine as it makes others have:
> She knows the sicknesse of that perfect place
> Hath yet such health, as it my life can save.

> But this she thinks, our paine hye cause excuseth,
> Where her who should rule paine, false paine abuseth.
>
>   (CS 11)

The lover of the *Certain Sonnets* generally refuses to play the role of humble servant. He never declares, as does Musidorus, that "her anger [is] my Instruction" (OA 28, 71). Rather, he asks, with obvious irony, whether his mistress considers his suffering to be mere pretense, and his marshalled, impetuous interrogatives are really a development of Philisides' belligerent methods:

> O faire, O fairest, are such the triumphs to thy fairnesse?
>   can death beautie become? must I be such a monument?
> Must I be onely the marke, shall prove that Vertue is angrie? . . .
>   (Philisides, OA 74, 31–33)

Despite similarities, however, the differences between the two are important. Philisides is never quite in full command of his situation: he is much too naive and too subject to his own uncontrollable feelings. If he reveals occasional flashes of a more sophisticated wit ("O sweet simplicitie"), he fails to sustain the tone. We are never really certain whether his arguments are earnest attempts at persuasion, clever tactics, or both. The lover of the *Certain Sonnets* presents no such difficulty. If the octave of his sonnet seems to sway indeterminately between controlled irony and uncontrolled resentment, the sestet resolves everything. Answering his own questions, he suggests that his lady knows precisely how much suffering she causes, and he then levels a final barb at her in the couplet. The argument has been thoroughly planned from the beginning. Everything is carried off with perfect assurance, and while the poem is not entirely graceful in its execution, it represents an extremely significant fusion: the dramatic energy of a Philisides has come together with the sophistication of an experienced courtly lover in a sonnet which manages to combine strong feeling, self-conscious wit, and complete control. The style is one of the middle range: it is responsive to the rhythms and pressures of a speaking voice, but it is also courtly in its balance, its verbal play, its concern for the surface of the verse. Essentially, it unites elements of both the high and the low styles examined in the

Arcadia, in the interest of creating a poetic version of courtly conversation: artificial and self-conscious, yet still fluid and natural;
witty, calculated, and strategical, yet also full of vigorous feeling. It
is, in fact, the mode of a courtier writing *in propria persona* for an
audience of friends and acquaintances, and it was to become
the conversational style of Astrophel himself: more poised than the
volatile manner of Philisides, and more complex and supple than the
ritual manner of Pyrocles and Musidorus. Thus while Sidney was
writing the *Arcadia* and adjusting his style to meet that book's varied
demands, he was equally able to write as "himself"—as a polished,
urbane devotee of Petrarch and Castiglione, a man whose poetry
(like his conversation) could be both formal and colloquial, ornate
and plain, witty and passionate. In the *Certain Sonnets*, of course, the
style is still far from its perfection, but a few quotations can perhaps
demonstrate its close relation to that of *Astrophel and Stella*. Compare,
for example, the octave of the sonnet quoted above (CS 11) with
that of AS 88. Or consider the method of CS 9:

> Wo, wo to me, on me returne the smart:
>> My burning tongue hath bred my mistresse paine,
> For oft in paine to paine my painefull heart
>> With her due praise did of my state complaine.
> I praisde her eyes whom never chance doth move,
>> Her breath which makes a sower answer sweete,
> Her milken breasts the nurse of child-like love,
>> Her legges (O legges) her ay well stepping feete.
> Paine heard her praise, and full of inward fire,
>> (First sealing up my heart as pray of his)
> He flies to her, and boldned with desire,
>> Her face (this age's praise) the thiefe doth kisse.
>> O paine I now recant the praise I gave,
>> And sweare she is not worthy thee to have.

The puns on "paine" in the opening lines may remind us momentarily of the *Arcadia*'s mode, but such verbal play never gains control
of the verse; it is done with a self-consciousness similar to that of
Astrophel's frequent word-juggling: "Sweet kisse, Thy sweets I
faine would sweetly endite, / Which even of sweetnesse sweetest

sweetner art" (AS 79, 1-2). In addition, the potential formality of the *blason* in the second quatrian of the sonnet is immediately modified by witty asides ("O legges") and by a sudden switch to the colloquial ("ay well stepping feete"; compare Astrophel's similarly "hyphenated" compound, "long with *Love* acquainted eyes" [AS 31, 5]). The tone throughout the sestet becomes increasingly playful, ending finally with the mock-solemn protest of the couplet. By this time, the personified figure of "paine" has begun to act extraordinarily like the Cupid of *Astrophel*:

> But finding these North clymes do coldly him embrace,
>> Not usde to frozen clips, he strave to find some part,
>> Where with most ease and warmth he might employ his art:
> At length he perch'd himself in *Stella's* joyfull face, . . .
>> (AS 8, 5-8)

Once such connections have been noted, one is in a better position to discover—throughout the *Certain Sonnets*—the full extent to which Sidney was already in 1577–1581 creating the manner and voice of Astrophel. Here, for example, are a number of lines which put colloquial diction and conversational phrasing to sophisticated uses in ways clearly foreshadowing the later poetry:

> Ah saucy paine let not they errour last, . . .
>> (CS 8, 13)

> No, no, she is too wise, she knowes her face
>> Hath not such paine as it makes others have: . . .
>> (CS 11, 9-10)

> Should Ladies faire be tyed to such hard lawes,
> As in their moodes to take a lingring pawse?
> I would it not, their mettall is too fine.
>> (CS 17, 23-25)

> Are *Poets* then the onely lovers true,
>> Whose hearts are set on measuring a verse:
>> Who thinke themselves well blest, if they renew
>> Some good olde dumpe, that *Chaucer's* mistresse knew,

And use but you for matters to rehearse?

Then good *Apollo* do away thy bowe: . . .

(CS 17, 31–36)

The syntax of these lines is relaxed, and the vocabulary of ordinary speech is handled in a casual, but self-conscious, way. Sidney has humanized the rhetorical gestures he was using so conventionally in the *Arcadia*. Apostrophe and interjection ("Ah," "No, no") are here delivered with light irony or are toned down by being juxtaposed with obviously informal and unrhetorical language ("Ah *saucy* paine"). An easy manner pervades, capable of mediating between the strict formality of a high style and the explosive qualities of the low. We find words that are close to slang ("good olde dumpe" or "saucy"), and there is a general tendency to transmute the vocabulary of courtly praise by placing it in consistently ironic contexts ("wise," "Ladies faire," "fine," "lovers true"). Indeed, the verse everywhere reveals the genial irony and spirit of banter which were typical both of Sidney's letters and of the *Arcadia*'s narrative asides. It is a spirit which relates directly to Astrophel's manner and tone, particularly to what one might call their antiheroic quality. "Saucy paine," "good *Apollo*," and "Some good olde dumpe, that *Chaucer's* mistresse knew" domesticate and diminish the venerable—very much as the "monster" pain (CS 8) was transformed into a kind of *putto* (CS 9). In CS 17, Apollo is called upon to supply "some sacred humour" (line 38). The tone becomes chatty, and the lover is seen mainly as a clever strategist with considerable control over his situation, capable of converting frustration into a form of wit. Cupid and the gods may occasionally bully him throughout the sequence, but he puts them—as much as possible—to his own uses. More than anything else, he speaks to them directly, in the tender, mocking, intimate, ironic tones which Astrophel later cultivates to such perfection:

Ah saucy paine let not thy errour last, . . .

(CS 8, 13)

Sweet, it was saucie *Love*, not humble I.

(AS 73, 8)

O paine I now recant the praise I gave, . . .
(CS 9, 13)

O Doctor *Cupid*, thou for me reply, . . .
(AS 61, 12)

Then good *Apollo* do away thy bowe: . . .
(CS 17, 36)

Good brother *Philip*, I have borne you long, . . .
(AS 83, 1)

I now recant the praise I gave,
And sweare she is not worthy thee to have.
(CS 9, 13-14)

And I do sweare even by the same delight, . . .
(AS 82, 13)

Tell me ô haire of gold,
If I then faultie be,
That trust those killing eyes, . . .
(CS 28, 17-19)

Then ev'n of fellowship, ô Moone, tell me
Is constant *Love* deem'd there but want of wit?
(AS 31, 9-10)

Not all the *Certain Sonnets* are quite so full of wit and self-dramatization as those I have just examined. Another group of lyrics shows signs of a still different kind of linguistic ease and fluidity, a more subdued, reflective, meditative kind:

When Love puft up with rage of hy disdaine,
Resolv'd to make me patterne of his might, . . .
(CS 2, 1-2)

Finding those beames, which I must ever love,
To marre my minde, and with my hurt to please,
I deemd it best some absence for to prove,
If further place might further me to ease.
(CS 21, 1-4)

5*

My ship, desire, with winde of lust long tost,
 Brake on faire cleeves of constant chastitie: . . .
                                    (CS 22, 55–56)

Oft have I musde, but now at length I finde,
 Why those that die, men say they do depart:
Depart, a word so gentle to my minde,
 Weakely did seeme to paint death's ougly dart.

But now the starres with their strange course do binde
 Me one to leave, with whome I leave my hart.
I heare a crye of spirits faint and blinde,
 That parting thus my chiefest part I part.
                                    (CS 20, 1–8)

Leave me ô Love, which reachest but to dust,
And thou my mind aspire to higher things: . . .
                                    (CS 32, 1–2)

We will find no verse like this in the *Arcadia*. A few poems there may
suggest the manner, especially the hymns of Philoclea and Basilius
(OA 18 and OA 38), or "My true love" (OA 45), or some of the
sonnets in the closing books (OA 51 and OA 69). They have, in
varying degrees, some of the same relative simplicity of speech and,
occasionally, even the same syntactical freedom (see the first stanza
of OA 38). But they are finally more patterned, more rhetorically
formal, more ritualistic than the poems quoted above. The lyrics
from the *Certain Sonnets* lack that higher pitch which is the distinguishing characteristic of the *Arcadia*'s high style. They avoid (or
tone down) apostrophe and exclamation, and although they sometimes use elaborate schemes and figures, they are rarely dominated
by them. The general quality of the diction, for example, and the
lack of syntactical inversion in the following two passages make them
comparable; yet their effects are utterly different:

And while ô sleepe thou closest up her sight,
(Her sight where love did forge his fayrest darte)
O harbour all her partes in easefull plighte:
Let no strange dreme make her fayre body starte.
                                    (OA 51, 5–8)

Oft have I musde, but now at length I finde,
   Why those that die, men say they do depart:
Depart, a word so gentle to my minde,
   Weakely did seeme to paint death's ougly dart.
                    (CS 20, 1–4)

The first passage is in every way more tightly and formally organized than the second. Every line has pointed alliteration ("sleepe"-"sight," "forge"-"fayrest"), every line is a unit in itself, and the repeated "O's" keep the tone close to that of ritual. Perhaps most striking, the anadiplosis of lines one and two ("sight, / Her sight") has the clear effect of a self-consciously used device or figure. The repetition has no special psychological function from the point of view of the speaker: its main use is to help maintain the general formality of style appropriate to the manner and mood of the poem. The anadiplosis of the second passage is very different. The repetition of "depart" at lines two and three is perfectly expressive of the lover's train of thought. He is "musing": why should dying be described as "departing"? He repeats the word as if to savor it again, to define its connotations for himself:

Depart, a word so gentle to my minde, . . .

The manner is still undeveloped, but the lines from the *Certain Sonnets* have in their method less in common with the *Arcadia* quatrain than they do with the musings of Hamlet:

'tis a consummation
Devoutly to be wish'd. To die—to sleep;—
To sleep—perchance to dream: . . .

In the *Arcadia* passage, we are immediately aware of the rhetoric; in the *Certain Sonnets*, only faintly so; in Hamlet, what was once the figure of anadiplosis seems simply the natural form of the mind's movement in reflection.

Other aspects of the quatrain from the *Certain Sonnets* need only be mentioned—the general lack of alliteration, the avoidance of apostrophe or invocation, the flexible movement from line to line. In general, one can see Sidney discovering a style for meditation or "musing" which was bound to have a deep effect on his style as a whole, and he put it to excellent uses, as will be seen later, in several of the *Astrophel* sonnets. If the style seems in some ways stiff and rather colorless—a fair criticism, indeed, of nearly all the *Certain Sonnets*—the fact suggests only that Sidney had still a great deal to learn. Part of his difficulty, of course, is prosodic. The meters are the steady, regular iambics of the *Arcadia*, and they are clearly inadequate for the particular kinds of supple, conversational verse he was experimenting with both here and in the *Arcadia* eclogues. Awkward inversions and "fill-in" phrases (noted by my italics) are the inevitable result:

> I deemd it best some absence *for to prove*, . . .
>   CS 21, 3)

> But *for all this* I can not her remove . . .
>   (CS 17, 4)

> Weakely *did seeme to* paint . . .
>   (CS 20, 4)

Sidney has simply not yet found the prosodic means of capturing the full swing of conversational speech and phrasing in verse.

Yet despite this and other weaknesses, the poetry of the *Certain Sonnets* reveals his "private" style in sufficiently developed form to distinguish it clearly from the fictional styles of the *Arcadia*. When the opening lines of a series of *Arcadia* sonnets are placed next to those of the *Certain Sonnets*, the differences are immediately apparent:

> Transformd in shew, but more transformd in minde,
> I cease to strive, with double conquest foild: . . .
>   (OA 2)

> Loved I am, and yet complaine of Love:
> As loving not, accus'd, in Love I die.
>   (OA 20)

> Since that the stormy rage of passions darcke
> (Of passions darke, made darke by beautie's light) . . .
>   (OA 39)

Harke plaintfull ghostes, infernall furies harke
Unto my woes the hatefull heavens do sende, . . .

(OA 40)

Howe is my Sunn, whose beames are shining bright,
Become the cause of my darke ouglie night?

(OA 42)

Do not disdaine, ô streight up raised Pine,
That wounding thee, my thoughtes in thee I grave: . . .

(OA 47)

O Stealing time the subject of delaie,
(Delay, the racke of unrefrain'd desire) . . .

(OA 53)

Beautie hath force to catche the humane sight.
Sight doth bewitch, the fancie evill awaked.

(OA 57)

*   *   *

When Love puft up with rage of hy disdaine,
Resolv'd to make me patterne of his might, . . .

(CS 2)

Wo, wo to me, on me returne the smart: . . .

(CS 9)

And have I heard her say, 'ô cruell paine!'

(CS 11)

A Satyre once did runne away for dread,
With sound of horne, which he him selfe did blow, . . .

(CS 16)

Oft have I musde, but now at length I finde,
Why those that die, men say they do depart: . . .

(CS 20)

Finding those beames, which I must ever love,
   To marre my minde, and with my hurt to please, . . .

(CS 21)

Leave me ô Love, which reachest but to dust,
   And thou my mind aspire to higher things: . . .

(CS 32)

The variety of openings in the second group, their relative casualness or sudden explosiveness, and their more serious use of the "I" in meditation should all be obvious. If one recalls that the lines from both groups of poems were written at approximately the same time, one can gauge the extent to which matters of decorum determined Sidney's various choices of style—particularly how much the *Arcadia*'s verse was deliberately fashioned to suit the book's special requirements. When Sidney was writing privately, as a courtier *in propria persona*, he turned quite naturally to a conversational style of the middle range and produced the *Certain Sonnets*. Throughout the sequence, he presents himself as a kind of suave Philisides: satiric, aggressive, witty, self-consciously strategical, erotic. Yet, while much of the poetry is urbane and clever, several of the lyrics strike much more serious, thoughtful chords, and the closing two sonnets are extraordinarily powerful in their depth of feeling. In other words, the collection as a whole contains all the essential elements for a substantial poetry of serious but sophisticated love. It has the suggestion of a plot, a variety of moods and tones, and strong intimations of an assured, controlling poetic voice. At every important level of form—phrasing, metrics, the lyric sequence—Sidney is just on the verge of the discoveries which will soon make *Astrophel and Stella* what it is.

CHAPTER IX

Sidney and Ciceronianism

❧❧

THE PREVIOUS four chapters have attempted to outline a new conception of Sidney's poetic development. Broadly speaking, they have argued against the view that the *Arcadia* is written in an overdecorative style which Sidney later repudiated for the plainer, dramatic manner of *Astrophel*. The evidence of the texts seems to support such an argument. The *Arcadia* eclogues contain verse that is as plain and dramatic as any passages in *Astrophel*, and the *Certain Sonnets*—composed at approximately the same time as the *Arcadia*—reveal a courtly, conversational poetry which is in fact the basis of *Astrophel*'s. Sidney was, at the very beginning of his career, a thoroughly sophisticated stylist, able to write the highly ornate double sestina of Strephon and Klaius, the rougher, unadorned verse of Geron and Philisides, and the more graceful, relaxed lines of the *Certain Sonnets*. Matters of decorum, not a commitment to "rhetoric" or "ornament," guided his choices of style. Like other Renaissance poets, he simply changed his manner to suit his matter.

Critics who have tended to oppose the *Arcadia*'s qualities and those of *Astrophel* have not, however, argued exclusively on the basis of the poetry. Starting with the assumption that the *Arcadia*'s "gorgeous eloquence" was a misguided eloquence, they have looked to the *Apologie for Poetrie* to substantiate their views. Myrick, for example, saw the *Apologie* as a work with inherent contradictions: it showed Sidney's concern both for "fitness" of style—that is, for unaffected plainness—and for rhetorical ornament; there was no way of reconciling the conflict:

> In the *Defence of Poesie* the classic principle of fitness leads the author to despise affection, but the Renaissance delight in ornament leads him to set a high value upon gorgeous phraseology.[1]

Sidney, Myrick felt, had not yet learned that "virtue is like a rich stone, best plain set."[2] "To use Sidney's own language, he has [in the *Arcadia*] 'cast Suger and spice uppon everie dish,'"[3] and he himself admitted in the *Apologie* that he was "sicke among the rest" of English poets:

> The poetic sincerity of *Astrophel and Stella*, and Sidney's dying wish to have the *Arcadia* burned afford a hint that he thought he had by no means "achieved perfection."[4]

In such passages, Myrick is really extending Hazlitt's criticism, particularly Hazlitt's use of the *Apologie* as a weapon with which to attack the *Arcadia*. Robert Montgomery has recently followed this line to its logical conclusion:

> Sidney's critical statements about lyric point in two directions. On the one hand, they seem to betray an intention to dismantle the principles of style implicit in the *Arcadia* poems. . . . The *Defence of Poesie* was probably composed after most, if not all, of the *Arcadia* verse was completed. As he lists his objections to over-decorative lyric, Sidney confesses himself "sicke among the rest." On the other hand, the *Defence* is echoed in a number of sonnets in *Astrophel and Stella* which argue against conventional devices in lyric ornament, and urge a plainer, more direct style, and had the sequence carried out this program with utter and obvious fidelity to its new principles, the work of the critic would have been simpler than it is.[5]

Montgomery goes on to place Sidney in a tradition of writers of the sixteenth and early seventeenth centuries who favored a plain style. Sidney rejected his early "Ciceronian" tendencies and, in the *Apologie*, announced a change of direction as radical as that which Gabriel Harvey proclaimed for himself in his *Ciceronianus* of 1577.[6] He became, in effect, part of a general movement which was to culminate in Bacon's eventual condemnation of Ciceronian prolixity and elaborateness. Myrick, again, had first framed this line of argument. He suggested that, although "Sidney, in school and university, could not have escaped . . . Ciceronianism,"[7] he was at least discerning enough to begin to distrust it. All Elizabethans,

> in their enthusiasm for choice language, too often conceived style as an end in itself, the ornament, not the inevitable expression, of thought. . . . But among English writers Bacon is only one of those

who, toward the end of the sixteenth century, were beginning to grasp more clearly than the Ciceronians the meaning of artistic form. . . . In this maturing of English taste, Sir Philip Sidney, had he lived, would doubtless have had an important part; . . .[8]

The chief difficulty of such views is their failure to appreciate the fact that Sidney's anti-Ciceronianism predated his composition of the *Arcadia* (ca. 1578–1580). This is abundantly clear from his correspondence with Languet and Robert Sidney. In 1573, he wrote to Languet asking for advice on problems of Latin style, and the older man replied:

> You ask me to tell you how you ought to form your style of writing. I think you will do well to read both volumes of Cicero's letters, not only for the beauty of the Latin, but also for the very important matter they contain. There is nowhere a better statement of the causes which overthrew the Roman Republic. Many persons think it very useful to take one of his letters and translate it into another language; then to shut the book and turn it back into Latin; then again to refer to the book and compare your expressions with Cicero's. But beware of falling into the heresy of those who think that the height of excellence consists in the imitation of Cicero, and pass their lives in labouring at it.   (Pears, 19–20)

Languet was warning Sidney about the dangers of Ciceronianism while the boy was still in his teens. Sidney, meanwhile, answered dutifully: "I intend to follow your advice about composition, thus; I shall first take one of Cicero's letters and turn it into French; then from French into English" (Pears, 23). This early letter contains no explicit comment on the Ciceronian issue, but one can scarcely doubt that Sidney had taken Languet's advice on the subject to heart. In October 1580, he told his brother Robert:

> So you can speak and write Latin, not barbarously, I never require great study of Ciceronianism, the chief abuse of Oxford, "qui dum verba sectantur, res ipsas negligunt." My toyful books I will send, with God's help, by February, . . .   (Pears, 201)

The passage is particularly interesting because it combines an expression of anti-Ciceronianism with a reference to the *Arcadia*, which Sidney was just bringing to conclusion.[9] It dramatizes, in short, the fact that Sidney's particular mode of anti-Ciceronianism was thoroughly compatible with the ornament and high rhetoric he was at that moment lavishing upon his pastoral-heroic romance. Ciceronians followed "words" and neglected "things" ("res ipsas"); Sidney, meanwhile, gives every indication that he considers neither himself nor his work—including specifically the *Arcadia*—to be guilty of such a charge. He "never" requires great study of Ciceronianism, and the "never" suggests a long-standing, well-formulated attitude on the subject. It suggests that his principles of style were settled long before he had undertaken the *Arcadia*, that they would never have tolerated a decorative preference for manner over matter, and that the *Arcadia* (indeed, all of Sidney's work) was very much the creation of a man who cared pre-eminently for the substantiality of "things themselves."

All of this, of course, confirms Myrick's and Montgomery's contention that Sidney was a part of the growing anti-Ciceronian movement of the sixteenth century. It argues, however, that he was so at least as early as 1573–74, and that his critical principles and ideas about style were essentially mature and fully developed by the time he came to write the *Arcadia*.[10] Unlike Gabriel Harvey, he was never a dedicated disciple of the sacred Tully, and consequently, he never suffered a radical change of creed comparable to that which Harvey announced in his *Ciceronianus* of 1577. His work, in this sense, was all of a piece.

Once such a view has been established, however, it is still important to define more carefully Sidney's precise relationship to the anti-Ciceronian currents of his age. Both Myrick and Montgomery, as I have indicated, tend to equate Ciceronianism with elaborate, ornamental rhetoric and anti-Ciceronianism with plainness. Yet this is far too schematic and uncomplicated a characterization. Not only did the meaning of Ciceronian (and hence of anti-Ciceronian) alter slightly as the sixteenth century progressed,[11] but a relatively wide range of acceptable styles was generally open to the man who professed anti-Ciceronianism. "Plainness" was indeed often recommended, but it was not the only possible response to the excesses of men like Nizolius and Bembo. Indeed, until the end of the century, the Ciceronian controversy was less concerned with specific stylistic prescriptions (although it inevitably dealt with them) than with the central issue of imitation and the related one of invention. A fuller discussion of these issues may help to locate Sidney's own position more accurately. Erasmus and Harvey are both satisfactory guides in the matter. Erasmus' Nosoponus, for example, is a brilliant satiric portrait of Ciceronian fanaticism in action:

No.– For seven whole years I have touched nothing except Ciceronian books, refraining from others as religiously as the Carthusians refrain from flesh.

Bu.– Why so?

No.– Lest somewhere some foreign phrase should creep in and, as it were, dull the splendor of Ciceronian speech. Also I have enclosed in their cases and removed from sight all other books lest I should sin inadvertently; and hereafter there is no place in my library for anyone except Cicero.[12]

Nosoponus has made an "alphabetical lexicon" consisting of bona fide Ciceronian words and phrases. He will use no others:

Bu.– What if a word is found in Terence or in an equally approved author? Will it be marked with a black mark?

No.– There is no exception. A Ciceronian he will not be in whose books there is found a single little word which he cannot show in the writing of Cicero: and a man's whole vocabulary I deem spurious just like a counterfeit coin if there is in it even a single word which has not the stamp of the Ciceronian die; ...[13]

Nosoponus is, of course, a parody, but he resembled actual Ciceronians closely enough to make Erasmus' dialogue effective as satire, and he was clearly the kind of man whom Gabriel Harvey ridiculed for being "a fowler after Ciceronian words, religiously following him in all the tiniest details, and childishly gathering a few pebbles from Cicero like pebbles on a beach, while trampling under foot the most precious gems of argument and pearls of philosophy."[14] Taken together, the passages from Erasmus and Harvey serve to expose the chief abuses of the Ciceronian breed: its sacrifice of substantive considerations to purely verbal ones, its narrow-minded devotion to a single master, and its spirit of pedantry. The Ciceronian neglected matter in an effort to produce superficially fine literary effects, and this disregard for the real substance of his theme or subject amounted to a gross distortion of Cicero's own conception of rhetorical procedure. For Cicero, the finding and full exploration of one's matter or argument—the whole process of "invention"—was the essential first step in composition, and it was just this step which sixteenth-century Ciceronians failed to take seriously. Perhaps the most brilliant moment in Erasmus' *Ciceronianus* occurs when Nosoponus admits that a Ciceronian would never be able to write about Christ or the Christian religion, since none of the words for such a discussion was used (and hence sanctified) by Cicero himself.

If the Ciceronian overlooked the importance of invention, he was equally culpable in his approach to the problem of imitation. He conceived of imitation as a form of copying—an attempt to reproduce the diction, phrasing, and rhythms of Cicero in such a way that the replica would be indistinguishable from its model. All individuality of temperament and intellect, all originality and sense of personal involvement with the subject at hand, would be obliterated. The posies or flowers or phrases of the master were to be culled, catalogued, and then "fit into" one's own writings. This, at least, is the concept of imitation which Nosoponus outlines. Bulephorus, meanwhile, expresses Erasmus' point of view in countering with a very different conception. He insists that a writer must follow the bent of his own nature and talent, that imitation does not involve a pedantic memorizing and copying of words and phrases, but a personal transmutation of them; it is

> that which culls from all authors, and especially the most famous, what in each excels and accords with your own genius, – not just adding to your speech all the beautiful things that you find, but digesting them and making them your own, so that they may seem to have been born from your mind and not borrowed from others, and may breathe forth the vigor and strength of your nature, . . . so that your speech may not seem a patchwork, but a river flowing forth from the fountain of your heart.[15]

Writers who imitated in this way were the rightful heirs of Cicero, and Bulephorus goes on to make clear the fact that anti-Ciceronianism did not necessitate a complete break with Cicero himself, but only with his narrow-minded Renaissance disciples. Indeed, one possible response to Nosoponus' brand of pedantic Ciceronianism was a "true" Ciceronianism which attempted to recapture the full spirit and power of the master:

> acknowledge him a Ciceronian who speaks clearly, fluently, forcibly, and appropriately, in harmony with the nature of the theme, the condition of the times, and the characters. . . . What pray is the fountain then of Ciceronian eloquence? – A mind richly instructed in general knowledge with especial care on those subjects about which you have determined to write, a mind prepared by the rules of rhetoric, by much practice in speaking and writing and by daily meditation, and what is the essential point of the whole matter, a heart loving those things for which it pleads, . . .[16]

Years later, Harvey followed Erasmus' lead:

> I found in Erasmus a Ciceronian not of the sort that these refined fellows foolishly imagine . . . rather I found the same kind of Ciceronian as P. Ramus had described, renewing and somehow recreating with the utmost effort and force of intellect the amplest glories of Marcus Cicero and all his virtues that were entirely worthy of imitation.[17]

A great many elements in Erasmus' and Harvey's treatment of Ciceronianism must have appealed to Sidney. Much of the *Apologie*, for example, is a hymn to the poet's extraordinary powers of invention,[18] and a similar emphasis falls upon the nature and potency of the poet's proper "matter." His duty to create notable images of virtue, moreover, is only the poet's first concern in this regard; inseparable from it, and equally important, is the care he must devote to both the details and the general conduct of his argument:

> For, there being two principal parts, matter to be expressed by wordes, and words to expresse the matter, in neyther wee use Arte or Imitation rightly. Our matter is *Quodlibet* indeed, though wrongly perfourming *Ovids* verse
>
> *Quicquid conabar dicere versus erat:*

never marshalling it into an assured rancke, that almost the readers
cannot tell where to finde themselves. . . . I [do] not remember to
have seene but fewe (to speake boldely) printed, that have poeticall
sinnewes in them. For proofe whereof let but most of the verses bee
put in Prose, and then aske the meaning, and it will be found, that
one verse did but beget another, without ordering at the first what
should be at the last: which becomes a confused masse of words,
with a tingling sound of ryme, barely accompanied with reason.

(*Apologie*, 50–51)

Sidney is perhaps expressing the fruits of his Ramist studies here,[19]
although there is nothing in the passage which he might not have
learned from Erasmus', Quintilian's, or Cicero's attitudes toward
composition. In any case, the desire to marshal things into an
"assured rancke," and the concern for "reason" and logical "ordering," are serious and deep-rooted in Sidney. His first allegiance is to
his subject matter, to invention, to the "sinnewes" of his work; and
this allegiance was not by any means a new one at the time of his
writing the *Apologie*. Even a perfunctory inspection of his earliest
verse and prose will reveal their manifest concern for tight logic
and rigorous order of various kinds.[20] There, as elsewhere, the influence of Ramus, Languet, and others showed itself in the clearest
possible ways.

Beyond such general considerations, the *Apologie* also comments
explicitly upon the principal issues of Ciceronianism, and here again
one feels Sidney's essential kinship with Erasmus and Harvey:

Truly I could wish, if at least I might be so bold to wish in a thing
beyond the reach of my capacity, the diligent imitators of *Tullie*
and *Demosthenes* (most worthy to be imitated) did not so much keep
Nizolian Paper-bookes of their figures and phrases, as by attentive
translation (as it were) devour them whole, and make them
wholly theirs.   (*Apologie*, 57)

Erasmus had urged that writers not simply add to their speech "all
the beautiful things that [they] find," but "digest" them and make
them their "own." Sidney agrees, and his disparaging allusion to
Marius Nizolius—probably the most notorious of all Ciceronians[21]
—makes equally clear his disapproval of "alphabetical lexicons"

like that which Nosoponus had compiled. He wants writers to "translate" into their own terms the flowers and phrases of others. Nizolian paper-books and similar Ciceronian aids to composition obviously inhibit such translation. They tend to encourage diligent, slavish copying, and the result is a literature that is uncreative and insubstantial. The point recalls Sidney's similar objections to "Herbarists" who rifle "all stories of Beasts, Foules, and Fishes" for similes, or poets who alliterate "as if they were bound to followe the method of a Dictionary" (*Apologie*, 57 and 58). In each case, Sidney quarrels with the lack of concern for the poet's personal, felt response to a given subject, and with the concomitant substitution of deadly, mechanical methods. It is not that the poet should be merely "original" but that he should absorb the substance and style of other poets in such a way that they become genuinely his own:

> But truely many of such writings, as come under the banner of unresistable love, if I were a Mistres, would never perswade mee they were in love: so coldely they apply fiery speeches, as men that had rather red Lovers writings, and so caught up certaine swelling phrases, which hang together, like a man which once tolde mee, the winde was at North West, and by South, because he would be sure to name windes enowe,—then that in truth they feele those passions: . . .   (*Apologie*, 57)

Erasmus counseled the poet that his speech should "not seem a patchwork, but a river flowing forth from the fountain of [his] heart," and Sidney echoes the sentiment. He calls for writers who "feele those passions," and the chief fault with the poets he sees about him is that they "coldely . . . apply" the speeches and "swelling phrases" they have found in other lovers' writings. Their verse is a patchwork or mosaic—remnants of other verses, pieced together without regard for what the words and phrases really mean. This is Ciceronianism of the most debilitating kind, and the result is simply incoherence: the wind at northwest by south.

In his general approach to the problems of invention and imitation, then, Sidney reveals himself to be in basic agreement with anti-Ciceronian humanists like Erasmus, Languet, and Harvey. He would have found nothing to quarrel with in Erasmus' concern for decorum ("acknowledge him a Ciceronian who speaks clearly, fluently, forcibly, and appropriately, in harmony with the nature of the theme, . . . and the characters''). He insisted on the pre-eminence of subject matter, on the necessity for imitating creatively, and on the importance of a writer's finding a personal style which declared the depth and vigor of his involvement with his theme. If he was wholeheartedly in accord with the humanists on these particular issues, however, he also tended to diverge slightly from them on others, especially on the complex question of stylistic plainness. Erasmus, for example, had prescribed an Attic plain style as an antidote to Ciceronian excesses.[22] While advocating a "true" Ciceronianism, he also declared for "something more severe, less theatrical, more masculine" than Cicero's usual manner. He doubted that such theatricality was "appropriate for Christians," who look "rather to living virtuously than to speaking ornately and elegantly." "Even granting that the eloquence of Cicero was useful once, what is its use today?" Erasmus asked.[23] Times and circumstances had changed. Cicero's rhetoric had been framed for a society whose legal and political matters were dealt with in large assemblies; public, formal modes of eloquence were appropriate in such settings. But sixteenth-century politics and law were far less public. Ornate rhetoric and the high style had, in effect, outlived the conditions which had created them—and they were in any case out of place in serious, devout, unpretentious Christian societies.

Erasmus' recommendations in this regard (and the similar ones of Vives) were congenial to several English writers of the period. Thomas Wilson's *Arte of Rhetorique* entered a strong plea on behalf of rhetorical restraint, and Bishop Jewel—in his *Oratio contra Rhetoricam* —asked scornfully: where can one "discover a better mode of speech than to speak intelligibly, simply, and clearly? What need of art? What need of childish ornament?"[24] Gabriel Harvey, meanwhile, preferred his own version of the Attic plain style, something "neat and pithy."[25] There was, in short, a tendency in England to advocate one or another mode of plainness and simplicity to combat the elaborateness and self-conscious finery of Ciceronian fashions. The champions of the plain style were not, of course, suggesting a wholesale rejection of rhetoric: the Attic manner had its own legitimate kinds of ornament, and its own kind of calculation, although its practitioners strived for an appearance of artlessness. As Wilbur Howell has rightly said of Jewel's *Oratio*, it "is not so much an attack on rhetoric . . . as an ingenious and ironical condemnation of what rhetoric had come to mean in the schools at Oxford."[26] What is equally important to note is the fact—rarely stressed—that the stylistic recommendations of men like Erasmus and Wilson went hand in hand with their fairly restricted range of literary concerns. The humanist critics of rhetoric were largely academics, religious controversialists, or civil servants, and they were interested in primarily those genres or forms which related to their professional activities. Jewel's *Oratio* was delivered to the fellows and students of Corpus Christi College, Oxford, and it was intended to correct the oratorical abuses of young men who would one day be public speakers of various kinds. The same is true of Harvey's *Ciceronianus*, which was first delivered as an undergraduate lecture at Cambridge. Erasmus based his arguments for the plain style partly on the fact that political and legal affairs had altered since Roman times, and the point would have been irrelevant unless he had expected his readers to be participating in such affairs. Wilson, finally, stressed the importance of rhetoric for men who "either shall beare rule ouer many, or must haue to doe with matters of a Realme."[27] In the light of such considerations, it is not surprising that the humanist rhetoricians urged their audiences to concentrate on the essential matter of their writing. That writing consisted mainly of pamphlets, letters, legal pleas, ambassadorial reports, political orations, and academic lectures or books. Few of the anti-Ciceronian humanists were deeply involved with either verse or prose fiction; and it is interesting that Harvey—perhaps the most deeply involved—certainly never expected plainness to be the norm in either poetry or heroic romance. Quite apart from his great admiration for Spenser, he urged that people

> Read the Countesse of Pembrookes Arcadia, a gallant Legendary, full of pleasurable accidents and proffitable discourses; . . . He that will Looue, let him learne to looue of him that will teach him to Liue, and furnish him with many pithy and effectuall instructions, . . . Liue euer sweete Booke, the siluer Image of his gentle witt, and the golden Pillar of his noble courage, and euer notify vnto the

worlde, that thy Writer was the Secretary of Eloquence, the breath of the Muses, the hoony-bee of the dayntiest flowers of Witt and Arte, the Pith of morall & intellectuall Vertues, . . .[28]

This passage is from *Pierce's Supererogation,* published in 1593, more than fifteen years after Harvey's own anti-Ciceronian conversion to plainness. It suggests, at the very least, that the high rhetoric and "flowers" of the *Arcadia* were as compatible with Harvey's kind of anti-Ciceronianism as they were with Sidney's.

Insofar as Sidney's range of literary interests coincided with that of the humanists, he tended to reflect their stress upon plainness. His own letters are invariably in an informal, offhand, sometimes careless manner. His translations and miscellaneous prose pieces vary rather with the occasion, but in nearly all of them, he cultivates an essential naturalness and conversational ease.[29] In addition, his conviction that a courtier's speech ought to be natural and un-affected[30] helped to shape the narrative voice he developed in the *Arcadia,* and the lyric voice of both the *Certain Sonnets* and the *Astrophel*—although Sidney's courtiers invariably possess a degree of wit, grace, and verbal polish which sets them off decisively from the personas of Wyatt, Surrey, and others. Finally, the remarks on diction at the end of the *Apologie* work to confirm Sidney's general practice. They recommend "playne sensiblenes" in writing, al-thought it is essential to notice the implicit qualifications which the context places upon that recommendation. Excepting three brief comments on the diction of poetry, Sidney addresses himself to "Prose-printers," "Schollers," and "Preachers" (*Apologie,* 57); he concentrates his energies upon "the diligent imitators of *Tullie* and *Demosthenes,*" on "certaine printed discourses," on "the pulpit," and on "professors of learning." His theme, momentarily, is prose dis-course (excepting fiction) and oratory, and it is in this context that he specifically recommends plainness:

> For my part, I doe not doubt, when *Antonius* and *Crassus,* the great forefathers of *Cicero* in eloquence, the one (as *Cicero* testifieth of them) pretended not to know Arte, the other not to set by it: because with a playne sensiblenes they might win credit of popular eares; which credit is the neerest step to perswasion: which perswasion is the chiefe marke of Oratory;—I doe not doubt (I say) but that they

used these knacks very sparingly, which who doth generally use, any man may see doth daunce to his owne musick: and so be noted by the audience, more careful to speake curiously, then to speake truly. (*Apologie*, 59)

Sidney is here discussing situations in which it is necessary to win credit from "popular eares," and his focus is upon genres or forms which have persuasive argument as their main purpose. There is no suggestion that his comments are to have a general applicability. Not all audiences are "popular," and not all compositions (particularly heroic romances and courtly-love lyrics) have the rhetorical purposes of prose pamphlets and public orations. Sidney, of course, would not have applauded those who spoke "curiously" in any context. But the criteria for judging curiousness (or plainness) varied from genre to genre and situation to situation, and they necessarily involved a consideration of the decorum of the work at hand.

Sidney's sensitivity to problems of decorum pervades the whole of the *Apologie*'s discussion of diction. He never objects to rhetorical ornament per se, but only to particular uses of ornament in particular contexts. He does not, for example, banish "*Similiter Cadences*" from use; he asks "Howe well store of *Similiter Cadences* doth sound with the gravity of the pulpit" (*Apologie*, 58): the question concerns the suitability of a given ornament to a given form of discourse. Nor does he banish "Herbarist" similes (although it is impossible to imagine his ever welcoming very many of them). Rather, he suggests that long lists of similes work to defeat the persuasive purposes of "printed discourses":

For the force of a similitude, not being to proove anything to a contrary Disputer, but onely to explane to a willing hearer, when that is done, the rest is a most tedious pratling: rather over-swaying the memory from the purpose whereto they were applied, then any whit informing the iudgement, already eyther satisfied, or by similitudes not to be satisfied. (*Apologie*, 58–59)

Finally, one ought not to overlook the careful qualifications introduced into a passage which is frequently cited to suggest Sidney's growing disenchantment with rhetorical ornament; he complains of Cicero's imitators and declares:

For nowe they cast Sugar and Spice upon every dish that is served to the table; like those Indians, not content to weare eare-rings at the fit and naturall place of the eares, but they will thrust Iewels through their nose and lippes, because they will be sure to be fine. *Tullie*, when he was to drive out *Cateline*, as it were with a Thunder-bolt of eloquence, often used that figure of repitition, *Vivit vivit? imo in Senatum venit &c.* Indeed, inflamed with a well-grounded rage, hee would have his words (as it were) double out of his mouth: and so doe that artificially, which we see men doe in choller naturally. And wee, having noted the grace of those words, hale them in sometime to a familier Epistle, when it were to too much choller to be chollerick.   (*Apologie*, 57–58)

Ornaments are altogether acceptable, indeed necessary, in their "fit and naturall" place, and decorum determines what is natural. Tully's repetitions are proper in forensic oratory (although they are to be used with discretion); it is when they are thrust into a "familier Epistle" that they become intolerable. Throughout this passage, and elsewhere, it is essentially a vulgar striving to be "fine" that Sidney objects to—the striving without any real sense of what may be suitable for a given subject or occasion. Sugar and spice should not be cast upon "every" dish, but the clear implication is that they will be perfectly appropriate for *some* dishes. Heroic verse is a case in point, and when Sidney comes to discuss it in the *Apologie*, he suggests the inability of mere plainness to deal adequately with its high themes:

I never heard the olde song of *Percy* and *Duglas*, that I found not my heart mooved more then with a Trumpet: and yet is it sung but by some blinde Crouder, with no rougher voyce then rude stile: which being so evill apparrelled in the dust and cobwebbes of that uncivill age, what would it worke trymmed in the gorgeous eloquence of *Pindar*?   (*Apologie*, 31–32)

Heroic tales or ballads are necessarily to be fitted out in the "gorgeous eloquence" of a high style, and Sidney is the first to demand this. He invokes Pindar—the exemplar of an ornate high style[31]—to transform the "rudeness" of Chevy Chase: not that the original does not move him, but that it might "worke" much more if it were written in a manner which suited its heroic matter. As always,

Sidney's evaluation of a given writer or piece of writing is grounded in considerations of decorum (and of methods of imitation and invention). Neither here nor elsewhere does he prescribe any single style—whether ornate, plain, or otherwise—as a regulating norm for himself and others. If he shared with the humanists the demands for a certain plainness in expository prose and oratory, his strong commitment to other prose forms and to poetry made his stylistic models more diverse, and his stylistic judgments rather more complex, than theirs.

Only when one has acknowledged the relative complexity of Sidney's attitudes toward style is it possible to consider properly the *Apologie*'s remarks on the diction of poetry. There, Sidney complains that the "honny-flowing Matron Eloquence" is

> disguised, in a Curtizan-like painted affectation: one time with so farre fette words, they may seeme Monsters, but must seeme straungers, to any poore English man; another tyme, with coursing of a Letter, as if they were bound to followe the method of a Dictionary: an other tyme, with figures and flowers, extreamelie winter-starved. *(Apologie,* 57)

The passage has sometimes been used to demonstrate Sidney's presumed antagonism to lyric ornament,[32] but this seems far too broad a reading of it. As usual, Sidney's comments are significantly qualified. He objects, not to alliteration itself, but to writers who alliterate "as if they were bound to followe the method of a Dictionary." Methodology, not ornament, is his target.[33] Similarly, he complains of "figures and flowers, *extreamelie winter-starved,*" and the qualifying phrase in apposition is crucial to his meaning. None of the Renaissance rhetoricians—not Erasmus nor Harvey—would have argued against culling figures and flowers from other writers, so long as one imitated them properly; as Sidney himself urged, writers should "not so much keep *Nizolian* Paper-bookes of their figures and phrases, as by attentive translation (as it were) devour them whole, and make them wholly theirs" *(Apologie,* 57). "Winter-starved" figures —that is, dead, uncreative, hackneyed ones—had obviously not been so devoured.[34] Finally, the caution against farfetched words is a reasonably traditional warning regarding inkhorn terms and Chaucerian affectations, and has no important bearing on the question of ornament itself.[35] In short, the *Apologie* passage on poetic diction essentially confirms Sidney's conception of rhetoric and style as I have tried to define it throughout this chapter. It does not argue against ornament in an effort to establish plainness; it argues, instead, against ill-used, misapplied, uninspired, mechanical ornament in favor of a more sensitive and creative approach to composition. This approach, too, is what Sidney surely has in mind when he later declares that poetry and oratory have "an affinity in this wordish consideration" (*Apologie*, 59). Their affinity lies, not in an indiscriminate antipathy to high rhetoric, but in their responsiveness to questions of decorum and methods of imitation and invention. As Sidney suggested in concluding his section on diction, the orator and the poet are alike in their need "to bend to the right use both of matter and manner" (*Apologie*, 59). That "right use" was a complicated affair, and involved much more than a policy of undeviating plainness.

A close reading of the *Apologie* suggests, then, that its statements about and attitudes toward style do not conflict with Sidney's actual practice in the *Arcadia*[36]—or, indeed, in any of his works.[37] He prescribes both Pindar's "gorgeous eloquence" and Antonius' or Crassus' "playne sensiblenes," and these apparently contradictory recommendations need only be related to Sidney's concern for decorum in order to be understood. It was a similar concern for decorum, as I have indicated in previous chapters, which determined Sidney's various choices of style in the *Arcadia* and the *Certain Sonnets*. Although the *Apologie* undoubtedly reflects the influence of writers like Erasmus, Vives, and Wilson, it is not primarily a plain-style document. Efforts to read it as such—like the efforts to identify Sidney completely with the plain-style movement—are bound to seem unsatisfactory in the end. Inevitably, they make it impossible for us to square the *Apologie* with the variety of Sidney's poetic practice or with the course of his poetic development. They ask us to ignore the fact that Sidney's anti-Ciceronian principles were established well before the time that he undertook the *Arcadia*; most important, they fail to explain the elaborate rhetoric and ornament in Sidney's last works—in those pieces which we know were composed after the *Apologie* discussion of plainness. The final result is to present Sidney as something of a paradox. Mr. Wesley Trimpi, for example, remarks that it is "strange that one of the earliest and finest criticisms of Petrarchan excesses should have been made by the man whom all courtly poets tried to imitate";[38] and he concludes by deciding that "Sidney . . . did not use the native plain style consistently or from principles that were firmly established."[39] Both statements recall similar remarks by other commentators on Sidney's style:

> the *Defence* is echoed in a number of sonnets in *Astrophel and Stella* which argue against conventional devices in lyric ornament, and urge a plainer, more direct style, and had the sequence carried out this program with utter and obvious fidelity to its new principles, the work of the critic would have been simpler than it is.[40]

> Sidney had not learned that "virtue is like a rich stone, best plain set." . . . He could not learn the lesson except by experiments like the *Arcadia*. The bad tendencies of the first version, to be sure, he did not correct in the revision. Mr. Mario Praz can even argue plausibly, if not so as quite to carry conviction, that "almost each sentence of the first draft has been subjected to a process of stucco decoration." Yet however firmly the mannerisms may have been fixed in Sidney's style, the path toward improvement could be found only by experience.[41]

Sidney's development does, of course, seem paradoxical if we try to link him too closely to Erasmus and Wilson, or if we view him as a harbinger of Baconian and Jonsonian plainness. We will be forced to see him as curiously inconsistent, lacking "firmly established" principles, writing ornately moments after a solemn declaration in favor of simplicity and plainness. Most of all, we will find it extraordinarily difficult to account for his revision of the *Arcadia*, which was almost certainly his last literary effort. Why, after so many apparent complaints about "decoration," should he have proceeded to make the *New Arcadia*'s style—as it undoubtedly is—even more elaborate and ornate than that of the original? If, however, we recall that he was also recasting his romance in an epic manner, adding nearly all its heroic and chivalric episodes, the puzzle disappears: he was simply writing according to decorum, as he had always done.

There are, one should add by way of conclusion, very good reasons why Sidney should *not* have conformed to the conceptions of style and ornament advocated by either Erasmus and Bishop Jewel or Bacon and Jonson. With all his deep concern for matter, for "playne sensiblenes" in certain contexts, for substance and solid argument in writing, Sidney—by virtue of his birth, temperament, and training—belonged to a world and milieu utterly different from that of either an Erasmus or a Bacon. He was the product of England's most brilliant court in its most romantic and Italianate period. His "realities" included a whole range of aesthetic, chivalric, and social values which were totally foreign to Erasmus, and which had effectively ceased to be viable in the time of Bacon and Jonson. Mr. Trimpi suggests at one point that the "Arcadian style of Sidney did not record the objectively real world in sufficient verisimilitude for Donne and Jonson."[42] It is true. But that style—with its wit, *sprezzatura*, grace, and delight in ornament—came much closer to recording Sidney's own world, or at least his idealized version of it. The high style had a meaning for him simply because it accorded with the high style of life which he lived. Whether he was thinking of heroic action in the Netherlands, or the "dignified ease" of Wilton, his vision of existence and experience could scarcely have been more different from Bishop Jewel's, Ben Jonson's, or Bacon's. That difference is precisely the reason why he never set out to banish ornament from lyric poetry, or why "he did not use the native plain style consistently." Yet it is obviously wrong to suggest that he lacked "principles that were firmly established." Rather, his principles centered upon a concept of decorum and a theory of imitation—both as ancient as Cicero and Quintilian—which allowed him a wide range of styles to be used as occasion and subject demanded.

CHAPTER X

Energia

✶✿✶

TO THIS POINT, I have argued that Sidney had, in effect, no development at all. The *Arcadia* and the *Certain Sonnets*, both written at approximately the same time, display a variety of styles which Sidney had developed for altogether different purposes; and in the poetry of both works, one can discover essential elements of *Astrophel*'s verse. The *Certain Sonnets*, particularly, developed a style that was both conversational—often colloquial—and courtly, sophisticated, ornamental. It combined the naturalness which Sidney (and Castiglione)[1] prescribed for a courtier's speech with equally necessary grace and polish. Out of this style, and out of the character Philisides, Sidney fashioned *Astrophel*. In its total conception, and in its quality, *Astrophel* is of course different from its antecedents. In this sense, one can indeed discover changes and developments in Sidney's work, although they consist largely of his learning to do more skillfully and effectively what he had already done before. His literary progress discloses no sharp breaks or sudden alterations of principle. *Astrophel* is considerably better poetry than anything he had previously written, but its success has nothing to do with new stylistic ideals, or a sudden preference for matter over manner. It has, on the other hand, everything to do with Sidney's development of new techniques, his growing interest in the sonnet as a potentially dramatic form, and his desire to reinvigorate the Petrarchan language of love. The following pages consider these developments in some detail, and they do so in relation to the rhetorical concept of energia, which Sidney mentions in the *Apologie*. Briefly, it will be suggested that the major changes which occur between Sidney's earlier love lyrics and those of *Astrophel* can best be understood in the light of this concept.

6+

Examining the *Certain Sonnets* closely, and keeping *Astrophel* in mind, one can scarcely avoid feeling their relative lack of vivacity, tension, and vitality. Some of them (especially CS 9–11 and CS 32) have feeling and drama, but the great majority are essentially tepid:

> Finding those beames, which I must ever love,
>   To marre my minde, and with my hurt to please,
> I deemd it best some absence for to prove,
>   If further place might further me to ease.
>
> (CS 21, 1–4)

> My mistresse lowers and saith I do not love:
>   I do protest and seeke with service due,
>   In humble mind a constant faith to prove,
> But for all this I can not her remove
> From deepe vaine thought that I may not be true.
>
> (CS 17, 1–5)

The difficulty with such verse is its lack of animus. It is "plain" and natural enough, and it suits the courtliness of its speaker, but it wants inner warmth and light. The stiff metrics are a major difficulty—the rhythms are not sufficiently supple and various for either the poetry's conversational manner or its range of feeling. Beyond this weakness, however, there is a more general lack of force, of compelling power, of that energia which Sidney valued so highly:

> But truely many of such writings, as come under the banner of unresistable love, if I were a Mistres, would never perswade mee they were in love: so coldely they apply fiery speeches, as men that had rather red Lovers writings, and so caught up certaine swelling phrases, which hang together, like a man which once tolde mee, the winde was at North West, and by South, because he would be sure to name windes enowe,—then that in truth they feele those passions: which easily (as I think) may be bewrayed by that same forciblenes or *Energia* (as the Greekes cal it) of the writer.
>
> (*Apologie*, 57)

Sidney's verses from the *Certain Sonnets* are not a patchwork of swelling phrases borrowed from other poets, but they do have all too little of that "forcibleness" which makes love poetry convincing and persuasive. Such forcibleness (or energia) cannot, of course, simply be learned. It derives as much from the poet's intense and imaginative involvement in his theme as it does from his skill in handling words and rhythms. But neither can it exist apart from specific skills and techniques—from "devices" and practiced habits of phrasing, structuring, and verbal gesturing which must first be discovered and then developed by training. No such training can endow a writer with the passion to write poetry like *Astrophel's*, but Renaissance rhetoric books could and did set out all the technical means necesary to help give passion effective and beautiful form. "For Poesie," Sidney wrote,

> must not be drawne by the eares, it must bee gently led, or, rather, it must lead. . . . a Poet no industrie can make, if his owne *Genius* bee not carried unto it; and therefore is it an old Proverbe, *Orator fit, Poeta nascitur*. Yet confesse I always that, as the firtilest ground must bee manured, so must the highest flying wit have a *Dedalus* to guide him. That *Dedalus*, they say, both in this and in other, hath three wings: . . . that is, Arte, Imitation, and Exercise. But these, neyther artificiall rules nor imitative patterns, we much cumber our selves withall. Exercise indeed wee doe, but that very fore-backwardly: for where we should exercise to know, wee exercise as having knowne: . . .   (*Apologie*, 50)

The following pages suggest that Sidney's development between 1580 and 1582 (when *Astrophel* was probably written) can be described largely as an effort to achieve energia within the decorum of the private, courtly-love lyric. Sidney took his own advice: he exercised in order "to know," developing the skills and techniques necessary to make the Petrarchan sonnet once again a vigorous, passionate, moving form of poetry. He accomplished this essentially by importing into the sonnet many of the devices and more general qualities of style he had first used in the *Arcadia* eclogues, and by improving generally upon the experiments begun in the *Certain Sonnets*. He also accomplished much more, but to understand precisely how much, a fuller definition of energia itself is needed.

Sidney's brief discussion of that quality suggests both its richness and its elusiveness. He glosses it as "forciblenes" and sees it as a kind of proof of passion: it convinces or persuades us that poets "in truth . . . feele those passions" which they purport to feel. Since persuasion lies at the heart of Sidney's entire theory of poetry, energia emerges as one of the most crucial of poetic qualities. Without it, poetry is superior neither to history nor to philosophy, and the love poems of courtiers are certain to languish unacknowledged. Effective expressions of passion, on the other hand, produce immediate, powerful response: young men are driven to emulate Ulysses and Aeneas, and young ladies believe and finally show mercy to their lovers. It is no accident, therefore, that Astrophel begins his sequence by searching (not always correctly) for a "feeling skill" (AS 2) to paint his passions; Stella will read his verse, and

> reading might make her know,
> Knowledge might pitie winne, and pitie grace obtaine, . . .
>
> (AS 1, 3–4)

The "Knowledge" of the poet's love which the lady is to gain will not simply be conveyed to her by a plain-speaking man. It must be communicated through the total activity of the verse itself. She must be made to see her lover's plight, to feel what he feels, and to respond with sympathy. Energia, although Astrophel does not use the term, is the chief means to that end.

Once the important role of energia in Sidney's poetic theory and practice is grasped, particularly its connection with the passions and its consequent power as an instrument of persuasion, one can see more clearly how thoroughly the concept pervades Sidney's discussion of poetry in the *Apologie*. He defined it loosely as "forciblenes," and the word (or its synonyms) occurs time and time again throughout the essay:

> For the question is, whether the fayned image of Poesie, or the regular instruction of Philosophy, hath the more force in teaching: . . . a fayned example hath asmuch force to teach, as a true example (for as for to moove, it is cleere, sith the fayned may bee tuned to the highest key of passion) . . .   (*Apologie*, 19 and 21)

> [The poet] yeeldeth to the powers of the minde an image of that whereof the Philosopher bestoweth but a woordish description:

which dooth neyther strike, pierce, nor possesse the sight of the
soule so much as that other dooth.   (*Apologie*, 17)

Poesie may not onely be abused, but that beeing abused, by the
reason of his sweete charming force, it can doe more hurt then any
other Armie of words: . . .   (*Apologie*, 41)

For as the image of each action stirreth and instructeth the mind, so
the loftie image of such Worthies most inflameth the mind with
desire to be worthy, . . .   (*Apologie*, 33)

Sidney responded to a great many qualities in poetry, but he was
most vitally interested in verse that stirred or inflamed the mind or
that could "bee tuned to the highest key of passion." The drama-
tization of strong feelings and the persuasive forcibleness or energia
in such verse were for Sidney the very essence of great poetry. Other
passages in the *Apologie*, moreover, give a fuller sense of the precise
ways in which energia might be expressed. David's Psalms, for
example, are declared to be "meerely [absolutely] poetical" in their
handling:

For what els is the awaking his musicall instruments; the often and
free changing of persons; his notable *Prosopopeias*, when he maketh
you as it were, see God comming in his Maiestie; his telling of the
Beastes ioyfulnes, and hills leaping, but a heavenlie poesie, wherein
almost hee sheweth himselfe a passionate lover of that unspeakable
and everlasting beautie to be seene by the eyes of the minde, onely
cleered by fayth?   (*Apologie*, 6–7)

David is seen as a passionate lover whose powerful feelings reveal
themselves in forcible verse, and Sidney has elaborated interestingly
on the details of that revelation. Some of the devices, at least, which
exhibit energia are apostrophe ("changing of persons"), prosopopoeia, and certain visual effects (including personification) which
make one "see" God coming or the hills leaping. In addition, there
is simply the obvious vitality of the actions mentioned—the animated joyfulness of the whole landscape. Nearly all of these elements
were mentioned by Aristotle in his discussion of ἐνέργεια ("actuality" or "activity") in the *Rhetoric*:

We have seen, then, that smartness depends on "proportional"
metaphor, and on "setting things before the eyes." We must now
explain what we mean by "setting things before the eyes," and
by what methods this is effected. This is my definition—those
words "set a thing before the eyes," which describe it in an
active state. For instance, to say that a good man is "four-square"
is a metaphor, since both the man and the square are complete;
but it does not describe an active state. This phrase, on the
other hand, "*in the flower of* his vigour"; or this, "at large,
like a sacred animal,"—are images of an active state. And, in the
verse—

"From thence the Greeks, then, *darting* with their feet,"

the word "darting" gives both actuality and metaphor—for it means
swiftness. Or, we may use the device, often employed by Homer,
of giving life to lifeless things by means of metaphor. In all
such cases he wins applause by describing *an active state*: as
in these words—

"Back again plainward rolled the *shameless* stone."
        "The arrow *flew*."
    "The arrow *eager* to fly on."
"The spears stuck in the ground *quivering* with hunger for the flesh."
    "The spear-point shot *quivering* through his breast."[2]

Sidney had translated at least two books, if not all, of the *Rhetoric*, and
he must have known this passage well.[3] It emphasizes "activity" and
the sense of things being present before one's eyes, as well as more
general visual effects. Words like "darting" or "quivering" have
the same animated, "present" quality as King David's "leaping"
hills. Energia may be in some ways elusive, but there are in fact
techniques for its expression, and Sidney clearly has studied them.
Moreover, Scaliger—whom Sidney mentioned several times in the
Apologie—enlarges considerably upon Aristotle's discussion, and his
comments are well worth considering. He defines energia (Latin:
efficacia) as "vigor of speech" and goes on to say that it can be
found in words, in things, or in actions.[4] He observes, in addition
to Aristotle's points:

Exclamations or addresses exhibit the greatest *efficacia*: "So great an
effort was it to found the Roman race!" . . . "You have conquered.

Lavinia is yours for a marriage partner." . . . "Cruel foe, why do you rattle on?"[5]

There is also such *efficacia* in apostrophe and interrogation, so that it makes the spirit of the listener leap up. When these are joined, the highest vigor is produced. For when I read these verses from Book Two [of the *Aeneid*], they banish all other thoughts from my mind: "Was it for this, dear parent, that you brought me to safety through missiles and fire?" . . . Or the line about Nisus: "What is he to do? With what force, what weapons, should he make bold to rescue the young man?" Cries, as we have said, and simple exclamations: "Joys pervade the silent breast of Latona, O thrice and four times blessed!" "O lucky ones, whose walls now rise!"[6]

And with greater effect, direction of speech to inanimate objects: "O spear, that has never frustrated my efforts!" And in the Twelfth Book: "Good earth, hold my sword."[7]

Exclamation, direct address, apostrophe, rhetorical questions, and "direction of speech to inanimate objects" are the main techniques which Scaliger focuses upon, and they have obvious qualities in common. Most important, perhaps, is the sense of vivid dramatic action they create. Nearly all of them initiate dialogue—they are nearly all forms of "address"—and Scaliger expands on this dramatic quality in his long discussion of the *Aeneid*. Particular objects, situations, or whole scenes can have the quality of energia for him, and he mentions specifically:

The flaming arrow of Acestes. Turnus shut up within the camp of the Trojans. . . . The helmet of Turnus. His sword broken. Rain at the burning of the ships.[8]

He continues, retelling the flight of Aeneas, Anchises, and Iulus, and adding his own responses to the developing action:

"I go under my burden" (i.e. "I take up my burden."). Indeed I seem to carry my own father, a man most brave. "Little Iulus entwined his hand in his father's and follows his father with unequal steps." Here I seem to be dragged along. For whatever "implicuit" means, the passage surely arouses pity in me. . . . Who would not accompany Aeneas in spirit there?[9]

Scaliger's asides are an interesting testimony to the moving powers of energia when it is effectively used. His discussion of Turnus and Aeneas, moreover, almost certainly influenced Sidney's in the *Apologie*:[10]

> Who readeth *Aeneas* carrying olde *Anchises* on his back, that wisheth not it were his fortune to perfourme so excellent an acte? Whom doe not the words of *Turnus* moove? (the tale of *Turnus* having planted his image in the imagination,) ...   (*Apologie*, 26)

Such a passage suggests not only Scaliger's probable influence on Sidney but also the great extent to which the *Apologie* is concerned with the concept of energia, even when it omits to mention the term itself. Sidney's discussion of Aeneas and Turnus reveals the same kind of response as Scaliger's to vivid scenes and compelling actions, although it goes a step further in showing how "being moved" leads to emulation. Both writers extend the notion of energia beyond the province of rhetoric (apostrophe, personification, etc.) to that of narrative and dramatic situations. They generalize Aristotle's dictum about setting things "before the eyes." "When I hear," writes Scaliger, "of Venulus in the arms of Tarchon, I see it too: 'Fiery Tarchon flies over the plain, carrying the man and his weapons.'"[11] And he jots down a series of vivid scenes and actions: "Shame in the case of Deiphobus, 'trembling and covering his horrid torments.' Wrath in the case of Turnus: 'Sparks come forth from all about his mouth as he speaks; fire gleams from his piercing eyes.'"[12] Sidney, too, offers a series of such vignettes and discusses their significance:

> Let us but heare old *Anchises* speaking in the middest of Troyes flames, or see *Ulisses*, in the fulnes of all *Calipso*'s delights, bewayle his absence from barraine and beggerly *Ithaca*. Anger the *Stoicks* say, was a short maddnes: let but *Sophocles* bring you *Aiax* on a stage, killing and whipping Sheepe and Oxen, ... and tell mee if you have not a more familiar insight into anger then finding in the Schoolemen his *Genus* and *difference*? See ... the sowre-sweetnes of revenge in *Medæa*; and, to fall lower, the *Terentian Gnato*, and our *Chaucers* Pandar, so exprest, that we nowe use their names to signifie their trades. And finally, all vertues, vices, and passions, so in their own naturall seates layd to the viewe, that wee seeme not to heare of them, but cleerely to see through them.   (*Apologie*, 18)

Energia is above all a means of giving feeling a visible form,[13] and Sidney suggests in this passage how poetry makes us see revenge, anger—indeed all passions—expressed in such a way that we understand them for what they are. The result is that "true lively knowledge" or "hart-ravishing knowledge" which only poetry can render: "an image of that whereof the Philosopher bestoweth but a woordish description: which dooth neyther strike, pierce, nor possesse the sight of the soule so much as that other dooth" (*Apologie*, 17). Knowledge and persuasiveness, I might add, are here synonymous. If the image is forceful enough, we will both understand and be moved. Finally, one should notice that Sidney returns several times in the *Apologie* to the importance of dramatic situation or plot ("tales") as a source of such persuasive images:

> [the poet] commeth to you with words set in delightfull proportion, . . . and with a tale forsooth he commeth unto you, with a tale which holdeth children from play, and old men from the chimney corner: . . .   (*Apologie*, 25)

> Whom doe not the words of *Turnus* moove? (the tale of *Turnus* having planted his image in the imagination,) . . . (*Apologie*, 26)

> *Menenius Agrippa*, who, when the whole people of Rome had resolutely devided themselves from the Senate, . . . came not among them upon trust of figurative speeches, or cunning insinuations; . . . but forsooth he behaves himselfe, like a homely, and familiar Poet. He telleth them a tale, . . .   (*Apologie*, 27)

Sidney comes very close at such moments to identifying poetry with what we would normally think of as either drama or fiction: it is, for him, not essentially rhyme or meter, but "that fayning notable images of vertues, vices, or what else" (*Apologie*, 12). He wrote to his brother Robert that poets painted "forth the effects, the motions, the whisperings of the people" (Pears, 200), and the remark has in itself a strong suggestion of the drama, activity, and energy which Sidney instinctively associated with poetry. Plato was a poet because in his work

> all standeth upon Dialogues, wherein he faineth many honest Burgesses of Athens. . . . Besides, his poetical describing of the circumstances of their meetings, as the well ordering of a banquet,

6*

the delicacie of a walke, with enterlacing meere tales, as *Giges*
Ring, and others, which who knoweth not to be flowers of Poetrie
did never walke into Apollo's Garden.   (*Apologie*, 4)

Poetry, in short, is defined largely in terms of dialogues, tales, the
motions and whisperings of the people, the "setting" of a banquet
or a walk, and the vivid scenes, actions, or images from dramatic and
narrative verse. And these, in turn, are essentially what Scaliger and
Aristotle describe as the main constituents of energia.

One final aspect of energia deserves attention before I turn to
Sidney's actual poetic practice. The *Apologie* passage on the Psalms
mentioned David's "awaking his musicall instruments," and in
another part of the *Apologie*, verse is praised because

> that can not be praiselesse, which dooth most pollish that blessing
> of speech, which considers each word, not only (as a man may say)
> by his forcible qualitie, but by his best measured quantitie, carrying
> even in themselves, a Harmonie . . . [Poetry is] the onely fit speech
> for Musick (Musick, I say, the most divine striker of the sences), . . .
>   (*Apologie*, 36)

We know that Sidney was exceptionally interested in and responsive
to music, and he expresses here the common Renaissance view that
music has extraordinary moving powers—it is the "most divine
striker of the sences." Like a great many writers of the period,
Sidney hoped that poetry might draw upon those powers. He was
intrigued by the idea of uniting verse and music, and this was certainly one of the motives which prompted his experiments with
Latin meters in English.[14] The well-known passage in the Queens
College manuscript of the *Arcadia* debates the music-poetry relationship, and Dicus there insists that the poet adapt his quantities to
music so that "every sem[i]brefe or minam" has its "silable matched
unto it with a long foote or a short foote" (Ringler, 390). Similarly,
at the end of the *Apologie*, Sidney declared that classical quantitative
prosody was particularly "fit for Musick, both words and tune observing quantity" (*Apologie*, 60). If he had ideas, however, about
reviving the classical fusion of poetry and music, he failed to work
them out in detail or put them into practice. He seems not to have
known enough about musical composition himself, and he appar-

ently developed no close working relationship with the skilled musicians to whom he had access. Instead, he gradually reconciled himself to English prosody and concentrated his energy on discovering a means of developing the "music" of poetry itself. He makes it clear on several occasions that he responded strongly to the melodic and expressive powers of verse, apart from its relationship to music:

> [Poetry] considers each word, not only (as a man may say) by his forcible qualitie, but by his best measured quantitie, *carrying even in themselves, a Harmonie* . . .   (*Apologie*, 36, italics mine)

> [Poetry] hath *in it self a kind (as a man may well call it) of secret musicke,* since by the measure one may perceave some verses running with a high note fitt for great matters, some with a light foote fitt for no greater then amorous conceytes.   (Ringler, 390, italics mine)

And the passage on prosody at the end of the *Apologie* declares that, although classical verses are more suited to music, English poetry,

> with hys Ryme, *striketh a certaine musick to the eare*: and in fine, sith it doth delight, though by another way, it obtaines the same purpose: there beeing in eyther sweetnes, and wanting in neither maiestie.
>   (*Apologie*, 60, italics mine)

This last statement is particularly interesting. It shows Sidney going beyond his earlier contempt for rhyming; it also emphasizes again that poetry has in itself "a certaine musick," and therefore that it might in itself be capable of some of music's moving, persuasive effects. Sidney assures us, in fact, that he is intrigued by meters (or rhymes) because they can "expresse divers passions," because they are expressive forms capable of communicating vivid feeling in a way that is analogous to the action of forms like prosopopoeia, apostrophe, narrative, and drama. They are, in other words, another potential means of achieving energia, that general vigor of language which reveals the passions of a writer. The fact is extremely important. It demonstrates the great extent to which Sidney conceived of the problem of style as a problem of persuasive expression, involving an effort to discover forms at every level of language—rhythm, sound, syntax, rhetoric, stanza, genre—forms which draw their energies from a writer's strong feelings and release them with such force as to move, convince, and teach (in the broadest sense) an audience. The music of poetry, in its ability to "expresse divers passions," was thus as potentially effective as prosopopoeia or dramatic action in communicating that "true lively knowledge" which Sidney conceived to be poetry's distinctive province.

Once a detailed idea of energia, and of the important role it plays in Sidney's conception of poetry has been gained, one can begin to see some of the ways in which it bears upon his actual writing. I should remark at the outset that energia makes its appearance in Sidney's work long before he discusses it in the *Apologie*. I pointed out in Chapter One that, when Pyrocles falls in love, he discovers, in effect, a new style:

> And Lorde, deare Cossyn (sayde hee) dothe not the pleasantnes of this place, carry in yt self sufficyent Rewarde, for any tyme lost in yt or for any suche daunger that mighte ensewe? . . . Doo yow not see the grasse, howe in Coloure they excell the Emeraudes every one stryving to passe his fellowe, and yet they are all kept in an equall heighte? And see yow not the rest of all these beutyfull flowers, eche of whiche woulde requyer a mans witt to knowe, and his lyfe to express? Doo not these stately trees seeme to meynteyne theyre florisshing olde age with the onely happynes of theyre seate beeyng clothed with a Continuall springe, bycause no beauty here shoulde ever fade? . . . Ys not every Eccho here a perfect Musick? and these fressh and delightfull brookes, how slowly they slyde away, as, lothe to leave the Company of so many thinges united in perfection, and with how sweete a Murmer they lament theyre forc[ed] departure: Certeynly, certeynly Cossyn yt must needes bee, that some Goddess this Dezert belonges unto, who ys the sowle of this soile, . . .
>
> (F, IV. 12–13)

Pyrocles' style is characterized essentially by its energia, by its animated, vivid, energetic expression of the new passions which he feels. Nearly all the key devices are present here: the apostrophes, the strong sense of a dramatic voice speaking in dialogue, the exclamations and emphatic repetitions, the mode of direct address, the "interrogations," the personifications (of the grass, the trees, the brooks), the "direction of speech to inanimate objects," and the eloquent rhythms of the whole. Everything breathes life; everything is animated and vivacious, in a state of activity, present "before the eyes." One could scarcely imagine a passage which crowded more densely into a few lines all the elements which Aristotle, Scaliger, and Sidney himself had enumerated in discussing the means for creating a forceful, persuasive language of the passions. Pyrocles, like David in the Psalms, "sheweth himselfe a passionate lover"; both lovers assure us that "in truth they feele those passions: which easily . . . may be bewrayed by that same forciblenes or *Energia*."

Much of the prose in the *Arcadia* reveals similar qualities. Hector Genouy long ago observed of the book's style: "La prose de Sidney . . . est aussi plus énergique, rappelant les fortes qualités des meilleurs prosateurs français du 16ᵉ siècle. Elle se distingue par le mouvement et le vigueur . . ."[15] Moreover, quite apart from the texture of the prose itself, a number of explicit remarks about style in the *Old Arcadia* (made both by the narrator and by various characters) suggest the extent to which Sidney valued, in even his earliest work, the persuasive power of "lively" descriptions and vividly expressed feelings:

> *Musidorus* did so lyvely deliver oute his inwarde greeffes, that *Cleophilas* frendly harte felt a great Impression of pity withall, . . .
> (F, IV. 38)

> yt seemes to my self I use not wordes enowe to make yow see, how they coulde in one moment bee so overtaken. But, yow worthy Ladyes, that have at any tyme feelingly knowne what yt meanes, will easily beleeve the possibility of yt, . . .   (F, IV. 45)

> Receyve here not onely an Example of those straunge Tragedyes, but one, that in hym self hathe conteyned all the particularityes of theyre mysfortune: . . . yow shall see I say, a Living Image and a present Story of the best Patern, Love hathe ever shewed of his worckmanship.   (F, IV. 114)

> yf by the bending together all my inward powers, they bringe forthe any Lyvely expressing of that they truely feele, . . .
> (F, IV. 207)

All of these passages stress the importance of "Living Images," "present" tales or stories, the need for vividly expressing what one truly feels and for making others "see" so that they may "feelingly know." In this regard, it is important to remember that Languet had "With his sweet skill" given Philisides a "feeling tast of him that sitts / Beyond the heaven" (OA 66, 26–27), and that Astrophel had sought "a feeling skill" to "paint [his] hell" (AS 2, 14). In short, Sidney's observations on style (and those of his various heroes) betray a common set of concerns: none of them—from the remarks in the *Old Arcadia* to those of Astrophel—leads us to believe that Sidney was ever interested in fundamentally decorative, mannered writing; all of them, rather, seem to insist that the final test of any style is its *efficacia* or energia, its ability to capture the substantiality of "things" so forcefully as to give the reader a "feeling tast" of them.

What is true of the *Arcadia*'s prose is equally true of the poetry. The lively speech of Philisides displays energia in its free rhythms, its colloquial diction, its satiric tone, and its air of passionate debate. I have already shown how the sestinas, in their stately but weighty movements, build toward powerful climaxes; and even the lower-keyed, ritualistic sonnets are crowded with apostrophes and exclamations. Perhaps the most vivid of all the *Arcadia*'s ornate verse, however, is Plangus' lament:

> Shall I that saw *Eronae's* shining haire
> > Torne with her hands, and those same hands of snow
> > With losse of purest blood themselves to teare,
> Shall I that saw those brests, where beauties flow,
> > Swelling with sighes, made pale with minde's disease,
> > And saw those eyes (those Sonnes) such shoures to shew,
> Shall I, whose eares her mournefull words did seaze,
> > Her words in syrup laid of sweetest breath,
> > Relent those thoughts, which then did so displease?
> No, no: . . .
>
> O eyes of mine, where once she saw her face,
> > Her face which was more lively in my hart;
> > O braine, where thought of her hath onely place;

O hand, which toucht her hand when we did part;
O lippes, that kist that hand with my teares sprent; . . .
(OA 30, 44–53 and 116–20)

Sidney's formal rhetoric, with its powerful repetitions and forceful rhythms, creates here a vigorously expressive poetry of passion which continually sets objects and vivid scenes before our eyes; we "see" not only Plangus' plight but Erona's, and we are made to concur in Boulon's reply:

Thy wailing words do much my spirits move,
They uttred are in such a feeling fashion,
That sorrowe's worke against my will I prove.
(OA 30, 125–27)

The *Arcadia*, then, possesses energia, but apart from the eclogues, its energia is of a special sort. Emotion is expressed in the elaborately ornate, conventional ways examined earlier—ways which suited the demands of Sidney's heroic romance, but which were clearly not transferable to other verse. The stylized gestures of formal rhetoric, the diffuse and incantatory techniques of the sestinas, the inflexible iambics, and the elaborate rhyme conventions worked well enough in a poetic world of high ideals, serious chivalry, and lamentation in a tragic key. A quite different tone and manner were necessary, however, for the love poetry of Elizabeth's court. In addition, all the sources of energia which the *Arcadia*'s prose narrative had supplied—the "tale," the clash of characters in argument, the vivid descriptions and actions—would no longer be directly available. Sidney's problem, in effect, was to discover ways in which the courtly-love lyric could be shaped to express something of the *Arcadia*'s vigorous drama of love, and yet do so with all the polish, ease, and wit required of a courtier among his familiars.

Sidney took the most natural way he knew. As suggested, he simply introduced into the sonnet and related lyric forms the ironic and intimate tones which were characteristic of the letters to Languet and the *Arcadia*'s narrative sections, the impetuousness and satiric aggressiveness of his fictional counterpart Philisides, and the general dramatic vigor typical of the *Arcadia* eclogues. The achievement of

the *Certain Sonnets* is that they come very close to fusing these diverse
elements—to establishing a dramatic, poetic voice which takes
courtly conversation for its norm, but which can rise easily to higher
strains of praise and grief, or fall to more colloquial outbursts of
anger and sarcasm:

> Sweet Ladie, as for those whose sullen cheare,
>   Compar'd to me, made me in lightnesse found:
> Who Stoick-like in clowdie hew appeare: . . .
>   (CS 17, 46–48)

> But now the starres with their strange course do binde
>   Me one to leave, with whome I leave my hart,
> I heare a crye of spirits faint and blinde, . . .
>   (CS 20, 5–7)

> Wo, wo to me, on me returne the smart: . . .
>   (CS 9, 1)

> Ah saucy paine let not thy errour last, . . .
>   (CS 8, 13)

> And have I heard her say, 'ô cruell paine!'
>   And doth she know what mould her beautie beares?
>   (CS 11, 1–2)

> O faire, O sweete, when I do looke on thee,
> In whom all joyes so well agree,
> Heart and soule do sing in me.
>   (CS 7, 31–33)

The voice is still unperfected, but it is Sidney's, and it manages the
transitions from more familiar tones of address ("Sweet Ladie") to
formal ones ("O faire, O sweete") to the abrupt challenges of rhetorical questions ("And have I heard her say") with no great strain.
The accomplishment was an important one. It made the speaker in
a group of lyrics the locus of a complex drama and gave him a
poetry both supple and various enough to express the conflicting

feelings of a courtier in love. It intimated that Sidney would search for his chief sources of energia in the situations, moods, and emotions of a single, fully articulated love story and, ultimately, in the conversational, dramatic speech of that story's hero.

Sidney's first steps in the new mode were tentative, and one need not exaggerate the quality of the verse in the *Certain Sonnets* to understand its importance. Despite the collection's suggestions of a plot, it is clearly not a genuine whole. And despite its considerable variety, most of the individual lyrics are simply pedestrian. Sidney has adopted the principle of using a dramatic voice—of approximating courtly conversation—as the main source of his poetic energy, but he is still far from working out the full implications of that choice in terms of style.

The change from the *Certain Sonnets* to *Astrophel* was prompted by his further reflection on the possibilities of the lyric as a form for the expression of those powerful and often conflicting feelings which lay at the center of all his writings on love. The commitment to a norm of courtly conversation in verse led him necessarily to seek a greater fluency, a closer approximation to the phrasing patterns of actual speech. It was this search which must have forced his invention of the new, irregular iambic line. He had for some time felt the general inadequacy of English prosody, and he must have been all the more keenly aware of this as he wrote the verse of the *Arcadia* eclogues. There, we feel in nearly every line the strain which a conversational idiom exerts on perfectly regular iambics. A similar awkwardness exists, as was noted, in the more dramatic lyrics of the *Certain Sonnets*. Such lines could hardly have satisfied the ear of a poet who knew the music of Petrarch and the complex harmonies of Vergil. If G. L. Hendrickson and John Thompson are correct, Sidney understood the subtle technique of counterpoint between accent and metrical ictus in Latin dactylic hexameter, and he successfully imitated the effect in his own experiments with that meter in English.[16] When his attempt to domesticate Latin quantitative measures was finally given up, Sidney managed to create a similar form of counterpoint in native iambics—the system of stress variation as we know it in late Elizabethan and post-Elizabethan poetry: the constant interplay between speech accent and the established metrical norm that gave the iambic line an internal dynamics it had never before possessed. Sidney's determination to invent forms which could "expresse divers passions" for persuasive purposes thus led finally to the discovery of a prosody which could communicate more subtle shades of feeling with different kinds of power than the system he had adapted and perfected in the *Arcadia*'s ornate verse. His lines could now accommodate the irregularities of ordinary speech, thereby adding variety to the music of his verse, and yet they might still retain (when desired) a high degree of courtly formality and stateliness of movement. Finally, a general freedom of syntax, a broadening of the usable range of vocabulary, and a bolder use of the sonnet were equally natural consequences once Sidney had decided to let his speaker's changing moods and feelings direct the flow of essentially dramatic verse. Indeed, Astrophel would alter the sonnet form in very much the same way that Philisides had transformed the *terza rima*.

If dramatic speech or conversation was to be the new poetry's main source of energia, however, Sidney did not at all want to forego the other sources of energia mentioned earlier in the analysis of the *Apologie*. The emphasis there was on the importance of dramatic situation, on tales, on what Aristotle called "setting things before the eyes," on the sense of activity and of things being "present," on characters like Medea and Ajax who act out their feelings of revenge or anger with such vividness that "wee seeme not to heare of them, but cleerely to see through them." The new poetry was to retain, if possible, all these other sources of drama as well, and Sidney's desire that it do so led to his invention of what was really a new form in English—the so-called dramatic lyric and its sequence. It is no accident that *Astrophel* is the most carefully plotted and the most overtly dramatized of all the English sonnet sequences. Sidney wanted a hero whose tale would be played out before us, whose love would be rendered with such immediacy that it could not help but move and persuade:

> Flie, fly, my friends, I have my death wound; fly,
> See there that boy, that murthring boy I say,
> Who like a theefe, hid in darke bush doth ly, . . .
>
> (AS 20, 1–3)

Alas have I not paine enough my friend,
    Upon whose breast a fiercer Gripe doth tire
    Then did on him who first stale downe the fire, . . .
                        (AS 14, 1–3)

Vertue alas, now let me take some rest,
    Thou setst a bate betweene my will and wit, . . .
                        (AS 4, 1–2)

O how for joy he leapes, ô how he crowes, . . .
                        (AS 17, 12)

Stella, whence doth this new assault arise,
    A conquerd, yelden, ransackt heart to winne?
                        (AS 36, 1–2)

With how sad steps, ô Moone, thou climb'st the skies,
    How silently, and with how wanne a face, . . .
                        (AS 31, 1–2)

Be your words made (good Sir) of Indian ware,
    That you allow me them by so small rate?
                        (AS 92, 1–2)

This night while sleepe begins with heavy wings
    To hatch mine eyes, and that unbitted thought . . .
                        (AS 38, 1–2)

Out traytour absence, darest thou counsell me,
    From my deare Captainnesse to run away?
                        (AS 88, 1–2)

We feel immediately the presence of energia in Sidney's lines. In *Astrophel*, the action is always present and the objects continually set before our eyes. The exclamations, sharp questions, apostrophes, abrupt openings, the "direction of speech to inanimate objects" ("ô Moone"), the sense of particular places and times ("This night while sleepe")—all of these have found their way into a lyric poetry which is fully dramatic. The whole is endowed with a lively "demonstrative" quality: the activity of Astrophel arguing, pointing, praising, gesticulating, and pleading. We know his voice, witness his tale, and accept the energia of his verse as the sign of his passion. As Lamb said long ago:

> [Sidney's sonnets] are not rich in words only, in vague and unlocalised feelings—the failing too much of some poetry of the present day—they are full, material, and circumstantiated. Time and place appropriates every one of them. It is not a fever of passion wasting itself upon a thin diet of dainty words, but a transcendent passion pervading and illuminating action, pursuits, studies, feats of arms, the opinions of contemporaries and his judgment of them. An historical thread runs through them . . . marks the *when* and *where* they were written.[17]

Sidney's achievement in *Astrophel* can hardly be overestimated. His hero is the first fully realized, poetically conceived character in modern English literature. Astrophel's irony and impetuousness are evident everywhere in his verse; the accents of his speech are recognizable from poem to poem, and are themselves the music of his poetry. In him, Elizabethan literature comes of age, and his creation —or that of someone like him—was essential to the theater of Shakespeare or the lyric poetry of Donne. He showed what might be done in the native tongue, and Sidney through him made available to the writers of the 1590's a necessary example of, and a source of techniques for, the realization of dramatic character in verse. The kind and quality of the achievement were what mattered, quite apart from what individual poets may have learned from it. A standard had been set, and a living personality who "conversed" in poetry had been created. The level of Gascoigne and Turberville, or even of Wyatt and Surrey, would never again seem the best that the new English literature could produce.[18]

In some ways, of course, Sidney had done nothing more than develop the suggestions of earlier writers like Wyatt and Surrey. The chief Tudor poets had established the norm of "good English speech" in the love lyric, and Wyatt especially had developed a

manner that was conversational and dramatic, although it was
scarcely courtly in Sidney's sense of the word. Wyatt saw, too, that
such a manner necessarily involved a transformation of the regular
iambic line and a more sensitive use of poetic forms than was generally typical of Tudor poets. He understood, in other words, that the
problem of style was a whole problem, that a new kind of love poetry
would not be able to get along on monotonous iambics or poulter's
measure or the charming but trivial forms of the villanelle and
rondeau. Sidney, with a greater talent, and a much more developed
poetic, managed to finish what Wyatt had left undone. His voice
was surer, he solved the metrical problem, he made the sonnet a
beautifully flexible medium for lyric expression and dramatic speech,
he gave the lyric a more vivid particularity of time and place, and
he made his hero the center of a tale that gave order to the otherwise
unrelated moments of drama which the verse recorded. Most of
these achievements had been suggested and partly anticipated by
English poets before Sidney. But none had approached the problem
of writing love poetry from quite his point of view, and none had his
complete grasp of the formal problem or his ability to pursue successfully its implications in terms of technique.

The motive of that pursuit, as I have suggested, was Sidney's
desire to write persuasive, moving verse, and he thought of energia
as the chief means to such persuasion. The quest for energia ultimately led Sidney to write a lyric poetry which was full of drama and
which brought new rhythms into English.[19] Interestingly enough,
his development was in some ways paralleled by other artists in other
forms during the sixteenth century. The Camerata group, especially,
brought about a revolution in Italian music which was motivated by
a similar desire to move an audience, and it too found its expressive
means in a combination of words, drama, and music.[20] Just as
Sidney decided that the "music" of his verse—its rhythms—should
be directed primarily by the tones of a speaking voice, so the
Camerata concluded that

> the meaning of the text was . . . of paramount importance: the
> rhythm of melody should be determined by the rhythm of the words.
> The harmony must suit their mood. Interest focused . . . on project-
> ing the meaning and intensity of the words.[21]

Projection was the key to persuasion. The singer was to act out, in effect, his song, imitating what the Camerata believed to have been the methods of the Greek theater:

> The "sole aim" of contrapuntal music "is to delight the ear," wrote Galilei, in his *Dialogo della musica antica e della moderna* in 1581, "while that of ancient music is to induce in another the same passion that one feels oneself." These emotions, he believed, . . . cannot be inspired in the listeners unless they are felt and acted by the performer. By words, gestures, affective control of voice, by intense feeling of the executor, rather than by harmony, the audience could be moved, . . .[22]

Galilei urged the singer to study the methods of orators and actors:

> let them observe . . . the petitioner who is entreating his favor; how the man infuriated or excited speaks; the married woman, the girl, the mere child, the clever harlot, the lover speaking to his mistress as he seeks to persuade her . . .[23]

The singer thus became a dramatic actor, and the result was the invention of recitative and, eventually, of opera. Sidney never pursued very far the possibilities of uniting verse, music, and drama. Instead, he concentrated on the music of verse itself, set to work on its metrical problems, and finally produced a poetry whose harmonies were inseparable from a dramatic speaking voice. While the dramatic lyric was thus being born in England, the dramatic song was invented in Italy. Both were produced by artists who believed that emotions felt and acted by performers or by the characters of a "tale" were the most powerful form of persuasion. Language, gesture, and music all cooperated to create an

> effect . . . of talking in harmony. Caccini wrote that he believed he had "approached . . . ordinary speech." Peri described his settings as "lying between the slow and suspended movements of song and the swift rapid movements of speech." The composer Gagliano called this style a manner "di recitare cantando"—hence the term "recitative."[24]

The aims of the Camerata were broadly moral in nature: the composers took their cue from Aristotle in particular and hoped generally to produce the cathartic effects he had discussed in the

Poetics. Sidney's intentions were equally (though rather differently) moral: he expected poetry to move men to "vertuous action," the "ending end of all earthly learning." It was the thoroughgoing application of this persuasive theory to the practice of the love lyric, however, that constituted Sidney's particular contribution. Astrophel would seek fit words to provoke, not Aristotle's cathartic pity, but a different sort which might "grace obtain." Interestingly enough, the self-consciousness of his persuasive methods is foreshadowed by that of the heroes of Arcadia, although the latter, in their use of musical instruments, seem almost to be versions of Camerata performers in action. When Musidorus sets about wooing Pamela, for example, he first recounts the moving tale of his ill-starred adventures. Like all tales in Sidney, this one has the hoped-for effect:

> *Dorus*, that founde his speeches had given *Alarum* to her Imaginacyons to holde her the longer in them, and bringe her to a dull yeelding over her forces, (as the nature of musick ys to doo) hee tooke up his Harp, & sange these fewe verses.

> > *My Sheepe are Thoughtes wch I bothe guyde & serve,*
> > *Theyre Pasture ys fayre Hilles of fruteles Love;*
> > *In barreyn sweetes they feede, and feeding sterve,*
> > *I wayle theyre Lott but will not other proove. . . .*

> The Musick added to the Tale, and bothe fitted to suche motions in her, (as nowe began ageane to bee awaked) did steale oute of the fayre eyes of *Pamela*, some droppes of Teares, allthoughe with greate Constancy shee would fayne have overmastered at least the shewe of any suche weykenes: . . . (F, IV, 101–102)

So Pamela yields, and so in part does Stella. In the *Arcadia* passage, however, the verse is appropriately decorous, and the tale and music work independently of one another. In *Astrophel*, verse, tale, and "music" fuse in a new poetry to which I must now turn.

CHAPTER XI

The Styles of Astrophel

❦

> Can doelful notes to measured accents set
> Express unmeasured griefs that time forget?
> No, let chromatic tunes, harsh without ground,
> Be sullen music for a tuneless heart.[1]

If the last chapter has stressed mainly the "chromatic" side of Sidney's work, this one ought to begin with a fitting act of contrition. For although it is correct to point out the dramatic and conversational qualities of his poetry, and to locate him (as opposed to Spenser, for example) in the tradition of Wyatt and Donne, he is clearly very different indeed from the latter two poets. His conversation and drama are not theirs, and his love poetry generally is separated from theirs by its courtly qualities, its playful wit and delight in ornament, its Petrarchan ceremoniousness, and its concern for chivalric or heroic values. That separation is, inevitably, a matter of style as well as of paraphrasable content. Sidney's rhetoric, his rhythms, his conception of form, and his grace and ceremony all serve to set him off from Wyatt's blunter tone and Donne's intellectual, febrile movement. Astrophel's conversational manner, in particular, is that of an Elizabethan courtier. Its wit and polish are the sign of his obligation to the sophisticated world about him; its relative formality and its proximity to the high style of ritual show his continual effort to direct feeling into rational and ideal forms. Since love is potentially a mode of aspiration for him (as it often was for the inhabitants of Arcadia), it should achieve its finest and most "natural" expression in the clear harmonies of fulfilled forms. What is socially correct—all the civility and concern for compliment which the Elizabethans valued—and what is spiritually refined ought ideally to come together in a poetry that combines exquisite manners with a purified expression of desire.

Such harmony, however, is rare in *Astrophel*—is rare in all of Sidney's work. In the *Arcadia*, love liberated the spirit and feelings of Pyrocles, but it was also a threatening, debilitating force. If it enriched life beyond measure, it also introduced tension and conflict into the lives of Sidney's heroes, and the *Arcadia* expressed that conflict in its various debates and dialogues, its high-pitched arguments in the eclogues, and its ironies of plot and tone. Nonetheless, a few lyrics there do suggest a more harmonious vision of love, and two of them provide a particularly important introduction to the love themes of *Astrophel*. The first is the duet which Pamela and Musidorus sing during their flight from Arcadia:

> *Pamela.* Like divers flowers, whose divers beauties serve
>   To decke the earth with his well-colourde weede,
>   Though each of them, his private forme preserve,
>   Yet joyning formes one sight of beautie breede.
>   Right so my thoughts, whereon my hart I feede:
>
>   Right so my inwarde partes, and outward glasse,
>   Though each possesse a divers working kinde,
>   Yet all well knit to one faire end do passe:
>   That he, to whome these sondrie giftes I binde,
>   All what I am, still one, his owne, doe finde.
>
> *Musidorus.* All what you are still one, his owne to finde,
>   You that are borne to be the worlde's eye,
>   What were it els, but to make each thing blinde?
>   And to the sunne with waxen winges to flie?
>
>   No no, such force with my small force to trye
>   Is not my skill, nor reach of mortall minde.
>   Call me but yours, my title is most hye:
>   Holde me most yours, then my longe suite is signde.
>
>   You none can clayme but you your selfe by right,
>   For you do passe your selfe, in vertue's might.

> So both are yours: I, bound with gaged harte:
> You onely yours, too farr beyond desarte.
>
> (OA 50)

Mr. Montgomery suggests that this lyric lays Sidney open to the
charge that "ornate verse unnecessarily duplicates 'similitudes.'"
In the first two stanzas,

> Sidney's careful separation of tenor and vehicle implies more than
> neatness: the tenor ("Right so my thoughts . . .") needs no simile to
> clarify it. Like the poem cited earlier [OA 47] this is clearly decora-
> tive.[2]

Manner is thus somehow in excess of matter. Yet one might well
make out a good case for the charming inseparability of the two in
this delicate, meticulously wrought lyric. The tenor of the second
stanza, for example, would be something very different without its
vehicle. By itself, it tells us merely of "partes," each of which possesses a "divers working kinde," and all of which are "well knit to
one faire end." But we learn what characterizes those parts and
defines their particular order only from the other terms of the simile.
Nothing else tells us, for example, that they are especially beautiful,
that they are associated with ceremony and grace ("serve / To *decke*
the earth"), and that they form an aesthetic order which is identified by implication with moral order ("Yet joyning formes one sight
of beautie breede"). Above all, nothing else relates Pamela's beauty
and harmony to the larger harmony of nature itself or suggests
(through the image of the flowers) her delicacy, chasteness, and
youthful freshness. Since her desire is pure, it finds perfectly fitting
expression in the metaphor of nature's beauty. The two stanzas together are an implicit statement about the identity of the moral and
aesthetic orders, and about the relationship between harmony in
man and in nature. Take away the first stanza—the vehicle—and the
statement simply disappears.

If the pure aspiration of Pamela's desire finds an appropriate
form in the metaphor of nature's harmony and beauty, it also finds
other forms in the careful patterning of the language, the restraint
of the syntax, the way in which each line and each stanza are
perfectly filled. No enjambement intrudes upon the first two stanzas,

and the simile which is begun in the first line waits until the last line
of the first stanza for its completing clause. All is then "well knit" in
the skillfully interwoven syntax of Pamela's final couplet:

> That he, to whome these sondrie giftes I binde,
> All what I am, still one, his owne, doe finde.

Sidney has also used the corona form (though modified) to give
added harmony and unity to the whole. Pamela's stanzas are joined
through this device, and Musidorus begins by echoing her final line:
the lovers are linked in their song, united in mutual love. The music,
however, is soon disturbed. Musidorus' questions break its graceful
movement: can he reach so high as to claim Pamela?

> What were it els, but to make each thing blinde?
> And to the sunne with waxen winges to flie?
>
> No no, such force with my small force to trye
> Is not my skill, . . .

The disruption of harmony is given very precise formal expression
here: the fluidity established by the corona device is broken, the
sharply repeated "No no" is placed at the beginning of the next
stanza, and the only enjambement of the poem carries us beyond the
end of that line to the heavily stressed "not" of the next. The lovers
are divided, and Musidorus has apparently refused Pamela's beautiful offering. But we soon learn that he has broken one harmony only
to establish another. Pamela's purity must be matched by his, and
his rebellion is really an act of restraint: tact, good manners, and the
need to control desire will not allow him to call Pamela "his owne."
Instead, he will be hers, and the lovers are again bound together in
another couplet which both echoes and alters Pamela's:

> So both are yours: I, bound with gaged harte:
> You onely yours, too farr beyond desarte.

It would be difficult to imagine a poetry that expresses better than
this the inseparable unity of matter and manner at every level of
style. Within the context of its *Arcadia* scene, and within the limits of
its chosen means, the poem makes every gesture significant. It expresses beautifully a charming moment in which desire has found its

ideal forms in language, in which desire has found an appropriate place in a love that acknowledges its responsibilities to reason. The formal rhetoric, the ornateness, and the respect for the shape of the stanzas all testify to the presence of those responsibilities and aspirations. Indeed, they embody them and work to create what Puttenham called that "lovely conformitie, or proportion, or conveniencie betweene the sence and sensible [which] nature her selfe first most carefully observed in all her owne workes."[3]

Such verse shows the extent to which rhetoric and all the uses of language have a strong symbolic character for Sidney. Astrophel's speech is of course not that of Pamela and Musidorus, but it shares a good deal of the formality of theirs:

> O eyes, which do the Spheares of beautie move,
> Whose beames be joyes, whose joyes all vertues be,
> Who while they make *Love* conquer, conquer *Love*,
> The schooles where *Venus* hath learn'd Chastitie.
>   O eyes, where humble lookes . . .
>
>   (AS 42, 1-5)

> *Stella*, the onely Planet of my light,
>   Light of my life, and life of my desire,
>   Chiefe good, whereto my hope doth only aspire,
> World of my wealth, and heav'n of my delight.
>
>   (AS 68, 1-4)

> Where be those Roses gone, which sweetned so our eyes?
>   Where those red cheeks, which oft with faire encrease did frame
>   The height of honor in the kindly badge of shame?
> Who hath the crimson weeds stolne from my morning skies?
> How doth the colour vade . . .   (AS 102, 1-5)

These lines are typical of much in *Astrophel*. The extraordinarily high pitch of the *Arcadia* is gone, as is the elaborate strictness of its patterns, but much of the "rhetoric" remains. The style of Sidney's new work reveals in one of its major tendencies a respect for the same social and moral values symbolized by the ornateness of the *Arcadia*'s poetry. Its implied ideal is a condition in which desire or love is

expressed with all the delicacy, control, and harmony detected in the
lyric of Pamela and Musidorus.

That ideal, however, is obviously rarely achieved. *Astrophel* is
clearly as full of tension and stress as Sidney's earlier work. We find
in it the same conflicts between passion and purer love, between the
life of action and the life of love, between wit and will.[4] In the
Arcadia, those conflicts were often embodied in the form of pastoral
dialogue, and one of those dialogues (between Geron and Philisides)
is particularly interesting from the point of view of *Astrophel*. It
juxtaposes, not only an impetuous lover and a highly moral counselor, but also two quite different styles. As noticed earlier, Philisides
speaks with the sarcasm, energy, and hotheadedness of youth; his
diction is colloquial, he avoids obvious rhetorical patterning, and at
one point he runs the stanzas of his *terza rima* together. Everything
connotes lack of control:

> And herein most their folly vaine appeares
> That since they still alledge, *When they were yong*:
> It shews they fetch their wit from youthfull yeares
> Like beast for sacrifice, where save the tong
> And belly nought is left, such sure is he, . . .
>
> (OA 9, 78–82)

Geron, by contrast, keeps within the bonds of his stanzas. He talks
plainly and vigorously, but always more sententiously. At the end
of the poem, he rises suddenly to a very different style:

> In hunting fearefull beastes, do spend some dayes,
> Or catch the birds with pitfalls, or with lyme,
> Or trayne the fox that traines so crafty laies.
> Ly but to sleepe, and in the earely prime
> Seeke skill of hearbes in hills, haunt brookes neere night,
> And try with bayt how fish will bite sometime.
> Goe graft againe, and seeke to graft them right,
> Those pleasant plants, those sweete and frutefull trees,
> Which both the pallate, and the eyes delight.
> Cherish the hives of wisely painfull Bees:
> Let speciall care upon thy flock be staid,
> Such active minde but seldome passion sees.
>
> (OA 9, 123–34)

The sudden rhetorical heightening here expresses well the ideal of orderly and purposeful activity in harmony with nature which Geron recommends to Philisides. Control is the keynote of the passage: all the lines but one are end-stopped, the phrasing is balanced, the alliteration and assonance trace patterns everywhere in the language:

> Ly but to sleepe, and in the earely prime
> Seeke skill of hearbes in hills, haunt brookes neere night, . . .
>
> Goe graft againe, and seeke to graft them right,
> Those pleasant plants, those sweete and frutefull trees, . . .

Like the lyric of Pamela and Musidorus, this is poetry which expresses the beautiful accommodation of energy to form that Sidney's ideal courtier—whether in love, in pastoral retreat, or in heroic action—aspired to. Philisides is placed over against that ideal. His colloquial vehemence is comic and charming, but it also comes to stand for what is unruly and disruptive. Unmanageable desire is juxtaposed with harmonious reason, and one of the central dichotomies of the *Arcadia* is thus given a significant stylistic expression within the form of pastoral dialogue.

In *Astrophel*, Sidney "internalized" such dialogues and included both voices (though obviously modified) within the character of Astrophel himself. This is to put the matter crudely. Essentially, however, Sidney extended his use of both the plain and the ornate styles from the *Arcadia* through the *Certain Sonnets* to *Astrophel*. Along the way, pastoral dialogue was converted into dramatic monologue, and a more natural, conversational voice was created, capable of moving easily to higher strains of rhetoric or to freer forms of direct speech. In effect, Sidney's development reveals just that pattern which Rosemond Tuve has traced in the development of Renaissance verse as a whole: the tendency of the lyric to absorb styles and modes which had previously been limited to other "kinds" or genres of poetry.[5] In Sidney, the styles are very often (but by no means always) juxtaposed with something of the same effect noted in the Philisides-Geron dialogue. They retain much of their symbolic value: the formal and colloquial are set against one another; control, aspiration, and reason are set against their opposites. One can see just such a juxtaposition in AS 47. Astrophel, frustrated by Stella's coldness, begins the poem on a note of self-reproach. Anger and humiliation join to produce a burst of sharp questions:

> What, have I thus betrayed my libertie?
>> Can those blacke beames such burning markes engrave
>> In my free side? or am I borne a slave,
> Whose necke becomes such yoke of tyranny?

Love for Astrophel (as for Philisides) is a disruptive experience, and the disturbance reveals itself in the exclamatory quality of their speech. Astrophel's confusion, however, suddenly turns to resolution at the beginning of the sestet:

> Vertue awake, Beautie but beautie is,
> I may, I must, I can, I will, I do
> Leave following that, which it is gaine to misse.
> Let her go. Soft, but here she comes. Go to,
>> Unkind, I love you not: O me, that eye
>> Doth make my heart give to my tongue the lie.

The turmoil of the preceding rhetorical questions is swept away by the near-comic call to arms. The strength of resolution expresses itself in the controlled clauses of the first line and the artificially marshaled syntax of the second. Sidney has created an intentionally hyperbolic high style of duty and heroic action. While Astrophel rides the wave of this style, Stella enters, and he plummets immediately into the direct speech and broken rhythms that indicate the force of her power over him. Heroic resolution disintegrates under the pressure of desire. We end, not with a harmonious adjustment of energy to form, but with a sharp contrast of forms or styles that symbolizes Astrophel's inability to resolve fully (for the poem does achieve partial resolution) the dilemmas created by his love.

Those styles are not, of course, precisely the styles of Philisides and Geron, but the principle of contrast is the same. The formal and the informal, the relatively structured and the relatively unstructured, are played off against one another in such a way as to dramatize the clash between Astrophel's contrary impulses. Such clashes occur frequently in *Astrophel*, although it would be a mistake to take them as a key to Sidney's style throughout the sequence. Rather, they appear at critical times of decision (e.g., AS 1–21 *passim*, and AS 71–72). They represent moments of extreme tension and self-division, and are almost as rare, though not quite, as the interludes of harmony and resolution. The two kinds of verse—that of sharp conflict and that of fulfilled harmony—are used to mark the opposing boundaries within which Astrophel's war of love takes place.

Astrophel's usual style, as has been suggested, is that of courtly conversation, and its great virtue is precisely its ability to express and yet control tension. It is alive with wit and sophistication; most important, its irony is a constant reminder of Astrophel's self-knowledge and self-consciousness, and these qualities assure us that, when other forms of control fail, intelligence at least remains. We sense this very strongly, for example, in the sonnet just examined. Throughout its several reversals, we feel altogether certain of the final outcome—and we feel that Astrophel himself is equally certain. He has long since affirmed his love to Stella in a way not to be doubted; he rather creates this particular crisis of conscience out of his sense of frustration, as well as out of a sense of his obligation to the "heroic" self which he left behind earlier in the sequence. The first lines of the sestet are consciously hyperbolic, the more so to increase the feeling of bathos when Astrophel finally collapses, and our response to his disintegration is mainly comic. He has, in effect, made himself an object of wit, and that wit is one of his chief ways of presenting and dealing with dilemmas which might otherwise prove intolerable. It is a courtier's way, and in the very last lines of the sestet we can detect the restoration of courtly control over the poem:

> Let her go. Soft, but here she comes. Go to,
> Unkind, I love you not: O me, that eye
> Doth make my heart give to my tongue the lie.

The sudden introduction of more fluid rhythms ("O me, that eye, etc.") after the preceding staccato, the pointed balance of "my heart" and "my tongue," and the strong sense of the couplet achieved by throwing emphasis on the rhyme words (especially "eye") all signify the return of Astrophel to his role as controlling courtly lover. Poetic order is re-established, and wit reconciles Sidney's hero to a situation that remains unresolved but at least has been rendered bearable. Significantly enough, Astrophel's solution here is exactly that which Sidney often relied on, both in the Languet letters and in the *Old Arcadia*. In particular, the bathetic spirit of the *Arcadia*'s sharp plot reversals—Musidorus' falling into love just after upbraiding Pyrocles, or lapsing into sensuality after swearing his purity of devotion to Pamela—is very like the reversal in sonnet forty-seven. Both convert potentially serious material into a source of comedy, and both suggest that a sophisticated response to the dilemmas of love is perhaps the only final means of exerting some control over them.

In *Astrophel*, then, Sidney has gone far toward re-creating situations and conflicts very like those discovered in the discussion of the *Arcadia*. In both works, contrasts of attitude on the subject of love are clearly reflected in contrasts of style, and the kinds of resolution offered are in some ways strikingly similar. Yet Astrophel's self-consciousness, if nothing else, separates him decisively from the heroes of Arcadia. He includes within himself, not only the voices of the Philisides-Geron dialogue, but also Sidney's as narrator of the *Arcadia*. Together, they endow him with an obvious complexity of character that finds expression in the equally complex tones of his courtly, dramatic speech. That speech, moreover, effects in itself a serious alteration of Petrarchan values[6] and constitutes a movement away from the ceremony and graceful harmony noticed in the Pamela-Musidorus duet (OA 50). As was suggested in Chapter Seven, Astrophel is closer in spirit to Philisides than to the major heroes of the *Arcadia*; he inherits much of the disruptive energy and satiric aptitude of the young shepherd-courtier, and the result is an inevitable loss in terms of purity of vision and aspiration in love. The humble pleading and the naive idealism of a Pyrocles or Musidorus are not his mode. If he is sometimes surprised by desire, he is never embarrassed by it. His tale, in fact, is structured as a sequence of choices, and when he elects to follow sensual desire instead of virtuous love, the act is fully self-conscious, decisive, and destructive of the highest Petrarchan values. Other values, however, survive, and although Astrophel's style is in one sense the signature

7+

of his ungovernable passion, Sidney also asks us to view both the style and the passion that informs it with a sympathetic understanding of their more positive values. As in the *Arcadia*, a double perspective is maintained, a double judgment of conviction and pardon. The pages that follow examine the nature of that judgment and discuss the vision of love in *Astrophel* as it relates generally to that of the *Arcadia*. As before, matters of technique—particularly Sidney's quest for energia—are as much a concern as matters of content. The effort is to show the inseparability of the two as they meet to create Astrophel's style of love.

CHAPTER XII

The New Poetry

ASTROPHEL'S WARS of love begin properly in the second sonnet of the sequence. Scarcely any other poem will reveal more about Sidney's new poetry or shed more light on the points of similarity and contrast between *Astrophel* and the *Arcadia*:

> Not at first sight, nor with a dribbed shot
> > *Love* gave the wound, which while I breathe will bleed:
> > But knowne worth did in mine of time proceed,
> Till by degrees it had full conquest got.
> I saw and liked, I liked but loved not,
> > I loved, but straight did not what *Love* decreed:
> > At length to *Love's* decrees, I forc'd, agreed,
> Yet with repining at so partiall lot.
> > Now even that footstep of lost libertie
> Is gone, and now like slave-borne *Muscovite*,
> I call it praise to suffer Tyrannie;
> And now employ the remnant of my wit,
> > To make my selfe beleeve, that all is well,
> > While with a feeling skill I paint my hell.

Astrophel begins by declaring his difference from the lovers of Arcadia. Love is no longer a sudden blow, a power to which one submits automatically and unresistingly. It comes to Astrophel, "Not at first sight," but gradually and in such a way that he can mark with some precision the stages of his slow involvement. Although Love is presented as a formidable antagonist, he is rather different from the omnipotent tyrant met in Chapter Five. Astrophel yields to him only after a long war of attrition in which Stella's beauty, her "knowne worth," and the passage of time join together to conquer him. Astrophel is deprived of his freedom, but not as Pyrocles, Musidorus, and Gynecia were. Rather, everything possible is done to suggest the activity of his own will and especially of his own critical intelligence as he proceeds to appraise Stella, approve her, and finally yield to her. The very lack of haste and the care of discrimination in the process do much to make the depth of Astrophel's love convincing. The shot was not "dribbed"; it went straight to the heart, and the wound will bleed so long as Astrophel lives. So the convention has it. But the convention here is backed up by other kinds of description which give body and meaning to it. In this regard, it is interesting that Sidney has used, as so often, the figure of anadiplosis to detail the process of falling in love:

> I saw and liked, I liked but loved not,
>   I loved, but straight did not what *Love* decreed:
>   At length to *Love's* decrees, I forc'd, agreed, . . .

But the figure is no longer managed as it was in the *Arcadia*. There, its clausal links were bound fast together to suggest the autonomous, irreversible quality of love's operation. Here, the form is broken down almost immediately by "but" and "not" so that its self-regulating and independent power is continually attenuated and redirected by the power of Astrophel's will and intelligence. He submits to rhetoric no more easily than he submits to Cupid.

Astrophel yields, then, but slowly and with reservations. Those reservations center primarily around his "lost libertie," and this particular complaint is not simply that of any lover who feels himself somehow less free after his capitulation. The military metaphors are important and functional, and they present Astrophel very much as a soldier—a courtier and man of action—whom love has humiliated and, so to speak, emasculated. From having been a warrior, he is now a slave; yet, because of Stella's beauty and virtue, he is something of a willing slave. The ambivalence of his feelings here relates strongly to the first long debate between Pyrocles and Musidorus in the *Old Arcadia*.[1] The conversion of Pyrocles from hero to Amazon portrayed vividly his withdrawal from the active life of combat, and Musidorus had protested to him that this effeminate love of a Woman, dothe so womanish a man, that, yf yow yeelde to yt, yt will not onely make yow a famous Amazon but a Launder, a Distaff spinner, . . . (F, IV. 17)

Pyrocles had staunchly defended himself on the grounds of Philoclea's virtue and love's transforming power, although later he lamented his transformation:

> Thus all my thoughts are slaves to one thought still:
> Thus Reason to his servants yeelds his right; . . .
> (OA 2, 10–11)

Astrophel's conflicting feelings echo those of the Musidorus-Pyrocles debate, and he stands divided within himself even as they stood opposed to one another. As with Pyrocles in OA 2, however, the emphasis in his sonnet tends to fall less on the positive aspects of love than on what has been lost. That "untrubled Tenor of a well guyded lyfe," of which Philisides and the princes of Arcadia had been deprived, is no longer Astrophel's either. He is left with a "partiall lot" and a "remnant" of his wit. Moreover, though he declares that he has ceased to "repine," his poem suggests that he is far from having overcome his reluctance to love. Despite his feelings for Stella, the self-reproach in "slave-borne *Muscovite*" (and other phrases) is much too great to allow us to think that the passage of his love will be altogether easy in the future. He will have to act out his decision and reaffirm his commitment to Stella more than once. In this respect, too, he is very different from the characters of Arcadia. For although they often lamented their conquest by love, they did so in the logical and self-determining forms analyzed in Chapter Five:

> Thus are my eyes still Captive to one sight:
> Thus all my thoughts are slaves to one thought still:
> Thus Reason to his servants yeelds his right;
> Thus is my power transformed to your will.
> What marvaile then I take a woman's hew,
> Since what I see, thinke, know is all but you?
> (OA 2, 9–14)

> In vaine, mine Eyes, you labour to amende
>> With flowing teares your fault of hasty sight:
> Since to my hart her shape you so did sende;
>> That her I see, though you did lose your light.
>
> .   .   .   .
>
>> And since in vaine I find were all my strife,
>> To this strange death I vainely yeeld my life.
>>> (OA 14, 1–4 and 13–14)

The heroes of Arcadia consistently prove to themselves the impossi-
bility of resisting love. To *decide* whether they should love or not, to
debate the question or try to cease loving, are never realistic alternatives for them. Astrophel, by contrast, is fundamentally a free agent
in spite of his "lost libertie." The first section of the sequence, especially, shows him arguing out the grounds of his love and coming
gradually to a final and irrevocable decision which has the greater
meaning because we have witnessed it.

If the self-division in Astrophel's second sonnet seems to portend
future difficulties, the main reason surely is that Sidney has by now
evolved a style capable of communicating feelings in such a way as
to suggest both their complexity and their depth. The poem is particularly interesting because its development resembles that of
several lyrics from the *Certain Sonnets* and the *Arcadia*, yet does so
only to exhibit its vast difference from them. The tone of the octave,
especially at the beginning, is relatively objective and descriptive.
Astrophel narrates the tale of his defeat in a voice that is full of discrimination and qualification, but not of emotion:

> Nŏt at fírst sìght, nòr with a dríbbed shót
>> Lòve gáve the wound, which while I breathe will bleed:
>> But knówne wórth did in mine of time proceed,
> Tìll by degrées it hád fùll cónquèst gót.
> I saw and liked, // I liked / but loved not,
>> I loved, but straight did not what *Love* decreed:
>> At léngth / to *Lóve's* decrées, // Ì fórc'd, / agréed,
> Yet with repining at so partiall lot.

The voice here is controlled, critical, judicious. All must be told
precisely, and the distinctions Astrophel continually makes force

italics upon important words—"Nŏt," "fĭrst," "drĭbbed," "knówne
wórth," "degrĕes." "It didn't happen this way, or that way, but
that way." "I did this, but not that, and finally *that*." The kinds of
metrical counterpoint Sidney was discovering in the *Arcadia* and the
Certain Sonnets have borne fruit here. In this "italicized" context, the
second line comes as a momentary lyric interlude, with its long
vowels and softened consonants:

> *Love gāve the wound, which while I brēathe will blēed:* . . .

This delicate stroke gives some brief intimation of the feeling that
lies behind the courtly narrative we are hearing. But Astrophel
moves quickly on, and only in the last lines of the octave do we begin
to notice very much tension. As the military metaphor is applied in
detail, we see Astrophel resisting with greater force, until the last
two lines:

> At length / to *Love's* decrees, // Ì fórc'd, / agreed,
> Yet with repining at so partiall lot.

The resistance is greatest in the first line here, where the constantly
interrupted rhythm tactfully conveys the lover's gradual but inevitable capitulation. He exerts continual pressure against the flow of
the line, and the deep reluctance of his surrender is nicely under-
lined by the isolation and added stressing of "I forc'd." He yields,
and we now first learn of his "repining," though the tone is controlled and even witty (qualities emphasized particularly by the
pointed alliteration). The resentment that has been more or less
under the surface to this point is then much more strongly re-
leased:

> Now èven thăt fóotstèp of lòst líbertie
> Is góne, and nów like sláve-bòrne *Múscovíte,*
> I cáll it prăise to súffer Tўrannié;
> And now employ the remnant of my wit,
>   To make my selfe beleeve, / that all is well,
>   Whíle / with a féeling skíll / I páint my héll.

The stressing of the first three lines here is essentially different from
that of the octave. It is more forceful, full of the stronger feeling

which the words demand. Astrophel has theoretically given up repining and has accepted love (the last "footstep"—his reluctance—
is even gone). Yet the language and rhythms tell us that he is anything but reconciled to his situation. All the tension latent in the
careful qualifications of the octave, combined with that in the military metaphors, now finds expression in a glaring paradox that sums
up the lover's condition to him:

> I call it praise to suffer Tyrannie; . . .

The poem appears to have reached its point of maximum tension,
and Astrophel has interestingly discovered that paradox, near-con-
tradiction, is the form most adequate to express his contrary feelings.
This was, of course, one of the principal forms of Arcadia's lovers,
although they employed it in a significantly different way. Pyrocles
may serve as an example:

> Loved I am, and yet complaine of Love:
> As loving not, accus'd, in Love I die.
> When pittie most I crave, I cruell prove:
> Still seeking Love, love found as much I flie.
> Burnt in my selfe, I muse at others' fire:
> What I call wrong, I doo the same, and more:
> Bard of my will, I have beyond desire:
> I waile for want, and yet am chokte with store.
>
> (OA 20, 1–8)

Unlike Astrophel, Pyrocles *begins* his lyric with paradoxes, and the
procedure is typical of a great many *Arcadia* poems.[2] The young
courtier-prince simply lists the various kinds of self-contradiction he
feels; he uses paradox as a mathematical formula to fix objectively
the particular condition in which he finds himself. Astrophel, on the
other hand, genuinely discovers his paradox in the process of defining and describing his love. It emerges gradually from a complex
of feelings which, at the beginning of the poem, are only half
realized. When he finds it, he thrusts it forth with a special vehemence—that extra power we feel in the pointed opposition and
strong stressing of "praise" and "Tyrannie."

Pyrocles' and Astrophel's sonnets have additional points of resemblance and contrast which are equally worth noting. Despite its static quality, for example, Pyrocles' lyric does in fact have a kind of development, and it reaches its most intense moment at a point that corresponds to a similar moment in Astrophel's sonnet:

> This is thy worke, thou God for ever blinde:
> Though thousands old, a Boy entit'led still.
> Thus children doo the silly birds they finde,
> With stroking hurt, and too much cramming kill.
> Yet thus much Love, O Love, I crave of thee:
> Let me be lov'd, or els not loved be.
>
> (OA 20, 9–14)

The sudden drama of the first line here leads to the relative violence of the fourth. Pyrocles' paradoxes have been gradually tightened, so to speak, to produce extra energy. Yet after the climax in "too much cramming kill," Pyrocles lapses into entreaty and concludes (in the couplet) with a perfectly balanced, unforceful appeal—a paradoxical request to match his paradoxical plight. Astrophel, similarly, had drifted toward a measured, balanced close:

> I call it praise to suffer Tyrannie;
> And now employ the remnant of my wit,
>   To make my selfe beleeve, that all is well,
>   While with a feeling skill I paint my hell.

After the first line here, the rhythms slack. The stressing is lighter, and we begin to slip easily toward the couplet. Although Astrophel's feelings are still unresolved, he seems to be moving in the direction of a controlled, verbal resolution. Our expectation, begging the reader's pardon, is something like this:

>   To make my selfe beleeve, that all is well,
>   While writing sonnets, that my sorrows tell.

This would round off the poem as Pyrocles' sonnet was rounded off, with the last two lines forming an anticipated paradox and with both more or less equal in the intensity of their feeling. Such is the method of the *Arcadia*. Astrophel's method, however, is clearly different. His

7*

final paradox has all the dynamic quality of the one he discovered earlier. Instead of settling into a quiet couplet, he kicks through the very bottom of the poem in the last line and reaches a depth of feeling we are not at all prepared for:

> To make my selfe beleeve, / that all is well,
> While / with a feeling skill / I paint my hell.

The pause after "While" (which allows its vowel to trail on), the admission of "feeling," the retardation of rhythm through the middle of the line, and the slow movement of the last four words with the climactic rhyme on "hell"—all combine to release the accumulated emotion of the poem. Astrophel's final conflict of feelings—unlike Pyrocles'—is *experienced* as a conflict in all of its intensity.

Part of the reason for the success of the last lines in Astrophel's sonnet is due to Sidney's extraordinary handling of the rhymes and sounds generally. Until this point in the poem, Astrophel's tones are mainly abrasive. He is critical, indignant, vehement, humiliated. He chafes. The stress patterns and sounds express the mood:

> Nŏt at fĭrst sìght, . . .
>
> a drĭbbed shót . . .
>
> it hád fùll cónqùest gót.
>
> to Love's decrées, Ì fórc'd, agreed, . . .
>
> thăt fóotstèp of lòst líbertíe . . .
>
> sláve-bòrne Múscovíte, . . .

Irregular or weighted stressing combine with a collocation of short vowels ("Not," "dribbed," "shot," etc.) and hard consonants (f, d, b, t, c, g) to make the texture rough. The rhyme words are of the same order: "shot," "got," "not," "bleed," "proceed," "decreed," "*Muscovite*," "wit," etc. One line—already mentioned—significantly breaks the pattern, and is echoed by the last lines:

Lòve gǎve *the* wōund, *which* whíle I brēathe *will* blēēd: ...

To máke *my* sélfe belēēve, *that* ǎll *is* wéll,

Whíle with a fēēling skíll I páint *my* héll.

The main consonants here are softened (w, l, v, th), and the vowels are predominantly long. Those that are not ("skill," "hell") are frequently lengthened by the consonants that follow them. The rhymes in the final couplet are now no longer clipped ("sho*t*," "agree*d*," "wi*t*") but concentrate the double "l's" that are so important here. The stressing is almost perfectly regular, and un-weighted. In short, everything is done to intensify the sense of a slow, deepened, strongly felt movement that suggests the reaches of emotion beneath the more courtly and critical surface of Astrophel's verse.

Finally, one might add that nothing much is done with the sonnet form per se here—nothing, at any rate, so dramatic as in the first poem of the sequence, where the last line is so vividly cut off from and balanced against the previous thirteen. But the lyric is almost the more impressive for that. The form is rather shaped and molded from within. The current of feeling sometimes erupts at a point where the form itself invites it—as at the eleventh line, where Sidney usually divides his sestet; sometimes it strongly defeats our expectations—as in the couplet, which is wrenched in two by the unexpected power of the last line. Sidney has essentially tunneled through the poem with a progressive exploration and revelation of Astrophel's feeling straight to the end, where he seems suddenly to break out of the form altogether.

The ways in which this poetry is different from Sidney's earlier work are almost too obvious now to require further comment, but a few general statements may nonetheless be helpful. First, it is a poetry of freedom insofar as it emphasizes the lover's conscious activity of evaluation, judgment, choice. Astrophel, at the beginning of the sequence, is torn between love and the "lost libertie" of the heroic or active life, and the conflict he feels within himself is, in effect, born of the *Arcadia* dialogue between Pyrocles and Musidorus. That conflict is expressed in verse which is pre-eminently dramatic in its subordination of all the major elements of style to the control of the speaker's voice. His fluctuating feelings and his changing tones govern the movement of the whole. The result is a poetry that is dynamic in the ways suggested above: it modifies rhetorical figures like anadiplosis, discovers others like paradox, and shapes the sonnet form from within. While it is conversational, it is so in a special way. Its norm is courtly, and it derives its tension, not from a free use of colloquial speech, but from various kinds of minor departure from the highly polished and well-regulated speech we normally expect of Astrophel. In the sonnet examined, we find neither the striking juxtapositions between structured and unstructured elements which were noted earlier, nor, obviously, the clear harmonies of resolution in love. Instead, the poem belongs to that broad range of Astrophel's verse which shows continual alterations in the balance of feeling. The norm established is the relatively formal, controlled, and mainly neutral poetry of the octave. A movement toward more vigorous, informal speech ("slave-borne *Muscovite*") increases the sense of Astrophel's active resistance against love; a more lyric quality (as in the last lines) suggests the full depth of his feelings. Both kinds of departure are easily within the reach of the courtier's voice. Despite the emotional strain they express, they never give the sense of a loss of control. Even in the final wrenched couplet, the half rhymes of "all"-"well" and "skill"-"hell," backed up by the full rhyme of "well"-"hell," force an important awareness of design upon us and remind us of the poet's calculating hand.

That calculation, however, seems always perfectly natural, and many of its effects are subliminal until they are touched into consciousness. The skillful handling of consonants and vowels, for example, and the contrast in rhyme sounds are very different in their method from the *Arcadia* examples noticed in Chapter Six. They are not at all so obtrusive. Alliteration is used relatively sparingly, and Sidney now concentrates much more on assonantal patterns; he groups correlative consonants (b-p, d-t) and relies much less upon identical ones. Often, as with the "l's", terminal consonants are far more important than initial ones.

Finally, in looking for the poem's main source of energia, one might do worse than to find it in the carefully articulated rhythms of the music. John Thompson, who has done most to define Sidney's prosodic achievement, has nonetheless suggested that the meters of *Astrophel* "do" very little:

> Can it be that this meter of Sidney's has only the strange merit of being supremely contrived? I think that is so. Earlier I made the claim that it was this recognition of Sidney's about meter which allowed him to practice his art with a new degree of sophistication. This sophistication is first the virtuoso technique; it is sophisticated because it involves the recognition that the poem is made of two things, pattern and language. . . . Sidney's recognition of the profound difference between art and experience often only encouraged in him his decorative fancies, and a silly kind of prettiness.[3]

One may perhaps question the sense in which any meter can be merely contrived, but Astrophel's, at least, seems to be anything but that. Thompson's comparison of Sidney and Donne[4] is perhaps more misleading, therefore, than helpful. Sidney's metrics simply do not work like Donne's. They are fashioned for a courtier's speech, and are absolutely right for that context: they strike just the necessary balance between stateliness and conversation, formality and informality—a balance that defines Astrophel's style as a whole. I have already described how some of the details of those metrics work. The rhythmic contrasts between the first and second triads in the sestet of AS 2 show the extent to which the music of the verse is one of its most affective and subtle powers. Astrophel moves in the course of his sonnet from speech that plays lightly, critically, against the metrical pattern ("Nŏt at fĭrst sìght," "But knówne wórth") to something much more abrasive ("sláve-bòrne *Múscovíte*") to something much more delicate ("Whĭle / with a féeling skĭll"). This is the very movement of the poem, of Astrophel's feelings, and the metrics are a continual notation of them.

The conflict revealed in the second sonnet of the sequence is played out primarily in the first twenty-one poems, and it may be helpful at this point to offer some preliminary observations on this section as a whole. It is carefully, if fluidly, structured, and it shows Astrophel doing battle on three fronts: against other courtly poet-lovers, against Stella's coldness, and against the various embodiments of Virtue that besiege him. Most of the poems in praise (or blame) of Stella focus on the adventures of Cupid, who is seen both as an ally and as an antagonist. The theme of love's tyranny and capriciousness—so important in the *Arcadia*—is here presented in a light and generally charming manner. The process of domestication which was taking place in the *Certain Sonnets* has been completed, and the blind god is now little more than a mischievous *putto*: noxious, but also potentially helpful as a sounding board for Astrophel's complaints. One might recall and compare, briefly, the treatment of "paine" in CS 9:

> Paine heard her praise, and full of inward fire,
> (First sealing up my heart as pray of his)
> He flies to her, and boldned with desire,
> Her face (this age's praise) the thiefe doth kisse.
> O paine I now recant the praise I gave,
> And sweare she is not worthy thee to have.
>
> (CS 9, 9–14)

> So when thou saw'st in Nature's cabinet
> *Stella*, thou straight lookst babies in her eyes,
> In her cheeke's pit thou didst thy pitfould set,
> And in her breast bopeepe or couching lyes,
> Playing and shining in each outward part:
> But, foole, seekst not to get into her hart.
>
> (AS 11, 9–14)

The Cupid sonnets are lyrics of both praise and complaint, and Astrophel's handling of them shows a slight development even in the opening stages of the sequence. The first three (AS 7–9) tell only of a wounded lover; after that (especially in AS 11–12 and AS 16) we see a more aggressive hero who is already complaining about Cupid's bungling (AS 11) and Stella's "disdaine" (AS 12). Astrophel thus shows himself from the beginning to be a descendant of both Philisides and the narrator of the *Certain Sonnets*. He has learned his tactics from poems like the epistle to Mira (OA 74) and the later sonnets on pain (CS 8–11), although he also aspires to Pyrocles' and Musidorus' clearer world of Petrarchan idealism:

Queene *Vertue's* court, which some call *Stella's* face
Prepar'd by Nature's chiefest furniture,
Hath his front built of Alablaster pure;
Gold is the covering of that stately place.

. . . .

The windowes now through which this heavn'ly guest
Looks over the world, and can find nothing such,
Which dare claime from those lights the name of best,
Of touch they are that without touch doth touch,
Which *Cupid's* selfe from Beautie's myne did draw:
Of touch they are, and poore I am their straw.

(AS 9, 1–4 and 9–14)

But while I thus with this yong Lyon plaid;
Mine eyes (shall I say curst or blest) beheld
Stella; now she is nam'd, need more be said?
In her sight I a lesson new have speld,
I now have learn'd Love right, and learn'd even so,
As who by being poisond doth poison know.

(AS 1, 69–14)

Both poems show very well the uncertain harmony of Astrophel's poetry of praise. The first sonnet, with its bejeweled *blason*, leads us expectantly toward either a tactful appeal (compare OA 13, 140–68) or a protestation of aspiring virtue. Instead, we discover a debilitated Astrophel, mildly self-pitying and registering only his disturbance. In the second sonnet, the effects are even more dissonant, though wittily so. At the beginning of the passage, we are led gradually toward Stella, but the parenthetical "curst" ruffles the line, and we come upon Stella's name placed abruptly after the enjambement in line two. A matter-of-fact question carries us into the final triad, where Astrophel learns "Love right." It is no heavenly love, however, and the last line upsets once and for all any hopes for a harmonious conclusion. Wit, mild impertinence, abrupt bursts of colloquial speech, and a structure of reversals have combined to create a poetry utterly unlike that of Pamela and Musidorus (in OA 50), with its delicacies of mutual compliment. The impatience of Astrophel's desire, his impetuousness and frustration, continually interrupt his gestures of high Petrarchan praise and promise no tale of simple love. Before examining the nature of that tale more carefully, however, I should turn first to a second group of poems in the opening part of the sequence: those which focus upon Astrophel's criticism of other courtly poets.

CHAPTER XIII

Astrophel as Poet

IF ASTROPHEL is uncomfortable in conventional postures of praise, he expresses some of that difficulty in a group of related sonnets that deal explicitly with problems of style (AS 1, AS 3, AS 6, AS 15, AS 55, and AS 74). They are a complex set, and offer no simple key to their interpretation. In them, Astrophel advances a critique of the Petrarchan mode, but one that is qualified both by his sense of the role he must play as a courtier in a courtly society, and by his genuine responsiveness to the social and moral values which the Petrarchan mode embodies. On the whole, he criticizes its aberrations, aspires to its excellences, and yet discovers himself to be incapable of fully realizing them.

Part of the difficulty of these sonnets lies in the variety of functions they seem to serve and the different kinds of recommendations they seem to make. Since they are partially anti-Petrarchan in spirit, they can be used to support readings which prefer to emphasize what is plain, or Senecan, or "sincere" in Sidney.[1] At the same time, since anti-Petrarchan protests were common well before the 1580's, the *Astrophel* poems lend themselves equally well to the purposes of critics who wish to stress their conventional and strategical aspects. From this point of view, the poems provide Astrophel with a way of urging the claims of his "real" love and make available to him a convenient means of flattering Stella:[2]

> For me in sooth, no Muse but one I know:
> Phrases and Problemes from my reach do grow,
> And strange things cost too deare for my poore sprites.
> How then? even thus in *Stella's* face I reed,

What Love and Beautie be, then all my deed
But Copying is, what in her Nature writes.

(AS 3, 9–14)

Astrophel consciously plays the role of naive poet here. He uses rich
art to confess his own poverty, and this is clearly a sophisticated
gambit intended for sophisticated ears. As courtier, he neither
desires, nor can he afford, to give up the artifice which is indeed
altogether natural to him. Yet he is being more than simply witty
here, and his sophisticated disavowal of "strange things" and
"Phrases and Problemes" differs significantly from the anti-
Petrarchan protests of earlier poets (such as Ronsard and du
Bellay).[3] If he is not wholly serious in his advocacy of poetic simplicity, neither is he merely copying a "conventional" tactic. His
comments are too detailed, too precise, and too closely related to
Sidney's own remarks in the *Apologie* to be considered purely as a
piece of clever strategy. Like the *Apologie* passages which I examined
earlier, however, the *Astrophel* sonnets on style reveal their significance only if close attention is paid to the precise ways in which they
qualify themselves. There is a sense in which they do in fact protest
against "Petrarchan excesses" (Montgomery's phrase), but dealing
in such general terms may lead to the conclusion that the poems are
a wholesale indictment of ornateness, and the sequence will become
a kind of stylistic puzzle. We will wonder how to account for Astrophel's own use of ornament, when he seems to disavow it altogether
in these opening sonnets; and we shall have to assume either that he
was being simply witty and tactical in his disavowals, or that he was
incapable of writing the plainer poetry he apparently admires.
Neither of these alternatives is very satisfying. What the following
pages suggest is that *Astrophel*, like the *Apologie*, never criticizes ornament itself, but only improper uses of ornament. The sonnets on
style do indeed offer a program for reform, but the reforms concern
methods of imitation and invention. No single style is prescribed.
Rather, Astrophel expresses a complex attitude toward style similar
to that which Sidney himself articulated in the *Apologie*: he calls for
a sensitive adjustment of manner to matter, of individual feelings to
the subject at hand, and for that kind of "naturalness" which can

include both unadorned plainness and high polish, depending purely upon the various and changing demands of decorum.

The very first sonnet of the sequence does a great deal to define Astrophel's views on style, and does so in highly dramatic terms. Sidney's hero begins his career as poet-lover by attempting to write in the manner of a "false" Ciceronian: not that he is pedantic, or that he reveres any single master, but that he works, as it were, from the outside in.

> I sought fit words to paint the blackest face of woe,
> Studying inventions fine, her wits to entertaine:
> Oft turning others' leaves, to see if thence would flow
> Some fresh and fruitfull showers upon my sunne-burn'd braine.
> But words came halting forth, wanting Invention's stay,
> Invention, Nature's child, fled step-dame Studie's blowes,
> And others' feete still seem'd but strangers in my way.
> Thus great with child to speake, and helplesse in my throwes,
>   Biting my trewand pen, beating my selfe for spite,
>   'Foole,' said my Muse to me, 'looke in thy heart and write.'
>
> (AS 1, 5–14)

Astrophel's compositional methods are faulty in several ways. He begins by seeking matter and inspiration in the pages of other poets, by looking for "ideas." Imitation has become little more than desperate (and comic) rummaging; as Astrophel practices it, it could scarcely be more different from the intense personal assimilation of other writers that Sidney described in the *Apologie*: "by attentive translation (as it were) devoure them whole, and make them wholly" yours. In addition, Astrophel is far too preoccupied with being merely ingenious, wittily complimentary, superficially showy. He studies "inventions fine" in order to "entertaine" Stella, and "fine" has the same ironic sense which it bore in the *Apologie*: "For nowe they cast Sugar and Spice upon every dish that is served to the table; like those Indians, not content to weare eare-rings at the fit and naturall place of the eares, but they will thrust Iewels through their nose and lippes, because they will be sure to be fine" (*Apologie*, 57–58). Astrophel, in short, begins by cultivating a false kind of ornament. His "inventions fine" are clearly related to the decadent "phrases fine" of the dainty wits (AS 3) and to the "choisest flowers" (AS 55) which he later regards with so much scorn. He is attracted by glitter, "sugars" his speech (AS 55), and misunderstands what is "fit" and natural. He is on the way to sounding like those poets who have only "red Lovers writings, and so caught up certaine swelling phrases."

These particular errors are, of course, bound up with others that Astrophel mentions: his failure to consider fully the content of his own feelings or to focus sufficiently upon Stella herself. Words without "Invention's stay" will inevitably be "halting," and attempts to imitate other poets before having discovered the substance of one's own themes will necessarily be stillborn. Astrophel's Muse corrects him in the final line of this opening sonnet, urging him to turn to more "natural" sources of inspiration. Yet (as recent criticism has rightly insisted) she recommends neither spontaneity nor naive simplicity of expression, only a fit subject for (and proper method of) invention. David Kalstone has pointed out, for example, that the heart—where Astrophel must now "looke"—conventionally lodged either the image of Cupid (Love) or that of the poet's lady. Mr. Kalstone concludes that the second of these alternatives is the "more relevant" one: Astrophel is commanded to focus upon Stella, and in doing so, he concentrates at last upon his true subject for invention.[4]

There is little to add to this interpretation, except perhaps a reminder that the poem's last line can also be read as a more general directive. It enjoins Astrophel from being merely "fine," ingenious, or entertaining and urges him not to neglect the passions of his own heart. He had begun his sonnet, after all, by declaring his intention to paint his "woe" and "paine" but had allowed himself to be distracted by the formulations of other poets. His Muse does little more than to recall him to his original purpose—that of giving expression to his feelings in order to move Stella and so win "grace" from her. Such an interpretation need not give way to more broadly "romantic" readings of either the poem or the sequence. Astrophel's primary goal remains an objective one: not self-exploration and self-expression as ends in themselves, but the expression of personal feeling for the purposes of rhetorical persuasion. The advice of his

Muse is, in this sense, an echo of that given by nearly all the major classical and Renaissance treatises on rhetoric:

> any diction is cold and dead that does not come from the heart.[5]

> not just adding to your own speech all the beautiful things that you find, but digesting them and making them your own, . . . so that your speech may not seem a patchwork, but a river flowing forth from the fountain of your heart.[6]

> Thus, in short, will the oration be alive only when it is born in the heart and does not float on the lips.[7]

To look in one's heart—to discover and give full expression to the feelings lodged there—did not in itself guarantee good writing, but failure to do so was invariably fatal. After this first sonnet, Astrophel sets off on a new course, hoping to keep his diction from being cold and dead, hoping to fashion a style which will persuade Stella that he "in truth . . . feele[s] those passions: which easily . . . may be bewrayed by that same forciblenes or *Energia* . . . of the writer."

Sidney's hero, having been schooled in composition, immediately feels ready both to satirize and to instruct other poets who have blundered in similar ways:

> Let daintie wits crie on the Sisters nine,
> That bravely maskt, their fancies may be told:
> Or *Pindare's* Apes, flaunt they in phrases fine,
> Enam'ling with pied flowes their thoughts of gold:
>   Or else let them in statelier glorie shine,
> Ennobling new found Tropes with problemes old:
> Or with strange similies enrich each line,
> Of herbes or beastes, which *Inde* or *Afrike* hold.
>   (AS 3, 1–8)

> You that do search for everie purling spring,
>   Which from the ribs of old *Parnassus* flowes,
>   And everie floure, not sweet perhaps, which growes
> Neare therabout, into your Poesie wring;
> You that do Dictionarie's methode bring
>   Into your rimes, running in ratling rowes:

You that poore *Petrarch's* long deceased woes,
With new-borne sighes and denisend wit do sing;
You take wrong waies, those far-fet helpes be such,
As do bewray a want of inward tuch:
And sure at length stolne goods do come to light.

(AS 15, 1–11)

The main complaints in these lyrics have nothing to do with ornament per se. They are aimed at poets who rely on various kinds of "far-fet helpes"—methods and devices used as substitutes for genuinely creative composition—and who care only for what is "fine" and "daintie." The dainty wits mask, enamel, or ennoble their thoughts, and each of those activities suggests a conscious effort to make something fancy out of patently poor materials. Their methods are like those of the writers whom Sidney had mocked in the *Apologie*: "Truly, they have made me think of the *Sophister*, that with too much subtlety would prove two eggs three; . . . So these men bringing in such a kind of eloquence, well may they obtain an opinion of a seeming fineness, but persuade few, which should be the end of their fineness" (*Apologie*, 58). Such poets are to be criticized, not because they are ornate, but because they are ornate in the wrong way. They are the nouveaux riches of poetry, casting sugar and spice on every dish, without regard for what is appropriate or fit or natural. They hunt for strange similes, gather "*everie* floure," use dictionary methods, and diligently search "*everie* purling spring." Lacking "inward tuch," they "ape" Pindar and ransack Petrarch, although Astrophel is confident that their "stolne goods" will come to light: not necessarily because their sources will be discovered, but because their verse effectively exposes itself. It is too obviously a patchwork of "swelling phrases, which hang together, like a man which once tolde mee, the winde was at North West, and by South." At bottom, of course, Astrophel's criticism of the dainty wits is directed at the quality of their love as well as of their style. The two are ultimately inseparable. These are poets, finally, who have in fact no feelings at all—no love, no matter to invent, no substance. Astrophel may have begun in their manner, but his own powerful passion soon persuaded him to take another way. That way, one should stress, does not at all preclude a proper use of ornament and artifice, or proper methods of imitating other poets. But choices of metaphor or figurative scheme or alliteration will arise naturally out of a poet's full consideration of the subject at hand, and other writers' phrases and flowers will meanwhile have been thoroughly digested so that they have become his own.[8] After Astrophel's first sonnet, he insists that he has ceased "Striving abroad a foraging to go" (AS 55), that he is "no pick-purse of another's wit" (AS 74). His tone in these and other passages is often ironic, but his criticism is simply too substantial and consistent not to have point, and his poetry—in all of its genuine originality—fully bears out his claims for himself. His point of view is very much that of the classical and humanist rhetoricians, and he echoes closely Quintilian's statement of the matter:

> as a rule, the best words are essentially suggested by the subject matter and are discovered by their own intrinsic light. But to-day we hunt for these words as though they were hiding themselves and striving to elude our grasp. And thus we fail to realize that they are to be found in the subject of our speech, and seek them elsewhere, and, when we have found them, force them to suit their context. . . .
> The usual result of over-attention to the niceties of style is the deterioration of our eloquence. The main reason for this is that those words are best which are least far-fetched and give the impression of simplicity and reality. . . . We borrow figures and metaphors from the most decadent poets, . . . we look upon everything that is dictated by nature as beneath our notice, and seek not for the true ornaments of speech, but for a meretricious finery, . . .[9]

There are, of course, differences between Sidney and Quintilian, and even greater differences between the demands of Roman forensic oratory and those of Elizabethan courtly lyrics. But both writers were alike in their love of "true ornaments" and their scorn for "meretricious finery."

I began this chapter by suggesting that Astrophel was uncomfortable in postures of Petrarchan praise, and that part of his discomfort found explicit expression in his sonnets on style. The source of that discomfort, as I have shown, has nothing to do with a proclaimed revolution against either ornament in love poetry or Petrarchan language and conventions generally. It concerns primarily the abuse of such things. Astrophel aims his barbs at the decadent, superficial, "fine" verse of the dainty wits—"dainty" itself obviously suggests their lack of passion and substance—and he begins his courtship of Stella by staking out a strong claim for his own genuine feeling and original poetry. His effort is not to reject the Petrarchan mode out of hand but to find a personal style of his own within its broad confines, a style that will transform or transmute the inherited language of love in such a way as to betray the sign of his own particular "inward tuch."

The fact that Astrophel also finds it convenient to play the roles of naive poet and plain-speaking lover is a separate (if related) matter, and must be related to the circumstances of his milieu as well as to the nature of his temperament. Stressing his plainness (or his originality) is an important way of emphasizing his difference from the dainty wits. It also allows Astrophel to "entertain" Stella by trying out the fashionable poses of the day. Moreover, he parodies rather than imitates plain speakers and naifs. The sestets of AS 3, AS 6, and AS 15 are ironic in their confession of "poore sprites" and self-consciously hyperbolic in their suggestion that one need only "behold" Stella in order to write well. They are anything but straight-faced defenses of unadorned simplicity. Far from supporting Astrophel's supposed advocacy of plainness, they intimate that Sidney's hero knows only too well that *mere* plainness and simplicity will get him nowhere with Stella. He will have to be courtly and artful and strategical, and yet also passionate. The difficulties of his situation are compounded, moreover, by his obvious uncertainty in the face of his desire; not that he distrusts its genuineness or substantiality, but rather, that it seems only too strong, sensual, and imperious. If Astrophel is prone to role playing and if his feelings have trouble accommodating themselves to traditional modes of Petrarchan praise and compliment, the cause has a great deal to do with the very equivocal nature of his love. When he attempts to follow the proper method of poetic invention, his verse never rises in the moving, persuasive strains of celebration and reverence which we find in Petrarch or even in the Pamela-Musidorus duet. He discovers, not a refined and virtuous desire which proclaims its own sincerity through the high lyricism of its style, but a powerful, disruptive, sensual passion which is struggling for quite different means of declaring itself.[10]

That discovery exerts continual pressure upon Astrophel's verse. His speech is courtly, but it shows everywhere the traces of that energy which love and desire have turned loose in him. An intimacy of manner, an aggressiveness in debate, an exclamatory impetuousness, and a strong satirical spirit all characterize him. Although he remains a humble, Petrarchan servant of love, and Stella is indeed aloof, Astrophel's constant drive is toward bringing his lady to his own level, where he may talk and debate with her. Indeed, the range of his style includes so much of the dramatic and colloquial, even as his love includes so much frank desire, that the traditional harmonies of the convention are appreciably altered by him. His speech, as suggested earlier, derives partly from the "rough" eclogues of the *Arcadia*, and that particular strain inevitably affects the texture of the whole. The sarcasm of a Philisides and the interrupted rhythms of pastoral quarrels are hardly native to the Petrarchan love lyric. A voice that can include them, along with the ironic wit and eroticism found in the *Certain Sonnets*, has gone far toward transposing the old music into a new key. Love, essentially a matter of worship in Petrarch, is now equally a matter of tactics, debate, play, and peremptory desire.

For all this, Astrophel creates no revolution. He accepts the convention and its basic style, partly because they define the terms in which he has learned to think of love, partly because he affirms their values, and partly because Stella forces those values upon him. He brings with him, however, his new and disruptive vitality. He modifies the convention from within, satirizing those who have abused its language, and questioning (implicitly) its high idealism. The very texture of his colloquial speech is itself a threat to the values embodied in Petrarchan lyricism and ceremony. It stands over against that ceremony very much as the style of Philisides was opposed to the resolved and delicate harmonies of Geron's pastoral verse in OA 9. Yet if that speech marks in one sense a falling off, it is also of positive value, particularly when considered in relation to the artificiality of Astrophel's courtly milieu. It is the medium for much of Astrophel's strongest feeling, and it validates, through its directness and relative naturalness, the sincerity and depth of his love. Late in the sequence, when his style is frequently more ceremonial and formal (e.g., Eighth Song and AS 94–103), that ceremony has the quality of something positively achieved or earned. Astrophel reinvigorates the convention's formal language of feeling, and does so all the more movingly because he had earlier spoken in such very different tones.

CHAPTER XIV

Dialogue and Debate

THE THIRD major group of poems in *Astrophel*'s opening section records with some precision the successive stages of Astrophel's commitment to love, and it reveals a number of important connections with both the *Arcadia* and the letters to Languet. No other sonnets in the sequence relate so clearly to the set of tensions or conflicts outlined in the first four chapters of this book, although Sidney has in *Astrophel* nothing comparable to the inclusive symbol of Arcadia, with its rich associations and inherent values, to provide a focal point for the development of his themes. Nor does he, obviously, have the scope and freedom of range which the form of prose narrative previously afforded him. Instead, the court serves as a background for Astrophel's romance, and our attention throughout is directed almost exclusively to the details of the love relationship itself. Despite such limitations, however—limitations imposed largely by the nature of a sonnet sequence—Sidney has clearly invested *Astrophel* with some of the diversity, amplitude, and sense of drama that had characterized the *Arcadia*, and these qualities are nowhere more apparent than in the group of sonnets now under consideration. Here, Astrophel is presented very much as a product of the Renaissance "heroic" school. Like Sidney's earlier heroes, and like Sidney himself, he feels his obligations to virtue, but he also finds it exceedingly difficult to steer the narrow course assigned to him. Love deflects him from his steadfast pursuit of duty, and the result is a series of poems which dramatize very effectively his sense of divided allegiance. He laments that he has "most idly spent" his wealth of talents (AS 18); like Pyrocles, he complains of his "young mind marde" (AS 21). At the same time, the attractions of love and beauty, of the same sensuousness which had subdued Pyrocles, finally outweigh Astrophel's devotion to heroic action. Irony and wit once more come to the defense of truancy, and Sidney's hero eventually regards his fellow courtiers as "fools" and "curious wits" committed to the "tedious business" of state affairs. The political problems which Sidney once discussed so seriously with Languet are now dismissed as inconsequential and annoying (AS 30). Astrophel retires from the activities of the court in such a way as to remind us of Sidney's remark that he himself was "entirely averse to the excitement and the fascinations of a court" (Pears, 184). That retirement is later made explicit, moreover, in the beautiful Eighth Song of the sequence, a pastoral lyric whose unaffected celebration of love and natural beauty re-creates once more, if only momentarily, the vision of Arcadia.

If AS 2 ("Not at first sight") presented Astrophel primarily as a soldier humiliated by defeat, this third group of sonnets among the first twenty-one touches upon slightly different aspects of his predicament. Echoes from a number of Arcadian dialogues filter through to us:

> *Vertue* alas, now let me take some rest,
> Thou setst a bate betweene my will and wit,
> If vaine love have my simple soule opprest,
> Leave what thou likest not, deale not thou with it.
>   Thy scepter use in some old *Catoe's* brest;
> Churches or schooles are for thy seate more fit:
> I do confesse, pardon a fault confest,
> My mouth too tender is for thy hard bit.
>   But if that needs thou wilt usurping be,
>   The litle reason that is left in me,
> And still th'effect of thy perswasions prove:
>   I sweare, my heart such one shall shew to thee,
>   That shrines in flesh so true a Deitie,
> That *Vertue*, thou thy selfe shalt be in love.
>
> (AS 4)

> It is most true, that eyes are form'd to serve
> The inward light: and that the heavenly part
> Ought to be king, from whose rules who do swerve,
> Rebels to Nature, strive for their owne smart.

It is most true, what we call *Cupid's* dart,
An image is, which for our selves we carve;
And, fooles, adore in temple of our hart,
Till that good God make Church and Churchman starve.
  True, that true Beautie Vertue is indeed,
Whereof this Beautie can be but a shade,
Which elements with mortall mixture breed:
True, that on earth we are but pilgrims made,
  And should in soule up to our countrey move:
  True, and yet true that I must *Stella* love.

(AS 5)

Both of these poems concern a "Vertue" that makes very great claims upon Astrophel. We hear of Cato, schools, churches and churchmen, souls, temples, and pilgrims. The range of reference is moral and religious, rather than military or heroic, and the kind of life suggested as a model has to do with Stoic control, learning, "rules," and a sober contemplation of those heavenly things that are alone worthy of attention. Love here is not so much a power humiliating masculine pride as it is a deeper threat to the serious religious journey "up to our countrey."

Yet the two poems treat these claims in very different ways. Despite his confession of fault in AS 4, Astrophel there takes a generally satiric view of his antagonist. With good-humored contempt, he recommends virtue to churches and schools and associates it with "some old *Catoe's* brest." The focus is on a morality that seems narrow-minded, unattractively spare, and begotten of old age. Astrophel presents himself, meanwhile, as youthfully "tender." He begins to dramatize once more, in other words, that witty conflict between youth and age discovered in the Languet letters and throughout the *Arcadia*. The most relevant texts in this regard are Sidney's good-natured caution that Languet "observe what Aristotle says of old men in his Rhetoric; namely, that they are cold in love, . . . as if they were nothing else but the smoke of youthful ardour" (Pears, 121); Sidney's half-serious apology (in the dedication of the *Arcadia*) for his "young head, not so well stayed as I would it were (and shall be when God will)"; and the Philisides-Geron dialogue, which demonstrates so clearly the ways in which Astrophel is the true legatee of Philisides' (more heavy-handed) sarcasm:

> O gods, how long this old foole hath annoi'd
> My wearied eares!
>
> .   .   .   .
>
> O noble age who place their only blisse
> In being heard untill the hearer dye . . .
>
> .   .   .   .
>
> thinke them olde, that have the oldest minde,
> With vertue fraught and full of holy feare!
>   (OA 9, 66–67, 69–70, and 94–95)

Geron, like Cato, is reduced to the role of tedious moralist "With vertue fraught"—someone too old and unsympathetic to understand the joys and values of love.

If it is easy to sympathize with Astrophel and Philisides against Cato and Geron, however, one should also remember the quite different perspective on this quarrel that Philisides himself gave in speaking of Languet:

> The songe I sange old Languet had me taught,
> Languet, the shepheard best swift *Ister* knewe,
> For clerkly reed, and hating what is naught,
> For faithfull hart, cleane hands, and mouth as true:
> With his sweet skill my skillesse youth he drewe,
>   To have a feeling tast of him that sitts
>   Beyond the heaven, far more beyond your witts.
>
> He said, the Musique best thilke powers pleasd
> Was jumpe concorde betweene our wit and will:
> Where highest notes to godlines are raisd,
> And lowest sinke not downe to jote of ill: . . .
>   (OA 66, 22–32)

Here learning ("clerkly reed"), a sober morality, and serious religious concerns stand in judgment upon "skillesse youth," and they are presented with much of the "sweet" fullness that leads men into their ways.[1] They are, moreover, accorded equal respect in the second sonnet quoted above (AS 5). There, Astrophel weighs without irony, and with considerable judiciousness, all that stands opposed to his love; the effect is to impress upon us the enormous implications of his decision:

> the heavenly part
> Ought to be king, from whose rules who do swerve,
> Rebels to Nature, strive for their owne smart.
>   It is most true, what we call *Cupid's* dart,
> An image is, which for our selves we carve;
> And, fooles, adore in temple of our hart,
> Till that good God make Church and Churchman starve.

Astrophel and the *Arcadia*, then, present the clash between virtue and love in very similar terms, and with a similar lack of resolution. Philisides and Astrophel are both attractive in the vigor of their commitment to love and in their ridicule of the narrow-minded who are "full of holy feare." Yet both, at other moments, are sadly aware of what their commitment forces them to surrender. Neither alternative is wholly satisfactory, and satire offers itself to them as a means of temporary relief as well as of protection. Philisides takes the offensive against Geron, and the bitterness of his attack betrays the depth of his own real disturbance. Astrophel is more complicated. He mocks Virtue (in AS 4), but he simultaneously casts himself— half-seriously—in the role of wayward youth. He makes concessions (as Philisides does not), cries out for rest from a battle that clearly exhausts him, and pleads that he is "too tender." In one sense, these are genuine expressions of a guilty conscience; yet they are obviously not to be taken at face value. Wit and role playing, in this case ironic "confession," provide an uneasy resolution for feelings that seem to permit no other mode of expression. Both the tactics and the tone clearly recall Sidney's own method of sparring with Languet: "Do you not see that I am cleverly playing the stoic? yea and I shall be a cynic too, unless you reclaim me. . . . I have now pointed out the field of battle, and I openly declare war against you" (Pears, 143–44).

The sestet of AS 4 presents a similar mixture of defensive and offensive tactics. Virtue presses its advantage and threatens to usurp the "litle reason that is left" to Astrophel. Astrophel had earlier warned Virtue to "Leave what thou likest not"; he is now driven, half-reluctantly, to stronger measures:

> I sweare, my heart such one shall shew to thee,
> That shrines in flesh so true a Deitie,
> That *Vertue*, thou thy selfe shalt be in love.

We learn the result of this move in the tenth sonnet of the sequence:

> Reason, in faith thou art well serv'd, that still
> Wouldst brabling be with sence and love in me:
> I rather wisht thee clime the Muses' hill,
> Or reach the fruite of Nature's choisest tree,
>   Or seeke heavn's course, or heavn's inside to see:
> Why shouldst thou toyle our thornie soile to till?
> Leave sense, and those which sense's objects be:
> Deale thou with powers of thoughts, leave love to will.
>   But thou wouldst needs fight both with love and sence,
> With sword of wit, giving wounds of dispraise,
> Till downe-right blowes did foyle thy cunning fence:
> For soone as they strake thee with *Stella's* rayes,
>   Reason thou kneel'dst, and offeredst straight to prove
>   By reason good, good reason her to love.

Astrophel expresses very little satisfaction but considerable resentment here: the victory over Reason (or Virtue) is essentially complete; yet it provokes anything but joyous response. The poem has its intentionally comic side, of course, but this aspect is just another reflection of Astrophel's ability to convert dismay into wit. He "rather wisht" for a different sort of denouement. Why did Reason insist on becoming involved? It ought to have known what would happen; now all has been lost.

The action I have described in this and the previous sonnets was, as suggested, central to the *Arcadia*'s poetry. There, however, love's progress was related in compact, recapitulative forms. The rigid causality of anadiplosis or of closely integrated narrative and logical forms plotted the inevitable movement from the conquest of sight to that of reason:

> For from without came to mine eyes the blowe,
> Whereto mine inward thoughts did faintly yeeld;
> Both these conspird poore Reason's overthrowe;
> False in my selfe, thus have I lost the field.

Thus are my eyes still Captive to one sight: . . .

(OA 2, 5–9)

Beautie hath force to catche the humane sight.
Sight doth bewitch, the fancie evill awaked.
Fancie we feele, encludes all passion's mighte,
Passion rebelde, oft reason's strength hath shaked.

(OA 57, 1–4)

In the first quatrain above, Pyrocles acknowledges his role in the action ("False in my selfe"), but the language of the poem is utterly neutral. Rhetorical and syntactical structures fully control a submissive human will. In *Astrophel*, however, everything resides in the tone with which actions are presented. Every step along the path from "first sight" to the defeat of "Reason" is qualified or shaded in an all-important way. Soldierly indignation and the pains of love burst forth in the second sonnet, where Astrophel's humiliation cuts across his carefully weighed appreciation of Stella's "knowne worth." Prolonged debate reveals signs of exhaustion in the lover of AS 4. Astrophel asks for rest, makes concessions that he qualifies with irony, resorts to ridicule, and threatens to use measures he would prefer to avoid. The tone of the sestet is very much that of a man who has been driven in a moment of weakness to say more than he wished. The quiet stubbornness of pure will closes the fifth sonnet, and the tenth shows a lover who has had his way but rather regrets it. Resentment here takes the form of half-comic finger wagging, as Astrophel berates Reason in a tone that one might adopt toward an imprudent puppy. Sense and will, aroused by sight, have finally conquered reason as they did in the *Arcadia* lyrics. But all has been done in such a way as to express with marvelous fidelity the witty maneuvers of a mind doing battle with itself. Astrophel's self-consciousness, his defensive role playing, his serious willingness to judge matters as they really are, and his persistent irony all emerge as aspects of a single, complex personality. Discriminating in his decision what has been simply willed, what has been impartially or judiciously decided, what has been precipitated by the feelings of a moment, and what has been merely rationalized is as difficult as it is in one's own decisions.

8+

Sidney is no Shakespeare, but he has here given us all that we expect from dramatic character in literature.

Matters seem settled at the end of AS 10. Reason has capitulated, and one expects Astrophel (like the Arcadian heroes) to settle, however reluctantly, into love. But if inner debate has stopped, Astrophel must still contend with the outside world. A friend assails him in AS 14—very much as Musidorus had assailed Pyrocles—and the wound is opened once again. The crisis provoked by this attack is dramatized in a carefully grouped series of poems (AS 14, AS 18–19, and AS 21) which ends with Astrophel's rejection of the friend's arguments and his final commitment to Stella. These sonnets are not at all a simple repetition of the earlier lyrics. Those had dealt with the conflict between virtue and love in much more generalized terms. Astrophel felt but did not spell out in personal terms the consequences of his choice. The fifth poem, for example, simply listed the general obligations of man to Virtue in order to demonstrate Astrophel's awareness of them; but AS 18 and AS 21 show with considerable intensity the plight of Astrophel's "wel-form'd soule" as it tabulates its deficits and considers the sad ruin of its hopes:

> to my birth I owe
> Nobler desires, least else that friendly foe,
> Great expectation, weare a traine of shame.
> For since mad March great promise made of me,
> If now the May of my yeares much decline,
> What can be hoped my harvest time will be?
> (AS 21, 6–11)

I need hardly point out how closely such verse is related, not only to the Pyrocles-Musidorus debate, but also to the Languet letters: "reflect how grievously you would be sinning against your excellent Father, who has placed all his hopes in you, and who . . . expects to see the full harvest of all those virtues, which your character promises so largely to produce" (Pears, 2). Astrophel is forced to take full account of such considerations, and he calculates the cost of his decision in personal terms: the squandering of his youth and of "those goods, which heav'n to me hath lent," the fear of being unable to render final account, the loss of that fine harvest of honor and achievement. The deep feelings that were earlier converted into various forms of wit now come to the surface and are permitted much fuller expression.

Yet for all this, Astrophel's final decision is less carefully justified than one might expect. He has defined love almost exclusively in terms of "sense" and "will," and he only once suggests how Stella's known worth might justify his love:

> with your Rubarb words yow must contend
> To grieve me worse, in saying that Desire
> Doth plunge my wel-form'd soule even in the mire
> Of sinfull thoughts, which do in ruine end?
> If that be sinne which doth the maners frame,
> Well staid with truth in word and faith of deed,
> Readie of wit and fearing nought but shame:
> If that be sinne which in fixt hearts doth breed
> A loathing of all loose unchastitie,
> Then Love is sinne, and let me sinfull be.
>
> (AS 14, 5–14)

Love can breed virtue and is itself a mode of aspiration. Astrophel here echoes Pyrocles' arguments to Musidorus (F, IV. 19), but he does so in lines that recall the phrasing and willfulness of tone noted in Philisides' quarrel with Echo:

> Tell yet againe me the names of these faire
> form'd to do ev'lls.   Dev'lls.
> Dev'lls? if in hell such dev'lls do abide,
> to the hells I do go.   Go.
>
> (OA 31, 49–50)

Astrophel's speech in the sestet of AS 14 is modified by that vehemence (of dubious purity) which Philisides represents, and his apology for love is heavily qualified both by his tone and by the circumstances in which he formulates it. Provoked by attack, he rises to a defense that suggests both the high ideal to which he aspires and the convenience of the ideal as a guard against assault from outside and inside alike. Moreover, his unwillingness to admit any of the dangers of desire is obviously uncandid and unconsidered. He has been eminently pragmatic and strategical in his wooing, and has

long since looked upon Stella as a citadel to be won. The power of the
"poison" that he feels (AS 16) points toward something rather
different from the "loathing of all loose unchastitie" that he boasts
of in AS 14.

Thus the grounds of Astrophel's love are not by any means fully
clear to him, and he relies for the most part on simple assertions of
the will. Despite the agitated feelings of AS 18, the sonnet concludes
with a controlled determination to lose all for love. In AS 19, Astrophel is already sufficiently distanced from the problem to give it
comic treatment:

> On *Cupid's* bow how are my heart-strings bent,
>   That see my wracke, and yet embrace the same?
>   When most I glorie, then I feele most shame:
> I willing run, yet while I run, repent.
> My best wits still their owne disgrace invent:
>   My verie inke turnes straight to *Stella's* name;
>   And yet my words, as them my pen doth frame,
> Avise themselves that they are vainely spent.
>   For though she passe all things, yet what is all
> That unto me, who fare like him that both
> Lookes to the skies, and in a ditch doth fall?
> O let me prop my mind, yet in his growth
>   And not in Nature for best fruits unfit:
>   'Scholler,' saith *Love*, 'bend hitherward your wit.'

The string of paradoxes here recalls more strongly than any other
poem in the sequence some of the poetic techniques of the *Arcadia*
(compare OA 20, OA 39, and OA 42). Contradiction in its various
aspects was a central part of the *Arcadia's* vision of love—a form that
defined the hopeless plight of characters coerced by a power beyond
their control. The pressure of such contradiction forced Gynecia into
ritual grief (OA 42) and Pyrocles into cries of outrage (OA 20).
Astrophel, however, absorbs such pressure and transforms it into a
source of comedy. The conceit of the heartstrings lightens the tone of
his sonnet, and playful hyperbole helps to deflate the potentially
oppressive power of love:

> My verie inke turnes straight to *Stella's* name; . . .

Astrophel's fall will be, not tragic, but bathetic—into a ditch—and he rather delights in the image. Finally, if the appeal in the closing triad seems suddenly more serious, it is so only to set up the reversal in the last line—a gambit similar to that of AS 47. Sidney's hero ends wittily as a "Scholler" sent off to study the book of love.

Paradox in AS 19, then, neither fixes characters in static predicaments over which they have no control nor comes with the force of dynamic discovery noticed in AS 2. Instead, Astrophel uses it self-consciously as a means of indicating the ridiculousness of his situation, of distancing and so diminishing its serious side. This technique gives him a kind of control and relief which the *Arcadia*'s lovers rarely achieved, but which Sidney, as narrator, exercised and so much enjoyed. In both cases (as I noted earlier) the method is that of a courtier, that of a mind sophisticated and witty enough to find comedy in the ambiguities of experience, even when they are painful ambiguties. Astrophel's actions, however, have consequences, and his ability to take the witty way out of the dilemmas that confront him is as potentially dangerous as it is liberating. Reason has just been defeated—at least partly—in this manner, and the chaste love to which he has now dedicated himself will later meet a similar fate. The courtier's sense of control and form that is evidence of his social and moral ideals and obligations thus slips easily into "courtliness," a witty form of control capable of subverting those ideals. Astrophel's style includes both kinds, and they are so closely related that much of the time we "One from the other scarcely can descrie" (OA 72).

The debates of the first section of the sequence come to an end in AS 21, and virtue—defined as the life of action and of learning—gives way to love. Astrophel rehearses all the arguments of the friend, credits them, and then simply dismisses them:

> If now the May of my yeares much decline,
> What can be hoped my harvest time will be?
> Sure you say well, your wisdome's golden mine
>   Dig deepe with learning's spade, now tell me this,
>   Hath this world ought so faire as *Stella* is?
>
> (AS 21, 10–14)

The touch of sarcasm in the last triad, and the quip of the final line, reveal the weaknesses of Astrophel's position as well as its strength. He is firm in his love, but he gives up "wisdome's golden mine" rather too flippantly. We do not hear the voice of a man who is absolutely sure of the quality and value of the love he is affirming. He has surrendered his true ground of certainty, surrendered the authority which fidelity to "the heavenly part" had given him. He has instead chosen to follow Stella, but his speech throughout the first twenty-one sonnets lacks generally the confidence of one who knows without question his new ground of praise. As a result, he adopts various roles—ironist, satirist, hapless victim, tender youth, military strategist, naive poet, dutiful lover, and fool. Some of these (though not all) were part of the convention's stock in trade, but they are given new meaning by the fact of Astrophel's fundamental uncertainty—by his search both for an adequate position of defense against the attacks of his friend and of his own conscience, and for a romantic role that will distinguish him from the dainty wits. In neither effort is he altogether successful. He relies heavily on wit and mere assertion in argument; on a pose of naiveté as poet; and on quite fashionable kinds of flattery, ruffled by evidences of unruly desire, in his poetry of praise. Astrophel himself mistrusts the quality of his love, and can give it no very pure expression, either through reasonable demonstration (AS 14) or through compliment and celebration (AS 16, *et al.*). Indeed, he tends to define love in terms of sense and will and hurls invective at Cupid for his tardiness in winning Stella. We never hear the graceful notes of Musidorus (OA 50) or the sure tones of a Petrarch balancing self-denial with a lyric hymn to high beauty and virtue. Instead, the sonnets of the sequence split open with exclamation and argument. Colloquial outbursts sabotage elegant rhetorical structures; juxtapositions and reversals turn all awry.

If Sidney asks us to be somewhat critical of Astrophel in this opening section, however, he also complicates our judgment of the situation. Astrophel may often be comic, crude, or too courtly, but he is also attractive in his impetuousness and his determined love. It is true that he often treats love as a game, a siege, a matter of ingenious compliment and persuasion; but he is obliged to entertain

Stella's wits, and he is necessarily formal and conventional in his first approaches to her. He is on the defensive, and consequently, he falls in rather with the fashion of courtly wooing and makes it possible for Stella to treat him like any other dabbler in love. Nonetheless, he is never merely one of the dainty wits. His poetry, even at its most conventional, has always the stamp of his own sensibility and passion upon it.[2] And here and there, we encounter more explicit expressions of the depth of feeling within him:

> *Love* gave the wound, which while I breathe will bleed: . . .

> While with a feeling skill I paint my hell.

> When trembling voice brings forth that I do *Stella* love.

Part of the task of the sequence is to give such feeling adequate expression in poetry that is full, moving, and sympathetic. Or, to put it another way, Astrophel must somehow discover his own voice for love, a style capable of expressing the powerful sincerity of his love in ways that are not mainly comic and disruptive. His search for that voice is, of course, partly self-conscious, and he himself raises the issue in his sonnets on style. Yet in spite of his proper methods of invention and imitation, his early solutions are inadequate, or at best provisional. His pose as naive poet, for example, will lead nowhere. It may do temporarily as a sophisticated way of urging his claims upon Stella; but, at bottom, it is a confession of his own inability to find (or use) a style that can include both his self-consciousness and his deep feeling without resorting to extravagant role playing. Sidney undertakes to provide him with such a style—of necessity, for it is all that can possibly redeem Astrophel's willful fall from virtue (AS 1–21) and virtuous love (AS 71–72). The plot of *Astrophel and Stella*, in its fundamentals, comes within an ace of being a sophisticated fabliau, a stock love triangle in which the husband is cuckolded. The poems on Lord Rich and on Stella's marriage (AS 24, AS 33, AS 37, and AS 78) keep this situation alive throughout the sequence. Yet Sidney has converted this potentially coarse material into something quite beautiful, and he has made Astrophel's devolution from heroic courtier to seducer acceptable and sympathetic.

He achieves this transformation only through style. Our harsher judgments of Astrophel and our sympathetic response to him are equally provoked by the kinds of poetry he writes. If we are critical of him in the beginning of the sequence, it is because the nature and spirit of his love seem often suspect. They mingle too easily with the superficial spirit of courtly love and alloy their purer element with a dangerous vehemence of feeling. Yet we see enough of them to know that they desire in earnest a language and forms worthy of them. The Petrarchan convention, in its broadest aspects, offers just such a framework, although we sense from the beginning that Astrophel will have to fashion the convention to suit the bias of his own sensibility. While it can give expression to his finest impulses, its mode of high praise and ceremony also inhibits the impetuousness and candor of his desire. The self-denial and harmony of restrained love in Musidorus' lyric (OA 50) will not be his. When Astrophel essays the manner, he sounds unconvincing, or else he simply breaks down (AS 9 and AS 25). His true form is not so much that of ceremony as of intimate, conversational speech, particularly of entreaty. He needs a style of direct address, just as he needs full response from Stella, simply because that is the stuff whereof his love is made. For various reasons, this style is not fully available to him at the beginning of the sequence. As time passes, however, the pressure of his frustration and isolation begins to tell upon him, and feeling finds expression in a language that is courtly but also direct, relatively simple, and altogether moving. Astrophel becomes increasingly frank in his expression of desire, and he finds authority for his candor in the pain he suffers, in his patient impatience, in his potency of feeling, which makes him more than a gamester, and in his knowledge of what he has given up for passion's sake. From this point of view, the prolonged debate in AS 1–21 is particularly important. It demonstrates the difficulty of Astrophel's decision in foregoing "Great expectation" and in suffering the humiliation of "Reason's audite." In other words, we come to measure the power of his love partly by what he feels compelled to surrender in its behalf.

Thus, a great number of factors finally endow Astrophel's poetry with a quality and spirit substantially different from those of his verse at the beginning of the sequence. They purify his desire and his entreaties—at least in part—and make them acceptable to us. Moreover, toward the end of the sequence, Astrophel's speech accommodates itself more easily to the ceremonial style of the convention and makes its timeworn forms vibrate with new feeling. But, again, Sidney does not simplify matters. Astrophel has other voices for his desire and his entreaties, and we are made to understand their relative crudity. We are not allowed to finish the sequence feeling that attempted seduction has been made attractive, but only that a particularly beautiful form of eros has triumphed over uglier forms.

CHAPTER XV

Astrophel in Love

❦

THE SONNETS between AS 21 and AS 41 reveal the first important signs of change in Astrophel's manner. The first of them, however, is precisely the sort that we are apt to pass over as being merely "conventional." It is so—a piece of quite ordinary courtly flattery which, were it typical of the sequence as a whole, would make Sidney's work witty but thoroughly undistinguished. Coming where it does, however, it has its point. The last lines of AS 21 are extremely direct, abrupt, conversational; they capture Astrophel in a natural posture, although it is one that has been adopted for debate. Next to this candid snapshot is placed the more formal, courtly pose that Astrophel still assumes when turning to Stella:

> Sure you say well, your wisdome's golden mine
>> Dig deepe with learning's spade, now tell me this,
>> Hath this world ought so faire as *Stella* is?
>>> (AS 21, 12–14)

> In highest way of heav'n the Sunne did ride,
>> Progressing then from faire twinnes' gold'n place:
>> Having no scarfe of clowds before his face,
> But shining forth of heate in his chiefe pride;
> When some faire Ladies, by hard promise tied, . . .
>> (AS 22, 1–5)

The "Sure" of AS 21 and its second-person form of address, among other things, remind us of the ordinary world and its modes of speech. Astrophel has accustomed us to these modes throughout the early part of the sequence, and we are meant to feel the sharp difference between their directness and the greater elaborateness of AS 22, which so inhibits the rich volubility of his feeling. AS 22 is the first poem to follow Astrophel's full commitment to Stella; carefully placed here, it reflects his first impulse in his career as confirmed lover and serves as a convenient standard by which to measure the stages of his progress.

The twenty-third sonnet, by contrast, is much more indicative of Astrophel's new mood:

> The curious wits, seeing dull pensivenesse
>> Bewray it selfe in my long setled eyes,
>> Whence those same fumes of melancholy rise,
> With idle paines, and missing ayme, do guesse.
> Some that know how my spring I did addresse,
>> Deeme that my Muse some fruit of knowledge plies:
>> Others, because the Prince my service tries,
> Thinke that I thinke state errours to redresse.
>> But harder Judges judge ambition's rage,
>> Scourge of it selfe, still climing slipprie place,
> Holds my young braine captiv'd in golden cage.
> O fooles, or over-wise, alas the race
>> Of all my thoughts hath neither stop nor start,
>> But only *Stella's* eyes and *Stella's* hart.

This is a steadier and more thoughtfully controlled voice than we have generally heard to this point. Astrophel stands outside the world of affairs represented by the friend of AS 14 and AS 21 and surveys it with the secret superiority that is the prerogative of new lovers. Its standards of "service" and "knowledge," so much a challenge to him before, now seem trivial. The satire has been toned down: one can contrast it with the hyperbolic gaiety of AS 3 and AS 6, or the harder punching of AS 4. In general, a mood of dull pensiveness appropriates the poem, and we feel this especially in the last triad. "Fooles" enters with none of the disruptive effect it possessed in AS 1 and AS 11; love has begun to be "long setled," and is (temporarily) past the time of sudden discoveries and unexpected explosions. Indeed, the closing lines have just the mixture of irony and

rue, naturally phrased and inflected, which is so "perfectly charac-
teristicall"—to use Lamb's phrase—of Astrophel. It is slightly
world-weary, tinged by regret and yearning, but with enough of the
abrasiveness of wit to give it strength and polish. Much of its success
derives from a complete mastery of the blend of formal, rhetorical
exclamatio and more informal speech that Sidney was experimenting
with in the *Certain Sonnets*. Consider, for example, the development
(marked by my italics) expressed in the following sets of lines.

> *Arcadia*: But yet, *alas*! *O* but yet *alas*!
>
> But *ah*! the more I hate, the more I thinke . . .
>
> *Certain Sonnets*: *Ah saucy* paine let not thy errour last, . . .
>
> *O paine* I now recant the praise I gave, . . .
>
> *Astrophel*: *O fooles*, or over-wise, *alas* the race . . .

The effect of this last line is difficult to define but is important. Despite the satirical context, "fooles" (and "over-wise") are used very
much like "saucy": they have almost the quality of being terms of
colloquial endearment. Above all they show Astrophel's tendency to
speak in familiar, direct forms of address, even to antagonists. At the
same time, the interjections (especially the elegiac "alas") bring
with them a touch of the formality and high style of which they are a
part. Directness and something like intimacy join with a dignified
plaintiveness to create a distinctive voice whose role becomes increasingly important as the sequence progresses.

Astrophel's mood holds, with some interruptions, through AS 31.
In general, he enjoys a consciously romantic interlude in which the
very isolation and privacy of his love are a source of satisfaction to
him. It is true that disturbance keeps bursting in upon him: he
begins, for example, to harass Lord Rich (AS 24), he confesses that
"I do burne in love" (AS 25), and he focuses once more upon
Cupid's energetic campaign against Stella (AS 29). The theme
most often returned to, however, is that of his insulation, so to speak,
in his new and more lyric world of love. Stella is still remote, and he
thinks of her very much as a young lover would. We see him bored by

conversation, irked by the inconsequential activities of the court, and thoroughly preoccupied with her image. Earlier struggles have subsided, and there is a momentary lull before the coming of others.

Astrophel's verse here is generally subdued by softer moods of melancholy and quiet pensiveness, and some of the poetry gives us a particularly clear picture of Sidney's new powers. The use of rhymes and other sound effects in AS 23, for example, is far beyond anything we can find in Sidney's earlier work:

> The curious wits, seeing dull pensivenesse
> Bewray it selfe in my long setled eyes,
> Whence those same fumes of melancholy rise,
> With idle paines, and missing ayme, do guesse.

Nearly all the vowels are carefully weighted and lengthened by the use of nasals, liquids, and sibilants to create that quality of slow fluidity which characterizes the movement of the lines. Sidney has chosen words that concentrate his important consonants (l, m, n, s, r) at terminal and interior points. The movement is away from the intentionally obvious and conventional techniques of the *Arcadia* toward methods that suit a poetry based on the norm of conversation. The rhymes of the sonnet are equally effective. Both rhymes of the first quatrain have been chosen to reinforce the important "s" sounds ("pensivenesse," "eyes"). As the tone changes in the sestet, one rhyme links with the octave through sibilants ("place"); the other makes a very slight transition to soft palatals ("rage"):

> But harder Judges judge ambition's rage,
> Scourge of it selfe, still climing slipprie place,
> Holds my young braine captiv'd in golden cage.

The usage here is too complicated to explicate in detail, but essentially, Sidney has increased the obviousness of his sound effects as Astrophel's satirical tone has increased. The "j" and "s" (a more hissing "s" than in the first quatrain) burst out into alliteration, and are backed up by a group of hard consonants (c, g, d, t, b, p). The sudden alliterative flurry here, as contrasted to the covert methods of the first quatrain, is very much in order. The poem began in the meditative haze of "fumes of melancholy." Imperceptible and quiet tactics were most appropriate to capture that mood. As Astrophel becomes more astringent, in turning to the "harder Judges," the sonnet gives the effect of waking into consciousness from the somnolence of its opening lines. Everything—including the sound—works for a moment to accentuate that consciousness before shading off into the quiet of the concluding triad.

The meditative quality that I noticed in a few of the *Certain Sonnets* comes closest, perhaps, to such poetry, but the differences between the two are enormous:

> Oft have I musde, but now at length I finde,
>> Why those that die, men say they do depart:
> Depart, a word so gentle to my minde,
>> Weakely did seeme to paint death's ougly dart.
>
> But now the starres with their strange course do binde
>> Me one to leave, with whome I leave my hart.
> I heare a crye of spirits faint and blinde,
>> That parting thus my chiefest part I part.
>
>>>>>>> (CS 20, 1–8)

> Because I oft in darke abstracted guise,
>> Seeme most alone in greatest companie,
>> With dearth of words, or answers quite awrie,
> To them that would make speech of speech arise, . . .
>
>>>>>> (AS 27, 1–4)

>>>> those Lampes of purest light,
> Whose numbers, wayes, greatnesse, eternitie,
> Promising wonders, wonder to invite, . . .
>
>>>>> (AS 26, 2–4)

The passages are particularly interesting because they show quite new ways in which Sidney's verse has gained power in the short time that has elapsed between the *Certain Sonnets* and *Astrophel*. The lines from CS 20, which are indeed natural in tone and fluid in movement compared to the *Arcadia* sonnets, now seem rather weak and over-formal. Although their phrasing and diction are close to a norm of ordinary speech, we can sense the pull toward balance and light pattern in them—a pull that becomes far stronger in the poem's sestet. "Musde" and "finde," "die" and "depart," "leave" and "leave," "parting" and "part," are all paired off, and although the lines are not too rigidly ordered, they do retain a certain stiffness. Some of the words and phrases are suggestive: "musde," "so gentle," "strange course," "crye of spirits, faint and blinde." As we touch upon them, we are asked, in effect, to penetrate beneath their surface; we experience a "feeling tast" of the sound, sight, or quality of actions and objects—not objectively described in imagist fashion, but filtered rather more vaguely through the speaker's mood. But this is managed too sketchily. For the most part, we are kept on the surface of the words and are consequently drawn to feel their pattern as pattern, as a verbal arrangement which is, in its way, formally satisfying and appropriate in view of the poem's decorum.

The stanzas from *Astrophel* are clearly different. There are still courtly balances (though not so pointed) and still some plays on words: "most alone" and "greatest companie," "speech of speech," "wonders, wonder." But the verse also pulls us away from these into the felt reality of Astrophel's world. The imagery is not particularly visual, but it is considerably rich in its use of suggestive detail: "darke abstracted guise," "most alone," "dearth of words," "Lampes of purest light," "numbers, wayes," "wonders." Sidney is concerned to find words that can capture more precisely the substance of feelings and moods ("darke abstracted") or the more diffuse quality of his lover's response to a beauty that is inviting yet also distant and full of the wonder of the heavens ("numbers, wayes, greatnesse, eternitie"). We are carried inside Astrophel and are made to share in his responses. Sidney has gone far beyond the method of the *Certain Sonnets*, and the growth is essentially one that has its motive in the quest for energia—in the desire to make us see things vividly as if they were present, to make us participate in their life. The narrator of the *Certain Sonnets* muses or "heare[s] a crye," but he does so quite in the void. The quality of Astrophel's musing, however, is much more precisely defined, and he is carefully set "alone . . . in companie." Place, objects, and mood unite to create a poetry which is immediately persuasive and which expresses the power of that "inward tuch" Sidney and Astrophel found lacking in the lyrics of other courtly poets.

Astrophel, then, is gradually presented to us more sympathetically, and we begin to participate in his feelings in a way we did not in the earlier section of the sequence. There, we tended to stand outside to observe the comedy of his role playing. Now, we mellow into his romance. Poems such as those on Lord Rich, however, remind us of the disruptive elements in Astrophel's love and intimate that he will not be very long content to think of Stella as a distant star. We feel this particularly strongly when we come upon the startling last lines of AS 30:

> How *Ulster* likes of that same golden bit,
> Wherewith my father once made it halfe tame;
> If in the Scottishe Court be weltring yet;
> These questions busie wits to me do frame;
> I, cumbred with good maners, answer do,
> But know not how, for still I thinke of you.

Astrophel's continual effort throughout the sequence, as suggested earlier, is to bring Stella to his own level, and this is one of the major implications of his conversational style. The sudden intimacy and frankness of the "you" in these lines are linked to the direct forms of address noticed in earlier sonnets—the imperatives of debate ("now tell me this") and the apostrophes of mild satire ("O fooles, or overwise"). For the first time, Astrophel speaks to Stella in the idiom of his daily life, though it obviously comes with a special tenderness we have not heard before. Most important, it demands a very different kind of response from Stella herself. Ladies who are sung to may stand apart and listen. Those who are talked to must sooner or later reply, if only to say "No, No." Astrophel's movement from relatively formal celebration and compliment to intimate conversation has thus a double value. It is related, on the one hand, to the urgency of Astrophel's desire, to the unruliness of "sense" and "will." On the other hand, it is a sign of his strength in love—his depth and poignancy of feeling which separate him so firmly from the more frivolous lovers at court, from Stella, and from his own "courtly" tendencies.

We begin to hear Astrophel's conversation with some consistency in the sonnets after AS 30, although it is rarely addressed directly to

Stella. It is, however, pitched in the minor key I have indicated developing between AS 23 and AS 30:

> With how sad steps, ô Moone, thou climb'st the skies,
>   How silently, and with how wanne a face,
>   What, may it be that even in heav'nly place
> That busie archer his sharpe arrowes tries?
> Sure, if that long with *Love* acquainted eyes
>   Can judge of *Love*, thou feel'st a Lover's case;
>   I reade it in thy lookes, thy languisht grace,
> To me that feele the like, thy state descries.
>   Then ev'n of fellowship, ô Moone, tell me
> Is constant *Love* deem'd there but want of wit?
> Are Beauties there as proud as here they be?
> Do they above love to be lov'd, and yet
>   Those lovers scorne whom that *Love* doth possesse?
>   Do they call *Vertue* there ungratefulnesse?
>
> (AS 31)

> I might, unhappie word, ô me, I might,
> And then would not, or could not see my blisse:
> Till now, wrapt in a most infernall night,
> I find how heav'nly day wretch I did misse.
>   Hart rent thy selfe, thou doest thy selfe but right,
> No lovely *Paris* made thy *Hellen* his:
> No force, no fraud, robd thee of thy delight,
> Nor Fortune of thy fortune author is:
>   But to my selfe my selfe did give the blow,
> While too much wit (forsooth) so troubled me,
> That I respects for both our sakes must show:
> And yet could not by rising Morne forsee
>   How faire a day was neare, ô punisht eyes,
>   That I had bene more foolish or more wise.
>
> (AS 33)

In the first sonnet, Astrophel casts himself playfully in the role of conventional lover. The poem's varieties of energia scarcely need to be stressed: its relatively vivid setting, its "direction of speech to inanimate objects," its quiet drama and dialogue. Light irony cuts across

a wistfulness that is full of poise: the melancholy mood reflected in
the slow climb of the moon, and paced by the carefully weighted
syllables of the first two lines, is soon qualified by the feigned surprise
and charming banter of the rest of the octave. The tone is very close
to quintessential Astrophel: lonely, that of an exile, but self-inclusive
in its irony, enlivened by a touch of satire, full of grace, and suggestive of serious feeling beneath. The perfect polish of the manner,
however, and the incidental details of the poem are carefully controlled by tactical motives. Like the lyrics on pain in the *Certain
Sonnets* (CS 8–11), Astrophel's sonnet moves obliquely toward a position that offers a convenient and effective avenue of attack against
the poet's mistress. When we reread it, every gesture seems to have
been determined by this general strategical aim. The poem's movement, in one sense so natural and offhand, is in retrospect thoroughly
artful. The air of intimacy, the easy familiarity, and the parenthetical asides here work to create a conversational poetry which—
despite its delicacy—has been fully pressed into obvious practical
service.

The second sonnet is rather different. It has the same informality
of manner, but its quality of privacy is more real. It is not designed
to be "overheard" by Stella in the way that AS 31 unmistakably is.
The voice is not so public, the stance not so self-consciously posed.
Instead, the repetitions, the emphatic rhythms of the opening quatrain broken by interjection ("ô me," "wretch"), and the italics of
regret ("mĭght"-"mĭght," "wŏuld not"-"cŏuld not") create the
effect of a sudden release of bottled-up feeling. Self-reproach and
resentment concerning the loss of Stella here provoke much more intense personal revelation on Astrophel's part than any we have so
far seen. The conventional machinery of AS 31 has been swept
away—the "busie archer," "arrowes," and "languisht grace"—and
we are given, instead, the details of a love situation that is altogether
real: a sketch of Astrophel's earlier failure to appreciate Stella's
worth, his worry over social delicacies, and his irrecoverable loss of
her to "No lovely *Paris*." Moreover, none of this occurred (as it
would have in the *Arcadia*) under the auspices of Fortune or a tyrannical Cupid. Force, fraud, and Fortune are absolved of any guilt, and
Astrophel insists: "But to my selfe my selfe did give the blow." Thus,

the course of the love, from the very beginning, is seen as having
been determined by choice, even as we have seen Astrophel himself
choosing in the early sonnets of the sequence.

Intimate conversation, then, has almost imperceptibly become
Astrophel's true language of feeling, the language of his most moving
love poetry. Whether it is in the service of strategy (as AS 31) or self-
revelation (as AS 33), it is clearly a very different language of love
from what we heard earlier in the sequence:

> When Nature made her chiefe worke, *Stella's* eyes,
> In colour blacke, why wrapt she beames so bright?
> > (AS 7, 1–2)

> Queene *Vertue's* court, which some call *Stella's* face,
> Prepar'd by Nature's chiefest furniture, . . .
> > (AS 9, 1–2)

> *Phoebus* was Judge betweene *Jove, Mars,* and *Love,* . . .
> > (AS 13, 1)

> In highest way of heav'n the Sunne did ride,
> Progressing then from faire twinnes' gold'n place: . . .
> > (AS 22, 1–2)

*   *   *

> O fooles, or over-wise, alas the race
> Of all my thoughts hath neither stop nor start,
> But only *Stella's* eyes and *Stella's* hart.
> > (AS 23, 12–14)

> I, cumbred with good maners, answer do,
> But know not how, for still I thinke of you.
> > (AS 30, 13–14)

> With how sad steps, ô Moone, thou climb'st the skies, . . .
> > (AS 31, 1)

> I might, unhappie word, ô me, I might, . . .
> > (AS 33, 1)

The formality, regular rhythms, public air, and flavor of courtly compliment in the lines of the first group contrast sharply with the more halting movement, relative simplicity, and direct feeling of those in the second. We can of course find colloquial and conversational speech early in the sequence, but it was there used either for high-spirited debate or for generally disruptive purposes. Now it has become the medium for Astrophel's most serious thoughts of love. These thoughts, moreover, center increasingly around the fact of Stella's inaccessibility. The sestet of AS 31 is important in this respect, for it shows the extent to which she thinks of love in terms of courtly play: she "love[s] to be lov'd," enjoys the conventional role of proud beauty, and refuses to take Astrophel's "constant *Love*" seriously. She is addicted to the game, although it should be remembered that in the early stages of the sequence Astrophel offered her a kind of poetry that all too often coincided with her expectations. In the meantime, however, he has discovered much more about the tenacity and strength of his desire, and he has learned very quickly that he must have a different and deeper kind of response from Stella. As he makes this discovery, the reality of his feeling breaks out of the more formal and public modes with which he had begun (e.g., AS 22) and finds its proper expression in the intimate and private conversation of AS 31 and AS 33. Even in the more mannered poems after AS 33, we respond to the essential naturalness and candor of feeling that motivate them. They are obviously much more moving and sympathetic than sophisticated compliment and wit, as well as more restless and imperative than Petrarchan praise and self-denial:

> Come let me write, 'And to what end?' To ease
> A burthned hart. 'How can words ease, which are
> The glasses of thy dayly vexing care?'
>
> (AS 34, 1–3)

> What *Nestor's* counsell can my flames alay,
> Since Reason's selfe doth blow the cole in me?
> And ah what hope, that hope should once see day,
> Where *Cupid* is sworne page to Chastity?
>
> (AS 35, 5–8)

The first that straight my fancie's error brings
   Unto my mind, is *Stella's* image, wrought
   By *Love's* owne selfe, but with so curious drought,
That she, me thinks, not onely shines but sings.
   I start, looke, hearke, but what in closde up sence
Was held, in opend sense it flies away,
Leaving me nought but wailing eloquence: . . .
                       (AS 38, 5–11)

Come sleepe, ô sleepe, the certaine knot of peace, . . .
                       (AS 39, 1)

The confidence of the early sonnets on style has by now entirely disappeared. The poet who was sure that "all my deed / But Copying is" has been reduced to debilitating self-questioning by "*Stella's* great powrs, that so confuse my mind" (AS 34). In AS 35, he tries a poem of formal praise, but he succeeds only in discovering the conflict (expressed in terms like those of the *Arcadia*) between his desire and Stella's chastity. He worries that "truth it selfe must speake like flatterie" and in the sonnet's sestet produces a very lame offering:

Honour is honour'd, that thou doest possesse
   Him as thy slave, and now long needy Fame
   Doth even grow rich, naming my *Stella's* name.
Wit learnes in thee perfection to expresse,
   Not thou by praise, but praise in thee is raisde:
   It is a praise to praise, when thou art praisde.
                 (AS 35, 9–14)

Nothing could demonstrate better than these lines how much the mode of Petrarchan celebration is alien to Astrophel. The passage is in no sense lyrical or hymnlike. The couplet involves itself in tedious logical distinctions and concludes with a flat formula. The poem ends by expressing, not so much a sense of aspiration toward the felt sweetness of beauty and virtue, as the crippling effect of Astrophel's frustrated desire upon his poetry of praise.

    That frustration comes out most strongly in AS 38 and AS 40. The shining image of Stella in AS 38 has some of the purity and harmony of a Petrarchan vision, but Astrophel is completely incapable of sustaining it. It arouses his desire, and his effort to possess the vision quickly dispels it. Its loss, moreover, does not provoke Astrophel to a meditation upon its miraculous beauty, or to thanks for the momentary gift of it. He finds himself left only with "wailing eloquence"—sorrow for the fact of having been deprived. The sonnet is managed, however, with extraordinary delicacy, and we are allowed to feel desire's urgency but none of its unpleasantness. Sidney focuses primarily upon the evanescence of beauty and harmony, and upon Astrophel's poignant attempt to recapture his vision:

> I start, looke, hearke, but what in closde up sence
> Was held, in opend sense it flies away,
> Leaving me nought but wailing eloquence:
> I, seeing better sights in sight's decay,
> Cald it anew, and wooed sleepe againe:
> But him her host that unkind guest had slaine.

The quest of the last lines expresses fully the twofold nature of Astrophel's love, for it is an act both of aspiration and of acquisitiveness. Its failure sums up the central action of the sequence as a whole: Sidney's hero is utterly deserted at the end, sustained neither by a vision of the ideal nor by the possession of Stella herself. The pathos of the situation is beautifully and simply evoked by the poem's economy of means. Scarcely anything is intellectualized, and we hear nothing of schematic conflicts between reason and passion. The method is narrative: the sonnet is primarily a record of the experience as it developed, communicated through the imagery and rhythms of the verse as they body forth Astrophel's journey into sleep, his sudden awakening, and his final, fruitless search for the lost vision of Stella. No better example could be found of Sidney's effort to write a poetry that sets moving images and actions before our eyes.

The last sonnet of this group (AS 40) is a direct appeal to Stella. It is particularly interesting because it represents a moment in which drama and ceremony, intimacy and formality, entreaty and praise, all meet:

As good to write as for to lie and grone.
  O *Stella* deare, how much thy power hath wrought,
  That hast my mind, none of the basest, brought
My still kept course, while others sleepe, to mone.
Alas, if from the height of Vertue's throne,
  Thou canst vouchsafe the influence of a thought
  Upon a wretch, that long thy grace hath sought;
Weigh then how I by thee am overthrowne:
  And then, thinke thus, although thy beautie be
  Made manifest by such a victorie,
Yet noblest Conquerours do wreckes avoid.
  Since then thou hast so farre subdued me.
  That in my heart I offer still to thee,
O do not let thy Temple be destroyd.

Astrophel here writes a new kind of poem to Stella. For the first time, except for the couplet of AS 30, he addresses her in the intimate terms he had previously used only in other contexts: "O *Stella* deare, how much thy power hath wrought, . . ." The frankness of this appeal asks for a return of feeling much deeper than the playful ambiguities of courtly flirtation to which Stella has so far restricted herself. Astrophel has been driven to bluntness by the power of his desire and the pain of his isolation. He thrusts the first line of the poem out with the force of sudden resolve. Frustration and inner debate come to an abrupt end, and feelings are permitted a free expression in language that is natural and direct.

If the poem begins with a sense of release, however, Astrophel soon alters its course. The intimacy of his speech has brought him momentarily close to Stella, but the gap between them widens considerably by the second quatrain. She is once again upon "the height of Vertue's throne," and the tone of address is thereafter determined by the decorum of the relationship as the convention traditionally defines it. Pain and humiliation ("my mind, none of the basest") had stimulated the opening gesture toward Stella. That spontaneity now vanishes, and Astrophel resorts to common Petrarchan arguments in order to persuade Stella to be merciful: "Weigh then . . . thinke thus . . . Since then." Noble conquerors should, after all, be merciful. Behind this formal framework, however, we sense the presence

of those feelings, peremptory and importunate, which provoke the
cry of the very last line. The sonnet ends with an appeal that is
tactical and conventional, yet also desperate in its helplessness and
need.

The group of lyrics from AS 33 to AS 40, then, steadily deepens our
sympathy for Astrophel and involves us in his suffering and growing
despair. If he seems driven more and more by the insistency of
desire, his impetuousness and occasional coarseness are redeemed by
the controlled pathos of his situation and by the greater simplicity
and candor of his speech. Role playing has for the most part ceased,
and we hear the voice of a private Astrophel in AS 33–34 and AS 38–
40. An intimate conversational style gradually becomes the medium
for his thoughts of love, and the seriousness of its tones undercuts the
superficiality of much of his earlier verse. His love begins to justify
itself, not because of any special purity, but because of the pain he
suffers; because of the quality of aspiration and devotion which is a
part of that pain (as in AS 38); and because the intensity of his feeling is such that it creates a style so direct in its means as to declare a
triumph over mere courtly dalliance and play:

> I, cumbred with good maners, answer do,
> But know not how, for still I thinke of you.

> I might, unhappie word, ô me, I might,
> And then would not, or could not see my blisse: . . .

> Come let me write, 'And to what end?' To ease
>   A burthned hart.

> I start, looke, hearke, but what in closde up sence
> Was held, in opend sense it flies away, . . .

> O *Stella* deare, how much they power hath wrought, . . .

This is of course not artless poetry, but it achieves indirectly the
kind of simplicity which Astrophel had claimed for himself in the
early sonnets on style. There, that claim was heavily qualified by his
role playing and by his own conventionally witty verse. Here, it is

substantiated unself-consciously and almost inadvertently. The abrupt dramatic openings, the sensitive rhythms that notate Astrophel's confusion and agitation as well as his more lyric moments, the imperatives and direct forms of address to Stella, and the diction and syntax of conversational speech combine to create a poetry that has the quality of being an immediate and spontaneous expression of feeling. No good verse ever is that, of course, and a glance at the rhetoric books will reveal that the second example above contains the figure epanalepsis, that the third example employs what Fraunce called "addubitation," and so on. The verse is full of "art," and we are not expected to forget that Astrophel is a courtier writing in a polished, graceful, courtly style. Many of the figures employed are so-called auricular schemes of repetition and sound play ("might ... me ... might"); yet they are generally made subservient to what Fraunce called

> the figures in Sentences, which in the whole sentẽce expres some motion of the minde. These are more forcible & apt to perswade, than those of words, which be rather pleasant and fit to delight. Generallie, as in tropes there is a certaine grace, in figures of words a kinde of delicacie, so in these sentences, appeareth force and maiestie.[1]

It is just this forcible rhetoric expressing "some motion of the minde" for the purposes of persuasion that Astrophel (and Sidney) use in the passages quoted. The figure in the second example may be epanalepsis, but the *effect* of its repetitions is what is primarily important. That effect is very like what Wilson claimed for another sort of repetition ("Doublettes"): "the oft repeating of one worde, doth muche stirre the hearer, and makes the worde seeme greater, as though a sworde were oft digged and thrust twise, or thrise in one place of the body."[2] Wilson called addubitation "Answering to our selfe" and showed that it was particularly apt for characters who were "much troubled and out of quiet."[3] I pointed out analogous uses of expressive rhetoric in my discussion of the *Arcadia*, but here the figures have been thoroughly adjusted to the conversational nature of the style. That conversation, moreover, has now more seriousness, more simplicity, more intimacy, and a greater appearance of spontaneity than that of Astrophel's earlier poetry of love.

Astrophel convinces us that "in truth [he feels] those passions, which easily . . . may be bewrayed by that same forciblenes or *Energia* . . . of the writer." And we are the more convinced because his new poetry comes as something of a triumph over the ingenuities of courtliness in love. It carries us through to a realm of feeling sufficiently deep to command respect and sympathetic response because it has managed to overcome more suspect forms of artifice and wit.

CHAPTER XVI

The Campaign Pursued

✣✣✣

THE SHAPE OF *Astrophel and Stella* is one of carefully maintained balance. Sidney continually qualifies and complicates our judgment of Astrophel. He exposes the unruliness of his desire, the uncertainty of his grounds for love, and the dangers of his tendency to resolve serious dilemmas in too sophisticated and courtly a way. Defensive argument (AS 14), disrupted praise (AS 9 and AS 25), conventional flattery of Stella (AS 13 and AS 22), and sudden bursts of uncontrollable colloquial energy (AS 1 and AS 11) are the main forms of that exposure. All of them show Astrophel's fundamental alienation from the purer idealism of Musidorus' or Petrarch's mode. His style retains an essential formality that implies a respect for the rational and ceremonial love so delicately expressed in the duet of Pamela and Musidorus. Yet although he partly affirms that ideal, his poetry reveals mainly his inability to achieve it. His speech continually pulls away from the harmonies of ceremony to the more irregular rhythms and colloquial vehemence that are the signs of his unmanageable desire.

As the sequence progresses, however, the forms that in the beginning suggested moral rebellion and disturbance take on more positive values. The colloquialism that had upset rational order and celebration in love begins to create exceptionally moving poetry— a poetry of "mundane" love in relatively mundane language. Broken rhythms now disclose the shape of passionate desire in such a way as to evoke our sympathy. Candor, simplicity, and tenderness are less than the idealism of Petrarch, but much more than the courtliness of dainty wits, and Astrophel's unadorned and unsteady speech becomes the medium for their expression. He begins to find a voice that is considerably different from the praiseful and high voice of the convention, yet one that is not merely a sign of his fall from that height. What he suffers and gives up in the fall helps to redeem him, as do the positive values of his love itself.

This rhythm of fall and redemption is one that Sidney pursues throughout the sequence. He repeats it twice after first establishing it in the long opening section (AS 1–40). Each time we are made aware of Astrophel's various (and often charming) failings, and each time he is purged at a crucial moment—not purged of desire, of course, but transformed in such a way as to make us respond strongly to the deep value of his love. The method, again, resembles that of the *Arcadia*: the maintenance of a double perspective on human desire, and the corresponding effect of a double judgment of conviction and pardon at the end.

The first repetition of this rhythm occurs in the group from AS 41 to AS 68, which ends with Stella's granting of grace to Astrophel. The appeal of AS 40 fails, and Astrophel now considers various alternatives: he thinks of turning back to the life of action (AS 47), decides momentarily to celebrate Stella's chastity (AS 42 and AS 48), but generally gives himself over to a bold campaign designed to win her—although it is not yet altogether clear what he expects the fruits of victory to be. The possibility of repudiating love is never deeply considered: a poem like AS 47 is only bathetic in its final effect. The moments of Petrarchan balance (AS 42 and AS 48) are more serious, but all too obviously precarious. Neither poem is particularly lyrical in its celebration of Stella, nor particularly joyous in its pledge of willing self-denial and control. Both are highly rational in their structure: they are governed by imperatives begging Stella not to depart, and expend much of their energy in offering "proofs" to restrain her. They have, therefore, a mildly tactical air about them, and are substantially different, for example, from Petrarch's sonnets in this manner. One should note that there is a similar group of lyrics in the *Certain Sonnets* (CS 23–26), and they come at an analogous point in the sequence. They follow the meditative poems of CS 15–22, and are an attempt to resolve the lover's frustration. They too are precarious, however, and soon give way to more rebellious and more demanding expressions of desire (CS 27).

Astrophel's desire grows, then, throughout AS 41–68, and he becomes increasingly aggressive. More particularly, he becomes extraordinarily self-conscious in using the persuasive powers of energia:

> Alas, if Fancy drawne by imag'd things,
> Though false, yet with free scope more grace doth breed
> Then servant's wracke, where new doubts honor brings;
> Then thinke my deare, that you in me do reed
> Of Lover's ruine some sad Tragedie:
> I am not I, pitie the tale of me.
>
> (AS 45, 9–14)

> he forst [me] out to find
> The thorowest words, fit for woe's selfe to grone,
> Hoping that when they might find *Stella* alone,
> Before she could prepare to be unkind,
> Her soule, arm'd but with such a dainty rind,
> Should soone be pierc'd with sharpnesse of the mone.
> She heard my plaints, and did not only heare,
> But Them (so sweete is she) most sweetly sing, . . .
>
> (AS 57, 3–10)

> Oft with true sighes, oft with uncalled teares,
> Now with slow words, now with dumbe eloquence
> I *Stella's* eyes assayll, invade her eares; . . .
>
> (AS 61, 1–3)

In the first example, Astrophel urges Stella to attend to his "tale" (as Musidorus had done with Pamela), but he meets with no success. Then Stella "sings" Astrophel's plaints, but they simply turn to tunes of joy (AS 57, 9–12). Finally, sighs, tears, words, and gestures are all called into action, only to disprove the validity of the Camerata's faith in the power of drama. Astrophel runs the entire gamut, and Stella continues to treat his verse and protestations like those of any other courtier: they are expected and received as part of a dalliance designed to entertain the wits of courtly ladies. She accepts all in the spirit of a game, and Astrophel is driven more and more to put on an antic disposition. The soulful verse produced by the crisis of AS 33–40 gives way to a poetry that is by turns frenetic, sophisticated, satiric, chatty, crude, charming, and simply weary.

These antics are in one sense forced upon Astrophel by Stella's unresponsiveness, but they are also embraced by him in the heat of his desire. He does much more than simply implore or write complaints. He shifts in and out of roles, playing the naive poet again (AS 54), berating a foolish courtier (AS 51), squabbling with Cupid (AS 46), affecting heroic poses (AS 47), and being reduced to foolishness when they fail (AS 53). Much of the vivacity and satiric spirit that was noticed in AS 1–21 returns in these poems, but the postures are more ridiculous, and the wit much more abrasive. Astrophel is no longer the harried and defensive hero of the first section, nor the passive sufferer of AS 33–40. Instead, he takes the offensive unabashedly, in the vigorous tradition of Philisides and the narrator of the *Certain Sonnets*. We see this most, perhaps, in the poems which begin to treat sexual desire far more openly:

> A strife is growne betweene *Vertue* and *Love*,
>> While each pretends that *Stella* must be his:
>> Her eyes, her lips, her all, saith *Love* do this,
> Since they do weare his badge, most firmely prove.
> But *Vertue* thus that title doth disprove,
>> That *Stella* (ô deare name) that *Stella* is
>> That vertuous soule, sure heire of heav'nly blisse:
> Not this faire outside, which our hearts doth move.
>> And therefore, though her beautie and her grace
> Be *Love's* indeed, in *Stella's* selfe he may
> By no pretence claime any maner place.
> Well *Love*, since this demurre our sute doth stay,
>> Let *Vertue* have that *Stella's* selfe; yet thus,
>> That *Vertue* but that body graunt to us.
>
> (AS 52)

The final rejection of virtuous love, which takes place unequivocally in AS 71–72, is clearly anticipated here. The predictions of the friend in AS 14 are well on the way toward being fulfilled, even as Astrophel half suspected they would be. We can see Astrophel solving the dilemma of virtue and desire in a way similar to (but cruder than) his solution of the earlier conflict between the active life and the life of love. Courtly wit and sophistication provide the basis for this solution, but they now take the form of false logic that Basilius first gave to them (in the *Arcadia*). In poems like AS 19 and AS 21, Astrophel relied ultimately upon simple assertions of the will, combined with a consciousness of the comedy of his situation. Now he is much bolder, undeniably charming, and considerably less admirable, as he uses elaborate mock logic to resolve his difficulties: Virtue may take the part of Stella it desires, and Astrophel will have the rest. The technique recalls Basilius' pleasant blasphemy:

> *Phaebus* farewell, a sweeter Saint I serve.
> Thou art farre off, thy kingdome is above:
> She heav'n on earth with beauties doth preserve.
> Thy beames I like, but her cleare rayes I love:
> Thy force I feare, her force I still do prove.
>
> *Phaebus* yeelde up thy title in my minde.
> She doth possesse, thy Image is defaste,
> But if thy rage some brave revenge will finde,
> On her, who hath in me thy temple raste,
> Employ thy might, that she my fires may taste.
>   And how much more her worth surmounteth thee,
>   Make her as much more base by loving me.
>
> (OA 38, 6-17)

Logic, like rhetoric, always tends to have a symbolic character in Sidney, and Astrophel here begins to place himself in the company of Basilius: both openly use perverted logic to flaunt a virtue which had previously claimed their allegiance. Earlier in the sequence, Astrophel either avoided rational defenses of his love (AS 5, *et al.*) or made a show of using logic properly (AS 14, 9-14). Now he gaily perverts it, and we are made to feel the difference.

Astrophel also in this sonnet (and throughout the group AS 41-68) puts the intimate manner of AS 33-40 to quite different uses. Stella is "ô deare name"; she is bandied about easily and, as it were, irreverently. Moreover, the argument of AS 52 is finished off with a "Well *Love*" that is rather too casual, and quite different from the debating tactics of AS 4, AS 10, and AS 21. In the early sonnets, we felt Astrophel's need to defend himself and appreciated the narrow-mindedness of some of his antagonists. But now he is on the offensive, and he uses a particularly chatty mode of address that inevitably alters the tone and spirit of his love:

> Faire eyes, sweet lips, deare heart, that foolish I
> Could hope by *Cupid's* helpe on you to pray; . . .
> > (AS 43, 1–2)

> Then thinke my deare, that you in me do reed
> Of Lover's ruine some sad Tragedie: . . .
> > (AS 45, 13–14)

> Yet Deare, let me this pardon get of you, . . .
> > (AS 46, 12)

> Deare, why make you more of a dog then me?
> > (AS 59, 1)

> Deare, love me not, that you may love me more.
> > (AS 62, 14)

Before AS 41, Astrophel addresses Stella directly only three times, and all the uses but one (AS 36) have a tender and moving quality. Astrophel has not relinquished the gain in intimacy he achieved in AS 33–40, but the special value of his relatively simple, direct speech in those poems has now been eroded away. Stella has become unceremoniously "Deare," and Astrophel's conversational style as a whole shows a marked change in the direction of sophisticated nonchalance, courtly patter, easy wit:

> Alas poore wag, that now a scholler art
> To such a schoole-mistresse, whose lessons new
> Thou needs must misse, . . .
> > (AS 46, 9–11)

> Let her go. Soft, but here she comes. Go to,
> Unkind, I love you not: O me, that eye . . .
> > (AS 47, 12–13)

On silly me do not the burthen lay,
   Of all the grave conceits your braine doth breed;
   But find some *Hercules* to beare, in steed
Of *Atlas* tyr'd, your wisedome's heav'nly sway.
                (AS 51, 5–8)

Cupid, having me his slave describe
   In *Marse's* liverie, prauncing in the presse:
   'What now sir foole,' said he, 'I would no lesse,
Looke here, I say.' I look'd, . . .
                (AS 53, 5–8)

'What he?' say they of me, 'now I dare sweare,
He cannot love: no, no, let him alone.'
                (AS 54, 7–8)

What, a whole weeke without one peece of looke, . . .
                (AS 56, 3)

A pretty case! I hoped her to bring . . .
                (AS 57, 12)

Then some good body tell me how I do, . . .
                (AS 60, 12)

O Doctor *Cupid*, thou for me reply, . . .
                (AS 61, 12)

We can find examples earlier in the sequence that approximate some of these, but very little that comes as close to the talk of prose as the lines from AS 47, AS 53, and AS 54, and no group of sonnets that is altogether as dense in its concentration of colloquial chatter as this one. Most important, Astrophel has never before been so fully theatrical and self-conscious in his gesticulation, so much like an actor commenting in soliloquy upon the last scene or appealing to the audience for response. This theatrical quality is especially true of AS 57, AS 60, and AS 61. Everything tends to suggest a courtship that is now frankly sensual in its motives, pragmatic in its methods,

9+

and thoroughly unceremonial in its manner and style. The lack of ceremony is perhaps the most telling fact of all. We have come very far from the exquisite manners, decorous self-restraint, and lyric ceremoniousness of Musidorus' aspiring poetry of praise (OA 50). Astrophel's verse shows at every level of style his distance from the ideal of virtuous love that he is in the midst of abandoning. His fall, however, is never unqualified, and Sidney refuses to let us be narrowly moral in our response to the action as it develops. Astrophel's charm never deserts him, and his wit remains as engaging as it is sophisticated. Polish, deftness, and grace control the verse, even when it is most theatrical and unceremonious. The tone is always complex: Astrophel's witty persuasions to love are never those of a mere seducer; his *crises de conscience* (AS 47) are so self-conscious and so close to self-parody that they prevent us from invoking similarly stiff moral standards in order to judge him; and, finally, his poetry always manages to persuade us of his strong, perfectly human love:

> and while I spurre
> My horse, he spurres with sharpe desire my hart:
> He sits me fast, how ever I do sturre:
> And now hath made me to his hand so right,
> That in the Manage myselfe takes delight.
>
> (AS 49, 10–14)

> *Stella*, the fulnesse of my thoughts of thee
> Cannot be staid within my panting breast,
> But they do swell and struggle forth of me,
> Till that in words thy figure be exprest.
>
> (AS 50, 1–4)

To moralize too easily is to place ourselves in the uninviting company of Geron. Sidney forces us to be more supple, and he never allows us to forget that many of Astrophel's own tactics are provoked by Stella's superficiality.

At this point in the sequence, Astrophel seems to have reached a position of stalemate. Direct appeals for mercy, sonnets of praise and devotion, and complaints about Stella's cruelty all sound no different to her from the verse of other courtiers, and Astrophel himself has tended to undermine his purer Petrarchan formulations (AS 42 and AS 48) by his own sophisticated bawdry (AS 52). He has not really defined the ground of his love, nor declared it in terms that have enough strength of conviction to move Stella. It is just at this moment that she herself suddenly offers him the opportunity he has been seeking. In AS 62, as Astrophel relates, she suggests that she does indeed love him,

> but loved a Love not blind,
> Which would not let me, whom she loved, decline
> From nobler course, fit for my birth and mind:
>   And therefore by her Love's authority,
>   Willd me these tempests of vaine love to flie,
> And anchor fast my selfe on *Vertue's* shore.
>   (AS 62, 6–11)

Stella's invocation of virtue and a "nobler course" at this point is of the utmost importance. It recalls the life and values that Astrophel had set aside in AS 18 and AS 21, as well as the struggle of his decision and the deliberate finality with which he had seemed to make it. It also makes clear the fact that Stella has no conception of the nature of his commitment to love. She considers him an interloper in the courts of Venus, professes to regret his departure from "*Vertue's* shore," and intimates that he might easily return to that safe harbor. Astrophel's immediate reply is both rueful and witty: his next poem (AS 63) is an exercise in high-spirited mock logic, proving that Stella's two negatives ("No, No") make a positive. Then all ceases. We hear the clear, harmonious notes of the First Song, followed immediately by two important, declarative, moving sonnets:

> No more, my deare, no more these counsels trie,
>   O give my passions leave to run their race:
>   Let Fortune lay on me her worst disgrace,
> Let folke orecharg'd with braine against me crie,
> Let clouds bedimme my face, breake in mine eye,
>   Let me no steps but of lost labour trace,
>   Let all the earth with scorne recount my case,
> But do not will me from my *Love* to flie.

I do not envie *Aristotle's* wit,
Nor do aspire to *Caesar's* bleeding fame,
Nor ought do care, though some above me sit,
Nor hope, nor wishe another course to frame,
But that which once may win thy cruell hart:
Thou art my Wit, and thou my Vertue art.

(AS 64)

Love by sure proofe I may call thee unkind,
That giv'st no better eare to my just cries:
Thou whom to me such my good turnes should bind,
As I may well recount, but none can prize:
For when, nak'd boy, thou couldst no harbour find
In this old world, growne now so too too wise:
I lodg'd thee in my heart, and being blind
By Nature borne, I gave to thee mine eyes.
Mine eyes, my light, my heart, my life, alas,
If so great services may scorned be: . . .

(AS 65, 1–10)

Both poems are significant because they persuade Stella of the reality of Astrophel's love and win for him the gift of grace in AS 69. Trying to account for their success is not easy. Richard Young states that "the effect here is of no role at all, the lover speaking in his own voice."[1] This suggests something of what we feel, although Astrophel is clearly not entirely free of certain kinds of posing. For the first time, however, he addresses Stella in verse that combines intimacy with strength, a colloquial and natural speech with the accents of authority and obvious seriousness. Defensiveness, satiric venom, high-spirited wit, and the broken rhythms of earlier despair have been swept away. Tactics, extravagantly self-conscious acting, and the chatter of AS 41–64 have momentarily ceased. Stella's suggestion that Astrophel return to a "nobler course" stirs him to an appeal that has the tenderness of importunity but the force of an imperative.

Astrophel derives his authority here primarily from the consciousness of his strong commitment to love, and from his sudden renewed determination to make love a source of heroic virtue. By challenging

Astrophel to return to "*Vertue's* shore," Stella has raised the one issue capable of spurring him to a rediscovery and articulation of the more serious feeling that motivated both his original departure from that shore and his subsequent perseverance in love. From his point of view, turning back has long since been impossible; exasperated by the fact that Stella either cannot or will not understand this, he speaks with uncalculated spontaneity in AS 64 and declares the fullness of his devotion: "Thou art my Wit, and thou my Vertue art." The declaration comes with a force and explicitness we have not heard before. It has been made possible mainly by the nature of Astrophel's experience of love: an experience involving difficult choice, renunciation of his expected "harvest," and prolonged fruitless entreaty. His consciousness of what love may cost him in terms of honor and fame makes Stella's suggestion particularly outrageous. He responds with sudden firmness and claims what he feels to be his due: "O give my passions leave to run their race." The language of that claim is particularly interesting, for Astrophel rehabilitates himself by presenting his love in consciously heroic terms. He swears to endure the enmity of "Fortune," "clouds," and "all the earth" for the sake of Stella. Aristotle's wit and Caesar's fame are dismissed with a flourish: he cares for neither. He speaks (in AS 65) of his "great services" and the gift of "my light, my heart, my life." In short, he casts himself in a hero's role, interpreting his fall from reason and virtue as an act of self-sacrifice, magnanimity, renunciation—as the willing martyrdom of a courtly Antony who has given up all for love. This interpretation is obviously only part of the truth. Throughout AS 64, the language strains with hyperbole, and the assertions of AS 65 are considerably qualified by Astrophel's own self-conscious resort to the gentle ironies of the Cupid convention. Yet his positive valuation of his conduct remains true in several important ways. His surrender of great expectation and his later exasperation, humiliation, and growing weariness have indeed involved giving up what constituted his light, his heart, his life. The entire experience has been in many ways one of frustrating trial and test, and it has brought to his voice the weathered tones of these climactic sonnets. The heroic quality is—at least in part—genuinely there, and Astrophel's awareness of it introduces into his poetry a note of authority that is quite new. Measured against Petrarch or Musidorus or Pyrocles, Astrophel is impatient, demanding, sensual, inadequate on almost every count. But measured against the dainty wits or Stella herself, he is powerful in his feeling and strong in his devotion. Whatever reservations we may have about him, both his power and his steadfastness go far to redeem the antic behavior of AS 41–63. The poetry of AS 64–65 retains all the intimacy of Astrophel's speech but endows it with compelling, new-found strength:

> When Nature made her chiefe worke, *Stella's* eyes,
> In colour blacke, why wrapt she beames so bright?
> (AS 7, 1–2)

> I, cumbred with good maners, answer do,
> But know not how, for still I thinke of you.
> (AS 30, 13–14)

> O *Stella* deare, how much thy power hath wrought, .. .
> (AS 40, 2)

> Then thinke my deare, that you in me do reed
> Of Lover's ruine some sad Tragedie: . . .
> (AS 45, 12–13)

> No more, my deare, no more these counsels trie, . . .
> (AS 64, 1)

> I gave to thee mine eyes.
> Mine eyes, my light, my heart, my life, alas, . . .
> (AS 65, 8–9)

One can here trace at a glance the permutations of Astrophel's style of love: from the conventional formality of a novice, to the first blush of suddenly addressing Stella, to helpless appeal, to the chatter of courtly persuasion, to the more potent tenderness of unanswerable entreaty.

Astrophel, then, is again rehabilitated. He manages to give his experience of love some meaning in terms of the trial and self-sacrifice it has involved, and he does this with sufficient conviction to persuade Stella that his love is indeed real. He spells out for her what love has cost him, and her belated recognition of that cost moves her as nothing else has. The critical issue has been that which Astrophel debated earlier—the question of "Vertue"—and this fact gives the sequence a special unity. Love for Astrophel was in the beginning a matter of deliberate choice, and the most persuasive claim he is finally able to make on Stella's affections relates directly to the difficulty, firmness, and consequences of that choice. The "great services" he mentions in AS 65 consist of nothing more— a fact which reveals both the limitations and the positive strength of his action. For if he wins Stella in AS 64–65 because of his strong feeling and firm commitment in love, we should also note that he makes no great effort to consider the relationship between these particular values and the higher, more inclusive ones which Stella urged upon him in AS 62. He simply follows the bent of his passion, never sifting fully his motives, or clarifying his expectations, or de- fining very scrupulously the precise nature of his desire. This fact, quite apart from his self-conscious irony in AS 65, forces us to look with some skepticism on his portrayal of love as service and self- sacrifice. Astrophel neglects to say—among other things—what sort of reward he expects in return for his service, and by now we know enough about the quality of his desire to regard him with some sus- picion. He has vacillated between moments of Petrarchan idealism (AS 42 and 48) and moments of frank sensuality (AS 52). The tide has been running in the latter direction for some time, however, and in AS 69–72 all our remaining doubts are thoroughly resolved. When Stella demands that Astrophel take a "vertuous course" in love (AS 69), he accepts the stipulation provisionally, and in AS 71 he attempts a full-dress poem of praise in Petrarch's best manner:

> Who will in fairest booke of Nature know,
>> How Vertue may best lodg'd in beautie be,
>> Let him but learne of *Love* to read in thee,
> *Stella*, those faire lines, which true goodnesse show.
> There shall he find all vices' overthrow,
>> Not by rude force, but sweetest soveraigntie
>> Of reason, from whose light those night-birds flie;
> That inward sunne in thine eyes shineth so.

And not content to be Perfection's heire
Thy selfe, doest strive all minds that way to move,
Who marke in thee what is in thee most faire.
So while thy beautie drawes the heart to love,
     As fast thy Vertue bends that love to good:
     'But ah,' Desire still cries, 'give me some food.'

The context of this poem is extremely important from a stylistic point of view. Since AS 66, Astrophel's voice has been full of excitement and anticipation. His passions have been given "leave to run their race," and the sonnets strain with abrupt questions and shouts of jubilation:

And do I see some cause a hope to feede . . .

Hope, art thou true, or doest thou flatter me?

I, I, ô I may say, that she is mine . . .

Cease eager Muse, peace pen, for my sake stay, . . .

Against this background of dramatic and colloquial speech, the lines of AS 71 issue forth with a formality of manner, a public mode of address, that we have recently ceased to associate with Astrophel. His style of love has become so much the style of conversation that we sense from the opening of the poem how far he is out of character. The measured pace, the restraint, the planned progressions ("Nature . . . Vertue . . . *Love* . . . *Stella*," in the first quatrain), the careful alliteration and assonance (especially in the second quatrain), and the syntactical parallelism that increases as the poem nears its end— all of these define a style more ceremonial and controlled than we expect Astrophel to sustain at this juncture. The sonnet in fact comes closer to the idealistic vision of Musidorus (in OA 50) than do any other of Astrophel's offerings. Aspiration seems finally to find a rational, graceful, fully articulated poetic form. That form is decisively shattered, however, when the voice of desire suddenly breaks through with the colloquial imperatives which have been the keynote of Astrophel's style. The sonnet breaks in two, and gives remarkably vivid dramatic expression to the central tension between reason and passion that I have noted throughout Sidney's work. That expression, moreover, as demonstrated in Chapter Eleven, relates directly to the *Arcadia*'s technique of dialogue or juxtaposition—particularly to the dialogue between Geron and Philisides. Colloquial energy and impatience are placed over against controlled, rational patterning as the two styles of the *Arcadia* confront one another in the character and voice of Astrophel.

Astrophel capitulates to desire, of course, and identifies himself with the conversational style of entreaty that I have defined as his own. Like Musidorus in the *Arcadia* (F, IV. 190), he is surprised by passion moments after protesting his commitment to virtuous love. Ironic plotting produces bathos of a kind in both cases. Astrophel, however, is much less ingenuous than Musidorus, and he simply accepts with some puzzlement (AS 72), but also with courtly sophistication, the facts that he had suspected all along. The stage is set for the final portion of his drama: Stella has at last responded to him, and he in turn has recognized and declared the fundamentally sensuous, impetuous nature of his desire.

CHAPTER XVII

Two Closing Songs

❧❧❧

IN THE SONNETS following AS 71–72, Astrophel undertakes an elaborate campaign designed to win Stella completely. Throughout it, Sidney continues to complicate our responses to the action, and he manages—in the Fourth and Eighth Songs—a final juxtaposition in the manner of the *Arcadia*. From AS 73 to AS 85, Astrophel grows increasingly bold: he steals a kiss (Second Song) and proceeds with a number of "celebrations" of Stella. These are in a self-consciously high style:

> She comes, and streight therewith her shining twins do move
>   Their rayes to me, who in her tedious absence lay
>   Benighted in cold wo, . . .
>
> . . . .
>
> She comes with light and warmth, which like *Aurora* prove
>   Of gentle force, . . .
>
> . . . .
>
> But lo, while I do speake, it groweth noone with me, . . .
>   (AS 76, 1–3, 5–6, and 9)

Ritual, classical allusion, elegant hexameters, and an apparatus of rhetorical figures are all marshaled here, only to be intruded upon by sexual pun and innuendo:

> No wind, no shade can coole, what helpe then in my case,
>   But with short breath, long lookes, staid feet and walking hed,
>   Pray that my sunne go downe with meeker beames to bed.
>   (AS 76, 12–14)
>
> Yet ah, my Mayd'n Muse doth blush to tell the best . . .
>   (AS 77, 14)

The style of ceremony is here wittily perverted, following its dramatic deflation in AS 71, even as Astrophel had previously perverted
his style of intimate conversation (AS 41–63) after the fruitless
appeal of AS 40. Lord Rich is playfully demolished in AS 78, the
theme of cuckoldry is trumpeted ("Is it not evill that such a Devill
wants hornes?"), and Astrophel ushers in a bevy of *baisers* to keep the
mood of dalliance afloat. These are in the manner of the Petrarchan
decadence, and they culminate in the high-spirited, erotic suggestiveness of the poem on Philip Sparrow (AS 83). We are then thrust into
the dramatic poetry of Astrophel's visit to Stella's house. An especially vivid kind of energia is here achieved, as Sidney uses individual sonnets (AS 84–85) to mark particular moments of time and
place ("I see the house"). He also begins to put his songs to narrative
uses, as lyric poetry generally gives way to more dramatic and narrative methods of telling a "tale." The verse, meanwhile, is "mad with
delight" (AS 81); as Astrophel hastens to his rendezvous, the
rhythms and rough syntax of his speech reveal both the eagerness of
his anticipation and the aroused urgency of his desire:

> I see the house, my heart thy selfe containe,
>> Beware full sailes drowne not thy tottring barge:
>> Least joy, by Nature apt sprites to enlarge,
> Thee to thy wracke beyond thy limits straine.

(AS 85, 1–4)

Throughout AS 73–85, Sidney has generally invited us to watch a
fallen Astrophel, governed by passions that are obviously frank in
their sensuality and coarse (for all Astrophel's suavity) in their
sexual innuendo. The whole momentum of this section leads us
toward an encounter that has the excitement—but also some of the
unpleasantness—of any assignation; at the same time, Sidney deliberately chooses a light stanza form, based on octosyllabic couplets, for
his climactic scene:

> Onely joy, now here you are,
> Fit to heare and ease my care:
> Let my whispering voyce obtaine,
> Sweete reward for sharpest paine:
> Take me to thee, and thee to me.
> 'No, no, no, no, my Deare, let be.'

Night hath closd all in her cloke,
Twinckling starres Love-thoughts provoke:
Danger hence good care doth keepe,
Jealousie it selfe doth sleepe:
Take me to thee, and thee to me.
'No, no, no, no, my Deare, let be.'

Better place no wit can find,
Cupid's yoke to loose or bind:
These sweet flowers on fine bed too,
Us in their best language woo:
Take me to thee, and thee to me,
'No, no, no, no, my Deare, let be.'

This small light the Moone bestowes,
Serves thy beames but to disclose,
So to raise my hap more hie;
Feare not else, none can us spie:
Take me to thee, and thee to me.
'No, no, no, no, my Deare, let be.'

(Fourth Song, 1–24)

The song is charming, and contains any number of fine, delicate strokes: "my whispering voyce," the twinkling stars, the moon's "small light," and the intimacy of Stella's repeated "my Deare." Yet the poem opens with a direct, eager request, and it never conveys a sense of that "sharpest paine" which Astrophel protests to feel. The present tense, the emphatically placed imperatives, and the insistence behind "now here you are" all serve to underline the impetuousness and quiet urgency of desire. The scene takes place at Stella's house, and we are reminded, however lightly, of the need for secrecy and deception ("none can us spie"). Love, now much closer to lust, is something to be stolen. The tone, nonetheless, is perfectly pitched, and it fuses the spirit of Ovid's Elegies with touches of Chaucerian humor and strains of Elizabethan lyricism:

That you heard was but a Mouse,
Dumbe sleepe holdeth all the house:
Yet a sleepe, me thinkes they say,

Yong folkes, take time while you may:
Take me to thee, and thee to me.
'No, no, no, no, my Deare, let be.'

Niggard Time threats, if we misse
This large offer of our blisse,
Long stay ere he graunt the same: . . .

Your faire mother is a bed,
Candles out, and curtains spread:
She thinkes you do letters write:
Write, but first let me endite: . . .
(Fourth Song, 25–33 and 37–40)

The vision of eros which Sidney offers us here is sophisticated and courtly—the game of love at its crucial moment. Astrophel pleads and argues in a way that is witty, tactical, clever, somewhat delicate, yet always single-minded in its designs. At the end of the poem, we learn abruptly and indirectly of his translation of desire into action:

Sweet alas, why strive you thus?
Concord better fitteth us:
Leave to *Mars* the force of hands,
Your power in your beautie stands:
Take me to thee, and thee to me.
'No, no, no, no, my Deare, let be.'

Wo to me, and do you sweare
Me to hate? But I forbeare,
Cursed be my destines all,
That brought me so high to fall:
Soone with my death I will please thee.
'No, no, no, no, my Deare, let be.'
(Fourth Song, 43–54)

The tussle in the first stanza here marks Astrophel's furthest point of departure from his earlier vision of virtuous love. The scene has its comedy and bathos, but it also suggests the extent to which Astrophel has alienated himself from the perfect grace and decorum of manner, as well as the self-restraint, which he once proclaimed to be the very essence of his love:

> If that be sinne which doth the maners frame,
> Well staid with truth in word and faith of deed,
> Readie of wit and fearing nought but shame:
> If that be sinne which in fixt hearts doth breed
> A loathing of all loose unchastitie,
> Then Love is sinne, and let me sinfull be.
>
> (AS 14, 9–14)

Astrophel ends the Fourth Song with a curse and a piece of callow self-dramatization ("Soone with my death I will please thee"), and these lead eventually to the ill-tempered "revenge" of the Fifth Song—a lyric, interestingly enough, which Sidney had apparently first written for Philisides.[1] The style of the poem hardly suits Astrophel, but it serves as a logical extension of the frustration and anger he displays at the end of the Fourth Song.

The first seduction scene of *Astrophel and Stella* thus comes to a close. In its entirety, it represents the lowest point in Astrophel's devolution from active hero, the perfect courtier, to rebellious sensualist, the epitome of courtliness. Sidney is not willing to leave matters there, however, and in the Eighth Song, precisely the same sequence of events is dramatized once again, but with a totally different effect. That song is the most beautifully lyric piece in the entire sequence, and it translates Astrophel's passion into a language that is altogether purer and finer than any we have heard before. It seems designed as a careful counterpoint to the Fourth Song: in its setting, its decorum, its technique of narration, and its portrayal of genuine love chastened by pain, it thoroughly qualifies the vivid, covert, insistent desire of its foil. Sidney carefully alters our perspective by using third-person narration and the past tense. This distances the lovers both in "space" and in time. The abrupt present-tense drama of the last group of poems has vanished, and we are asked to see Astrophel and Stella washed, as it were, of all their thoughtless haste. Their love now has a history, and a history that includes some self-denial and considerable pain. The setting, moreover, is pastoral.

The scene takes place in daylight, not the night of the Fourth Song, and all is open, fresh, candid. There is no Ovidian atmosphere of deception or seduction. We fall gently into a love song:

> In a grove most rich of shade,
> Where birds wanton musicke made,
> May then yong his pide weedes showing,
> New perfumed with flowers fresh growing,
>
> *Astrophil* with *Stella* sweete,
> Did for mutuall comfort meete,
> Both within themselves oppressed,
> But each in the other blessed.
>
> Him great harmes had taught much care,
> Her faire necke a foule yoke bare,
> But her sight his cares did banish,
> In his sight her yoke did vanish.
>
> Wept they had, alas the while,
> But now teares themselves did smile,
> While their eyes by love directed,
> Enterchangeably reflected.
>
> Sigh they did, but now betwixt
> Sighs of woes were glad sighs mixt,
> With armes crost, yet testifying
> Restlesse rest, and living dying.
>
> Their eares hungry of each word,
> Which the deere tongue would afford,
> But their tongues restrained from walking,
> Till their harts had ended talking.
>
> (Eighth Song, 1–24)

The excitement here is altogether different from that generated by the Fourth Song: not the headlong rush of passion brimming with anticipation, but the hushed tension of deep feeling restrained because of its very depths. The lines put into ritual form the silent articulateness of conversant hearts, and Sidney uses the technique of repetition and parallel syntax (especially in the third stanza) that he first developed in "My true love hath my hart" (OA 45). The mutuality of love and woe is beautifully rendered with harmonic formality: the delicacy of the alliterative and assonantal patterning is something we do not find at all in the Fourth Song, as are the softening feminine rhymes that here close each stanza. Before, a refrain threaded through the song, setting the imperatives of desire over against the resistance it encountered, and emphasizing the division between the lovers—one line for each:

> Take me to thee, and thee to me.
> 'No, no, no, no, my Deare, let be.'

Now we find a syntax that includes them both and offers us the images or emblems of their union:

> But her sight his cares did banish,
> In his sight her yoke did vanish.
>
> While their eyes by love directed,
> Enterchangeably reflected.
>
> With armes crost, yet testifying
> Restlesse rest, and living dying.

Donne may very well have noticed the image of the second couplet above and kept it for "The Extasie"—indeed, the whole idea of using octosyllabic quatrains as the proper form for his similarly fragile moment of love may also have derived from here. At any rate, Sidney's lovers are now presented with the utmost sympathy, and in their mixture of joy and pain, they give new life to the worn oxymorons of Petrarch: "Restlesse rest, and living dying."

I need not examine the entire song in such detail, though nearly every stanza reveals fresh and unexpected things. Most important, Astrophel's speech to Stella has obviously been carefully prepared for and set in a context of exquisite order. When he addresses her, the poetry is both tender and formal:

> '*Stella* soveraigne of my joy,
> Faire triumpher of annoy,
> *Stella* starre of heavenly fier,
> *Stella* loadstar of desier.
>   (Eighth Song, 29–32)

The verse thus rises to a song of pure Petrarchan praise, and its harmonies melt easily into the poetry of entreaty that is distinctly Astrophel's:

> 'Graunt, ô graunt, but speech alas,
> Failes me fearing on to passe,
> Graunt, ô me, what am I saying?
> But no fault there is in praying.
>
> 'Graunt, ô deere, on knees I pray,
> (Knees on ground he then did stay)
> That not I, but since I love you,
> Time and place for me may move you.
>
> 'Never season was more fit,
> Never roome more apt for it;
> Smiling ayre allowes my reason,
> These birds sing: "Now use the season."
>
> 'This small wind which so sweete is,
> See how it the leaves doth kisse,
> Ech tree in his best attiring,
> Sense of love to love inspiring.
>
> 'Love makes earth the water drink,
> Love to earth makes water sinke;
> And if dumbe things be so witty,
> Shall a heavenly grace want pitty?'
>
> There his hands in their speech, faine
> Would have made tongue's language plaine;
> But her hands his hands repelling,
> Gave repulse all grace excelling.
>
> (Eighth Song, 45–68)

The broken rhythms of Astrophel's conversation of love, rhythms I first noted in my discussion of AS 33–40, enter the poem in the first two stanzas here, but are not at all disruptive. Rather, they are purified by song and taken up into the larger ritual order of Astrophel's appeal: the periodic "Graunt, ô graunt" that begins each of the first three couplets, and the perfect decorum of gesture ("Knees on ground he then did stay"). The invitation to love, meanwhile, has nothing of "Niggard Time" and haste about it but invokes all the accumulated harmonies of the pastoral tradition. We arrive at it only after the long and ceremonious prelude—after Sidney's opening picture of the lovers, and after a decorous poem of praise to Stella. Nature itself points the way:

> 'Love makes earth the water drink,
> Love to earth makes water sinke; . . .

Finally, in the last stanza, Astrophel reaches toward Stella, but is refused with a gesture that in itself excelled "all grace." There is no tussle, and Astrophel accepts Stella's will. The central action of the Fourth Song, desire at its crucial and potentially most unruly moment, has been repeated in every detail and has been beautifully purified. Astrophel's disruptive speech, the conversational idiom that had toppled over Petrarchan idealism, has been redeemed and restored by its subordination to other kinds of order—the order of gesture, ritual, ceremony, and "fit season." Entreaty, so threatening to the highest Petrarchan values, has been made to express much of what is best in the kind of eros that presses for response: "That not I, but since I love you, / Time and place for me may move you." The distinction that Astrophel draws is an important one. Seduction has to do with one will persuading another; union with a free response to the fact of being loved. Astrophel asks for union.

Stella of course refuses and has her one moving moment. Her tenderness here is, one should not forget, a triumph for the quality of Astrophel's love. It is that love, with all its imperfections, which has brought her from superficiality and coquettishness to a level of feeling we scarcely expect of her. Indeed, both lovers here share a victory over artificiality of every kind, over the entire apparatus of the game of love, as their speech and their feeling achieve a quality of formality which is in its context perfectly simple and natural. Again, measured by Petrarch, Astrophel has failed. Measured by the dainty wits, he triumphs, and in very much the same way that the Elizabethans themselves preferred to believe that the innocence and harmony of the pastoral were finer than the polish of the court. For Sidney has managed throughout this song to endow Astrophel with much of that innocence and to present sexual love as its natural expression. Every trace of cleverness and mere sophistication has been refined away, and Astrophel's speech is now infinitely closer to genuine naiveté than was that of the naive poses he had previously adopted:

> 'Graunt, ô graunt, but speech alas,
> Failes me fearing on to passe,
> Graunt, ô me, what am I saying?
> But no fault there is in praying.

Finally, after Stella's last words, we find no curse like that of the Fourth Song:

> Therewithall away she went,
> Leaving him so passion rent,
> With what she had done and spoken,
> That therewith my song is broken.
> (Eighth Song, 101–104)

Astrophel's pain, echoing the pain described in the poem's opening, quietly concludes the verse, as he accepts Stella's will.

In the Fourth and the Eighth Songs, then, Sidney has given us two strongly contrasting views of Astrophel's love: the one exposing its impetuousness and unthinking haste, the other inviting sympathetic response to the positive values it contains. Those values, as I noted earlier, derive largely from the simple fact of Astrophel's genuine depth of feeling, his strong commitment to Stella and the cost that commitment entails, his conquest over coarser values, his intimacy and candor, which in the Eighth Song take on the character of innocence, and his suffering in love's behalf. In many ways, these values are not very different from those which Sidney affirmed at various moments in the *Arcadia*. Indeed, the two songs from *Astrophel* offer two perspectives on eros that recall those noticed in Chapter Three:

So that rysing softely from her overmastered with the fury of delighte (having all his Sences parciall ageanst hym self, and enclyned to his wellbeloved Adversary) hee was bent to take the vauntage of the weykenes of the watche, and see whether at that season hee could

wynn the Bullwarck before tymely help mighte come. And now hee
began to make his aproches when to the just punishment of his
broken promyse, . . . there came by a Doszen Clownish villeynes . . .

(F, IV. 190)

then every way enraged *Musidorus* rase from her enraged, betuixt
the repentant shame of his promyse breaking attempt, and the
tyrannicall fyer of Lust, whiche (having all redy caughte holde of so
sweete and fitt a fewell) was past the Calling back of Reasons
counsell, . . .   (F, IV. 286)

turning the passed greeffes and unkyndenes, to the excess of all
kynde Joyes (as passyon ys apte to slyde into all Contrary) beginning nowe to envy *Argus* thowsand eyes *Brierius* hundred handes,
feighting ageanst a Weyke resistance whiche did stryve to bee overcome; Hee gives mee occasyon to leave hym in so happy a plighte,
least my Penn mighte seeme to grudge, at the due Blisse of these pore
Lovers, whose Loyalty had but smalle respite of theyre fyery
Agonyes.   (F, IV. 226–27)

Sidney's wit is operative in both situations, and certainly one ought
not to take the "just punishment" visited upon Musidorus too
solemnly. But the difference of emphasis in the two scenes nonetheless remains: in the first, Musidorus' sudden "fury of delighte"
(compare AS 81: "mad with delight") leads to near rape, and the
language calls attention to lust, to the lack of "Reasons counsell," to
Musidorus' rage, and to Pamela's defenselessness. The narrator,
with all his sophistication, feels obliged to call in the "Doszen
Clownish villeynes" by way of fit chastisement. The third passage,
meanwhile, elicits a very different response from Sidney. Pyrocles
and Philoclea come together in "due Blisse"—"pore Lovers" who
are dignified and made sympathetic by their naiveté, by their
loyalty, and by the pain they have suffered. In both *Astrophel* and the
Arcadia, then, the heroes betray the purer vision of idealistic love to
which they—in varying degrees—aspire, and their fall provokes a
double judgment: "just punishment" for their display of incon-
stancy and lack of restraint, pardon for their tenderness, their burden
of pain, their intense feeling and loyalty. In the two *Arcadia* passages

and the two songs from *Astrophel*, Sidney thus gives us in sharp juxtaposition a summary of the complex, ambivalent, witty attitudes toward love that we find in all of his writings, and that had provoked the double verdict of conviction and pardon at the end of the *Arcadia*.

After the Eighth Song, Sidney generally maintains his double perspective on Astrophel, underlining the dangers—the disorder—of desire, stressing Astrophel's fidelity to Stella, and demanding sympathy for the pathos of his situation. Resentment and anger break out in the Ninth Song, only to be quickly qualified by the beautiful comment on parting in AS 87:

> When I was forst from *Stella* ever deere,
> *Stella* food of my thoughts, hart of my hart,
> *Stella* whose eyes make all my tempests cleere, . . .
>
> (AS 87, 1-3)

We hear of a "fault" (AS 93), and we see Astrophel again impatient and sarcastic (AS 92), or full of sexual longing (Tenth Song). Yet the theme of his attraction to other women (AS 88 and AS 91) is sounded mainly to underline his fundamental constancy (especially in the effective sestet of AS 88), and after AS 93 the sequence settles into a mood of grief that persists substantially to the end. It is true that Astrophel never reaffirms the idealistic, spiritual vision of love with which he had begun.[2] The choice he made in AS 71-72 has been a decisive one, and little remains to sustain him once Stella herself has left him. His despair is not relieved by the memory of her beauty and virtue, but only intensified by his physical separation from her. In this sense, he is very much passion's slave, committed to a love that involves a rejection of both kinds of virtue that the sequence has defined: heroic or public action, and idealistic love.[3] He has finally been able to affirm neither the style of purposeful activity which Geron recommended to Philisides, nor that of humility, restraint, and praise which Musidorus achieved momentarily with Pamela. His friend's early suggestion, which Astrophel had contested so vigorously, seems in retrospect to have been prophetic:

> with your Rubarb words yow must contend
> To grieve me worse, in saying that Desire
> Doth plunge my wel-form'd soule even in the mire
> Of sinfull thoughts, which do in ruine end?
>
> (AS 14, 5–8)

Yet, for all this, Sidney refuses to let us see Astrophel in the narrowly moral terms of the friend. With minor exceptions, the sonnets between AS 94 and 102 are in a high, ritualistic style analogous to that of the *Arcadia*: we find repeated invocations, some stricter rhetorical patterning, a general avoidance of dramatic effects, and a freer use of interjections and verbal repetitions:

> In night of sprites the gastly powers stur,
> In thee or sprites or sprited gastlinesse:
> But, but (alas) night's side the ods hath fur, . . .
>
> (AS 96, 10–12)

> Only true sighs, you do not go away,
>   Thanke may you have for such a thankfull part,
>   Thanke-worthiest yet when you shall breake my hart.
>
> (AS 95, 12–14)

One should notice that these poems repeat in considerable detail the images, themes, and poetic forms of the *Old Arcadia* lyrics 39–43. They recall Sidney's earlier use of correlative forms (AS 100 / OA 43), his restricted rhyme schemes (AS 89, "night"-"day" / OA 39, "darcke"-"light"), and his pervasive imagery of day and night (AS 89, 91, and 96–99 / OA 39–43). A rather different sonnet discloses some very striking particular echoes:

> Ah, is it not enough, that I am thence,
>   Thence, so farre thence, that scarcely any sparke
> Of comfort dare come to this *dungeon darke*,
> Where rigrows exile *lockes up all my sense*?
>
> (AS 104, 5–8, my italics)

> Since that the stormy rage of passions darcke
> (Of passions darke, made darke by beautie's light)
> With rebell force, hath *closde in dungeon darke*
> *My minde* ere now led foorth by reason's light: . . .
>
> (OA 39, 1–4, my italics)

In many ways, this poetry allies Astrophel with the Pyrocles and Gynecia of the *Arcadia*'s cave scene (F, IV. 169–74). He, as they did, chooses night over day, dark over light, passion over reason, and we are continually reminded of this. Yet, in the context of the sequence, Astrophel's ritual style lends him an important dignity and preserves him from mere frenzy or whining. It bodies forth the quality and depth of his grief in a way that is consonant with the depth of feeling achieved in the Eighth Song. In both cases, he rises to the high ceremony of the convention's main style and reinvigorates its forms of praise and complaint with the reality of his own feelings:

> Sigh they did, but now betwixt
> Sighs of woe were glad sighs mixt,
> With armes crost, yet testifying
> Restlesse rest, and living dying.
>
> . . . .
>
> 'Stella soveraigne of my joy,
> Faire triumpher of annoy,
> Stella starre of heavenly fier,
> Stella loadstar of desier.
>
> (Eighth Song, 17–20 and 29–32)

> O Teares, no teares, but raine from beautie's skies,
>   Making those Lillies and those Roses grow,
>   Which ay most faire, now more then most faire show,
> While gracefull pitty beauty beautifies.
>
> (AS 100, 1–4)

In AS 94–102, then, Astrophel uses the rhetorical artifice of conventional complaint unself-consciously, restoring to the high style that dignity which he had previously managed to subvert (AS 76–77, *et al.*). If in one sense these last sonnets declare the debilitating and destructive power of his passion, they also give sustained and elevated expression to his sorrow, a fit ceremony for the failure of a love that has been movingly portrayed. Some of the lyrics are relatively unsuccessful, but enough of them are sufficiently effective to show Sidney's general intention (e.g., AS 94, AS 97, and AS 99). One can perhaps best gauge their cumulative effect by trying to imagine the end of *Astrophel and Stella* if the sequence had consisted purely of poems like AS 88, AS 92, and AS 104:

> Out traytour absence, darest thou counsell me,
> From my deare Captainnesse to run away?
>
>   (AS 88, 1–2)

> Be your words made (good Sir) of Indian ware,
>   That you allow me them by so small rate?
>
>   (AS 92, 1–2)

> Envious wits what hath bene mine offence,
>   That with such poysonous care my lookes you marke, . . .
>
>   (AS 104, 1–2)

Astrophel would then have quit the scene abruptly and indecorously, leaving behind no finer expression of love than that which satire, impatience, and impetuousness can articulate.

Finally, one last gesture of the sequence balances the positive values in Astrophel's love against the disorder it creates. In the Eleventh Song, the lovers meet for a last time:

> 'Why alas, and are you he?
> Be not yet those fancies changed?'
> Deere when you find change in me,
> Though from me you be estranged,
> Let my chaunge to ruine be.

> 'Well in absence this will dy,
> Leave to see, and leave to wonder.'
> Absence sure will helpe, if I
> Can learne, how my selfe to sunder
> From what in my hart doth ly.
>
>   (Eleventh Song, 6–15)

Astrophel gains considerably by contrast with Stella here: his love is presented in terms of its fidelity, its capability of withstanding time and absence,[4] whereas hers has clearly consisted of little more than those "fancies" that have already changed. Stella has retreated to the safer world of courtly values and the noncommittal dalliance of the game, and Astrophel's own triumph over courtliness is under-lined by the comparison. Throughout the sequence, he has moved between the twin poles represented on the one hand by the dainty wits, on the other by a rational ideal of virtue. More admirable than "*Pindare's* Apes," through his constant love and deep feeling he forges a style characterized by its energia, its forcible expression of passion that does indeed persuade us. At the same time, however, that passion and its energetic conversation are themselves the greatest threat to the positive values implicit in them. They resist restraint and menace with disruption all that they have earned through intensity of commitment. Their moments of harmony are brief and unfulfilled. At the end of the sequence, Astrophel is given over to complaint, the emblem of both his strong love and his alienation from the life of reason.

Conclusion

❦

IF THIS BOOK may be said to have a single theme, it might be summarized briefly and simply by saying that Sidney was a sophisticated stylist from the very beginning of his career, and that he developed several different manners for very specific purposes long before he came to write *Astrophel and Stella*. The *Arcadia*'s ornate verse, far from revealing a young poet's sheer delight in "decoration," or an immature preference for manner over matter, was deliberately framed for the courtly, romantic, pastoral world which that book's heroes and heroines inhabit. Sidney perfected its stylized, conventional mode in a handful of memorable sonnets, in Plangus' powerful lament, in the elaborate corona *dizaine* of Strephon and Klaius, and in their inimitable double sestina. There is nothing experimental about such verse, nothing in it to suggest mere poetic exercise on Sidney's part. One can scarcely imagine that it is in any sense a preparation for other work to follow. It does precisely what it sets out to do, defining its own range and means of expression with a clarity and developed precision that are always impressive and often moving, and that certainly show no trace of hesitation, uncertainty, or amateurishness on Sidney's part. Whatever may be the limitations of such verse, they are the limitations of a deliberately chosen medium, not those of Sidney's talent or sensibility.

In retrospect, one can see that Sidney's truly experimental verse was the plain poetry of the *Arcadia*'s eclogues and of the *Certain Sonnets*. This was a dramatic verse, governed by the movements and tones of a speaking voice, using a wide range of vocabulary, rhythms, and rhetorical figures in its creation of vivid dramatic character. Sidney's first efforts in the manner were only too obviously stilted.

If one is to discover development in his work, it must be in terms of his efforts to perfect this early dramatic style: he invented a metrics for it, transformed the sonnet to suit its purposes, refined away its syntactical awkwardness, and experimented more generally with various means of creating the energy and vitality—the *energia*—which he strived for in all his writing:

> Fy man, fy man, what wordes hath thy tonge lent?
>
> (OA 10, 61)

> Fy, schoole of Patience, Fy, your lesson is
> > Far far too long . . .
> >
> > (AS 56, 1–2)

One can watch in passages such as these the direct transfusion of the rougher and more vivid speech appropriate to pastoral eclogue into the lyric forms of a waning Petrarchan tradition. Among other things, that transfusion helped to create the so-called dramatic lyric, as later developed by Donne and Herbert. Astrophel opens his sonnet abruptly, *in medias res*, and that burst marks the beginning of a new kind of love poetry in English: its energetic dialogue, its revolutionary prosody, and its high-spirited tone of satiric bravado were to set the style for much that would be written within a decade after Sidney's death.

Before hastening to stress what is plain and direct in Sidney, however, and to assimilate him into the tradition of Wyatt and Donne, it would be well to remember the content and context of the lines just quoted from *Astrophel*. For those lines dramatize Astrophel's banishment of "Patience" and restraint in love, and they associate his colloquial vigor very clearly with his rebellion against the ideal, spiritual values of the Petrarchan mode. Those Petrarchan values, moreover, are themselves given clear expression in the formal, ceremonial poetry which Astrophel writes at other moments:

> O Eyes, which do the Spheares of beautie move,
> Whose beames be joyes, whose joyes all vertues be, . . .
> > (AS 42, 1–2)

> *Stella*, the onely Planet of my light,
> > Light of my life, and life of my desire, . . .
> >
> > (AS 68, 1–2)

> Who will in fairest booke of Nature know,
>   How Vertue may best lodg'd in beautie be, . . .
>   (AS 71, 1–2)
>
> *Stella* soveraigne of my joy,
> Faire triumpher of annoy,
> *Stella* starre of heavenly fier,
> *Stella* loadstar of desier.
>   (Eighth Song, 29–32)

Astrophel has its high style—formal, ornate, patterned rhetorical
language that is analogous to the carefully patterned verse of the
Arcadia. Its symmetry and order embody the social and moral values
to which the content of its lines gives more explicit definition. Yet all
of the lyrics just quoted maintain at best an uncertain harmony, and
two of them are later intruded upon by the quite different, colloquial accents of imperious desire. They all bear witness to the strong
tension existing between Astrophel's efforts to impose order upon
language and feeling and his subsequent disruptions of that order.
The underlying form of much of his verse is that of a steady rise toward a climax of praise or resolution that is undermined at the very
last moment. Aspiration is persistently exploded by unmanageable
desire, and the plots of the *Old Arcadia*, of *Astrophel*, and of many
individual lyrics dramatize a precipitate fall which is both serious
and bathetic. In one sense, they constitute poignant summaries of
that "first accursed fall" that Sidney touched upon in the *Apologie*:
"sith our erected wit maketh us know what perfection is, and yet our
infected will keepeth us from reaching unto it" (*Apologie*, 9). The
plain style is very often the emblem of that fall, particularly as
Philisides and Astrophel use it; but while it is undeniably associated
with rebelliousness, it is equally the vehicle for a vigorous, spirited,
and frequently tender poetry of love, with positive virtues and values
of its own. It was Sidney's achievement, in other words, to create a
complex style—or set of styles—whose functions were intimately
related both to his complex vision of love and to the complex
characters who give body and form to that vision. What is ornate in
Sidney cannot be understood except in relationship to what is
plain: each derives its significance from contexts in which the other
is an essential, "functional" part.

Beyond matters of style, this study has also tried to suggest the extent to which nearly all of Sidney's work shares the same central concerns: much of his verse and prose was composed in just those years when he was reflecting upon the problems of duty and retirement in his correspondence with Hubert Languet, and that correspondence in fact relates very closely to the *Arcadia* and *Astrophel*. Sidney's tentative defence of relaxation and withdrawal (particularly in his letter of March 1578) found an echo in Pyrocles' similar arguments against Musidorus, as well as in Astrophel's battles with Virtue, Reason, and the anonymous "friend" of several of the sonnets. Geron and Philisides (in OA 9), Boulon and Plangus (in OA 30), and Philisides and Languet (in OA 66) offer still different but related versions of this central debate. In each case, spokesmen for reason and duty vie with much younger champions who have played truant in the name of love or leisure. For the most part, Sidney stresses the lively drama, the irony, and even the comedy of these encounters. Pyrocles, Musidorus, Geron, Philisides, and Astrophel are all presented with a great deal of wit. Neither the aged moralists nor the youthful rebels are allowed an unequivocal victory, although Sidney endows his young heroes with sufficient charm, virtue, and prowess to win our approval of them. Love and leisure invariably lead to trouble, whether in Arcadia or in the courtier's world of *Astrophel*; but they are also celebrated in such a way as to remind us of Sidney's own pleasure in Wilton's life of "dignified ease" and his remark (to Languet) that he was beginning to "relax without reluctance." A double perspective is thus maintained throughout Sidney's work—a simultaneous approbation and condemnation of his young truant-heroes, neatly summed up in the final scene of the *Arcadia*, with its initial conviction and subsequent pardon of Pyrocles and Musidorus. No strictly biographical reading of the *Arcadia* or *Astrophel* can hope, of course, to illuminate the full complexity of either composition. But the events of Sidney's life in 1578–1580, and the evidence of his correspondence, do at least help us to understand the source of some of the major tensions in his writing; and the playful, defensive, often sly tones of Sidney's letters to Languet do provide us with an important introduction to the dominant tones of nearly all his verse and prose.

Appendices

❦

Notes

❦

Index

The Unity of the Certain Sonnets

❧❀❧

THE ARGUMENT FOR the unity of the *Certain Sonnets* rests upon both internal and external evidence. Mr. William A. Ringler, Sidney's editor, has noted:

> the similarity in the order of the contents of [manuscripts] C1 and the original of 98 . . . indicates that [Sidney] tried to maintain the poems in a preferred sequence. He could not provide the collection with a middle, but his overriding sense of structure at least led him to give it a beginning and an end, for as finally arranged it opens with 'I yeeld, ô Love, unto thy loathed yoke', and after playing a number of variations on the theme of unfulfilled desire it concludes with 'Leave me ô Love, which reachest but to dust'.
>
> (Ringler, 425)

Mr. Ringler has also discovered that the first two sonnets of the collection were apparently written specifically to complement the last two; for although they were written *last* of all the poems, Sidney did not place them at random within the sequence (or at the end), but he carefully put them where the logic of his plot demanded them:

> it appears that all except the first two *Certain Sonnets* were written in 1581 or earlier, and that the first two were added to the collection late in 1581 or in 1582.   (Ringler, 423)

My own contention that the *Certain Sonnets* have a higher degree of unity than has been previously noted, or than Mr. Ringler allows, takes its cue from Mr. Ringler's manuscript evidence. If Sidney kept his lyrics in a "preferred sequence," and if he carefully added two lyrics at the beginning of the sequence to balance and complement two at the end, one has good reason to suspect that the collection will disclose other kinds of order within itself. Everything we know generally about Sidney's work leads us to expect that structure and form were indeed of extraordinary importance to him. External evidence suggests that they were equally important to him in the arrangement of the *Certain Sonnets*, and the internal evidence seems to me to bear out this suggestion.

I should first of all make it quite clear what kind of unity the *Certain Sonnets* seem to me to comprise. They are obviously not as coherent a work as the *Astrophel*. They were written at various times over a period of years, were apparently kept by Sidney in a loose-leaf notebook, and constituted his own private anthology of miscellaneous poems he wished to preserve. The most we can expect, therefore, is that the lyrics were "arranged" by Sidney according to theme and/or form. I have given in the main text a synopsis of the collection's plot or movement, and there is no need to repeat that here. What may be helpful, however, is some more detailed suggestion of the way individual poems, and groups of poems, do in fact link together. Quite apart from the prosodic arrangement noted in Chapter Eight—an arrangement that coincides generally with the thematic order of the sequence—we find obvious kinds of surface connections throughout. It is surely no accident that the Latin translations are placed together, that a poem by Dyer (CS 16a) is followed by a reply by Sidney (CS 16), that a poem on farewell (CS 20) is followed by one on returning (CS 21), that the opening two sonnets balance the last two, and that no poem mentions the dissolution of love until CS 27, when it becomes the major theme of five of the last six poems in the collection:

> Now thy sweetnesse sowre is deemed,
> Thy haire not worth a haire esteemed:
>
> . . . .
> No more in thy sweetnesse glorie,
> For thy knitting haire be sorie: . . .
>   (CS 27, 9–10 and 17–18)

The lover here rebels against the lady's cruelty; the next poem, CS 28, finds him forsaken and picks up the image of her golden hair as well:

Tell me ô haire of gold,
   If I then faultie be,
   That trust those killing eyes, I would,
   Since they did warrant me.
                 (CS 28, 17–20)

CS 30 then announces jubilantly:

Ring out your belles, let mourning shewes be spread,
   For love is dead;
      All Love is dead, infected
      With plague of deepe disdaine:
      Worth as nought worth rejected,
      And Faith faire scorne doth gaine.
                (CS 30, 1–6)

CS 31 and 32 conclude the collection:

Desire, desire I have too dearely bought,
With price of mangled mind thy worthlesse ware, . . .
              (CS 31, 1–2)

Leave me ô Love, which reachest but to dust, . . .
              (CS 32, 1)

In considering the fact that no poems before CS 27 entertain in any sense the notion of giving up love, and that five of the last six do so very explicitly, one may be willing to concede some care of arrangement to the collection. Similarly, the group from CS 15 to CS 27 is also carefully arranged. CS 15–22 are poems of doubt and hesitation in which the lover puzzles out the alternatives confronting him. Should he give up love or push on and be bold (CS 16)? The following passages set the general tone:

Like as the Dove which seeled up doth flie,
   Is neither freed, nor yet to service bound, . . .
             (CS 15, 1–2)

Even thus might I, for doubts which I conceave
   Of mine owne wordes, my owne good hap betray,
And thus might I for feare of may be, leave
   The sweete pursute of my desired pray.
             (CS 16, 9–12)

The restfull Caves now restlesse visions give,
   In Dales I see each way a hard assent: . . .
                          (CS 18, 9–10)

If I could thinke how these my thoughts to leave,
   Or thinking still my thoughts might have good end:
   If rebell sence would reason's law receave;
   Or reason foyld would not in vaine contend:
      Then might I thinke what thoughts were best to thinke:
      Then might I wisely swimme or gladly sinke.
                          (CS 19, 1–6)

Oft have I musde but now at length I finde,
   Why those that die, men say they do depart: . . .
                          (CS 20, 1–2)

Finding those beames, which I must ever love,
   To marre my minde, and with my hurt to please,
I deemd it best some absence for to prove,
   If further place might further me to ease.

      .   .   .   .

      Faire choice I have, either to live or dye
      A blinded Mowlle, or else a burned flye.
                          (CS 21, 1–4 and 13–14)

My ship, desire, with winde of lust long tost,
   Brake on faire cleeves of constant chastitie:
   Where plagu'd for rash attempt, gives up his ghost,
   So deep in seas of vertue beauties ly.
      But of his death flies up a purest love,
      Which seeming lesse, yet nobler life doth move.
                          (CS 22, 55–60)

All the lyrics of this group are meditative in quality, and the lover continually rehearses his doubts aloud. He is paralyzed both by the lady's aloofness and by the impurity of his own desires (CS 19). His state of suspension is captured in several important lines that have a parallel syntactical structure: he is neither free nor bound (CS 15), he can neither "swimme" nor "sinke" (CS 19), and he has only the choice of being a "blinded Mowlle" or "burned flye" (CS 21). A resolution comes in the long poem, CS 22, in which the lover announces that he will give up desire and pursue a "nobler life": that is, in Petrarchan terms, he will accept the fact of the lady's chastity, and be content to exercise self-restraint so long as he can continue to enjoy her presence. CS 23–26 show the lover doing precisely this, and his state is depicted in the traditional terms of a "living death," a willing sacrifice of his own desire to her purity:

> She never dies but lasteth
>   In life of lover's hart,
>   He ever dies that wasteth
>   In love, his chiefest part.
> Thus is her life still guarded,
>   In never dying faith:
>   Thus is his death rewarded,
>   Since she lives in his death.
>
> Looke then and dye, the pleasure
>   Doth answere well the paine:
>   Small losse of mortall treasure,
>   Who may immortall gaine.
>   (CS 23, 9–20)

> For me alas I am full resolv'd,
> Those bands alas shall not be dissolv'd,
>   Nor breake my word though reward come late,
>   Nor faile my faith in my failing fate,
>   Nor change in change, though change change my state.
> But always one my selfe with eagle eyde trueth to flie,
> Up to the sunne, although the sunne my wings do frie:
>   For if those flames burne my desire,
>   Yet shall I die in *Phaenix* fire.
>   (CS 24, 19–27)

> Gladly my senses yeelding,
> Thus to betray my hart's fort,
> Left me devoid of all life; . . .

Yet, yet, a life to their death,
Lady you have reserved,
Lady the life of all love;

For though my sense be from me,
And I be dead who want sense,
Yet do we both live in you. . . .

Thus do I fall to rise thus,
Thus do I dye to live thus,
Changed to a change, I change not.

(CS 25, 9–11, 18–23, 27–29)

No man doubts, whom beautie killeth,
  Faire death feeleth,
And in whome faire death proceedeth,
  Glorie breedeth:
So that I in her beames dying,
  Glorie trying,
Though in paine, cannot complaine. No, no, no, no.

(CS 26, 27–33)

In addition to the living-dying theme, there are some striking verbal echoes among the poems. CS 23 begins, "*Who hath* his fancie pleased," and CS 24 answers its optimism with a different comment on love that opens, "*Who hath* ever felt the change of love." CS 24 then plays on the word "change": "Nor change in change, though change change my state." And CS 25 obviously echoes this: "Changed to a change, I change not." Finally, CS 23 and 26 both play considerably on the words "mortal" and "immortal." As with the other groups of poems I have isolated, this one reveals a striking degree of internal order, and none of its particular themes or its verbal play appears significantly in any other poem of the collection.

In the poems I have analyzed here, one can see the meditation of CS 15–22 giving way to a temporary Petrarchan resolution (CS 23–26), and concluding finally with the dissolution and end of love (CS 27–32). The earlier part of the sequence is in some ways more obviously and mechanically organized. The first seven poems generally introduce the love affair and its difficulties; CS 8–11 are a group of sonnets which Sidney himself asks us to see as a unit ("made when his Ladie had paine in her face"); and CS 12–14 are adaptations from the Latin, showing the lover's general discontent and bitterness.

However one wishes to characterize the *Certain Sonnets*, they seem certainly to be more than the "number of variations on the theme of unfulfilled desire" which Mr. Ringler found. Their "middle" is not so carefully structured as that of *Astrophel*, but it shows a degree of coherence which simply could not have been accidental. Moreover, the various groups of poems do form a logical plot. The indecision of the middle section follows the opening gambits, and is in some ways not unlike the verse of *Astrophel*'s middle (see especially AS 23–38). Petrarchan self-sacrifice is the next step in both works: AS 42 and 48 attempt the same accommodation as CS 23–26. Finally, desire reasserts itself in both works. In *Astrophel*, it leads the hero to press his claims upon Stella; in the *Certain Sonnets*, it leads to a formal "cursing" of the lady (CS 27–29), paralleled by *Astrophel*'s Fifth Song, and a final recantation (CS 31–32).

The Date of Sidney's Psalms

✤✤✤

NONE OF THE external evidence for dating the *Psalms* is in any sense conclusive. Mr. Ringler notes that Scipio Gentili dedicated his own translation of the Psalms to Sidney in 1584, but failed to mention any version by Sidney in his dedication (see Ringler, p. 501). Yet this fact does not necessarily argue for a date later than 1584. As Mr. Ringler himself admits, Scipio may simply not have known of Sidney's own efforts. This would not be surprising. Although Scipio's brother Alberico resided in London, Scipio himself lived on the Continent, and does not seem to have been in particularly close touch with Sidney's literary activities. For an interesting discussion of the relationship between Sidney and the brothers Gentili, see John Buxton, *Sir Philip Sidney and the English Renaissance* (London, 1954), pp. 152–58. A more compelling piece of evidence is Mr. Ringler's suggestion that "Thomas Moffet, a member of the Pembroke household, stated that Sidney began his work on the Psalms after he had composed his *Stella* and *Arcadia*" (see Thomas Moffet, *Nobilis*, trans. V. Heltzel and H. H. Hudson [San Marino, 1940], p. 12). The difficulty here is that Moffet's chronology, such as it is, cannot be trusted. Although it seems certain that Moffet knew Sidney (see *Nobilis*, p. xvi), he did not become a member of the Pembroke household until 1592–93, and his knowledge of Sidney's writings is sketchy at best. He offers no dates whatsoever, and he fails to mention the existence of either the *Apologie for Poetrie* or a second version of the *Arcadia*. He discusses *Astrophel* before the *Arcadia* and gives no indication that he knew they were written in the reverse order. He assigns both the *Arcadia* and the *Astrophel* to Sidney's *adolescentia* (Sidney was actually twenty-four to twenty-eight when he wrote them) and stresses the fact that Sidney later turned to more "serious" and devout themes with his translation of du Bartas and the Psalms. Finally, he discusses *all* of Sidney's writings before he mentions the young man's career at Oxford and leaves the reader with the impression that Sidney's literary activities were either university or preuniversity escapades. As Heltzel and Hudson, Moffet's editors, remark: "Moffet's implication that all of Sidney's literary work, or at least the *Astrophel and Stella* and *Arcadia*, belonged to his *adolescentia*, may give a false view of the situation, especially because Moffet completes this part of the story before taking Sidney to Oxford. . . . Moffet's relegation of these works to their author's early years is part of the general tactics of Sidney's apologists to discount the importance of them and to excuse them by the author's youth at the time of their composition" (*Nobilis*, p. 116). Moffet's suggestion that Sidney wrote the *Psalms* after the *Arcadia* and the *Astrophel* may still, of course, be correct, but we need a more scrupulous witness than he to persuade us. This we do not have.

In the absence of incontrovertible external evidence, it remains important to take into account the literary quality of the *Psalms* in trying to date them. Judgments on general stylistic grounds are admittedly difficult in Sidney's case, since he was very capable of putting off one style for another as occasion demanded. But metrical tests are more decisive. No one, I believe, has pointed out that the metrics of the *Psalms* are the perfectly regular, essentially inflexible metrics of the *Arcadia*, even though the dramatic style of the poems frequently cries out for something more supple:

> I did not them frequent
> Who be to vaineness bent,
> Nor kept with base dissemblers company;
> Nay I did even detest
> Of wicked wights the nest,
> And from the haunts of such bad folks did fly.
> (XXVI)

> Thus did I think: I well will mark my way,
> Least by my tongue I hap to stray;
> I mussle will my mouthe . . .
> (XXXIX)

Poets often and willingly change their styles in the interest of decorum, but it seems highly unlikely that anyone who had learned to write the marvelously flexible lines of *Astrophel* would ever have voluntarily retreated to the awkward, humdrum manner of the lines just quoted. Sidney had invested a great deal of energy in experimenting with both Latin and English meters. He was deeply dissatisfied with the rigid, relatively inexpressive native prosody he had inherited, and he managed finally to transform that prosody in *Astrophel*. If the *Psalms* were indeed composed after *Astrophel*, we can only regard them as an unaccountable lapse on the part of a highly accomplished and—by that time—fully mature poet. A date of 1580–81, on the other hand, would place them in the general stylistic (and prosodic) context of the *Arcadia* and the *Certain Sonnets*, and would still be consonant with Mr. Ringler's suggestion that Sidney was influenced by the 1580 edition of Beza's *Psalmorum Davidis*.

Notes

❦

Preface

1. *The Complete Works of Sir Philip Sidney*, ed. Albert Feuillerat, 4 vols. (Cambridge, 1912–1926), IV, 207–208. All quotations from the *Arcadia* prose and from *The Lady of May* are from this edition. Future citations are listed as, for example: "F, IV. 207–208." The punctuation of this first quoted passage has been slightly amended for the sake of clarity. Elsewhere, however, Feuillerat's text has been faithfully reproduced, except for the following alterations. The sign [~] is regularly omitted, and its corresponding letter is inserted, as: spokẽ becomes spoken; letters in raised type have been standardized, as: wᵗʰ becomes wth.

2. The fictional situation here is, of course, complicated. Cleophila is in reality Pyrocles (who has disguised himself as an Amazon), and Pyrocles is understandably doing everything possible to keep Basilius at a distance. But the dilemma which the passage poses is nonetheless a central one in Sidney: Astrophel, in particular, finds himself confronted by it.

3. A detailed discussion of the entire problem can be found in Chapters Five through Nine of this book. Mr. David Kalstone's recent study stresses in a persuasive way the thematic unity of Sidney's work, qualifies the view of Astrophel as "rebel," and includes a sympathetic, illuminating treatment of the *Arcadia*'s poetry. For a summary of his conclusions, see his *Sidney's Poetry: Contexts and Interpretations* (Cambridge, Mass., 1965), pp. 1–5 and 124–32.

The extent of my own indebtedness to Mr. Kalstone's work is apparent in the succeeding chapters of this book. Mr. Kalstone, however, does not deal explicitly with the problem of ornament in Sidney's poetry, nor with the larger issues raised by a consideration of Sidney's relation to the stylistic controversies of his time. It is essentially with these questions, as well as with the overriding problem of tracing Sidney's poetic development, that the present study concerns itself.

4. I have included no discussion of Sidney's translation of the Psalms, essentially because they do not bear directly upon the pastoral and Petrarchan themes which form the core of this book. In general, I tend to agree with those critics who see the *Psalms* as a relatively early work, probably written at the time of the *Arcadia* and the *Certain Sonnets*. This was the view of Theodore Spencer, and it has received tentative reinforcement recently by Mr. J. C. A. Rathmell: see *The Psalms of Sir Philip Sidney and the Countess of Pembroke* (New York, 1963), pp. xv–xvi. Mr.

William Ringler argues for a later date (ca. 1585), and his conclusions are summarized in *The Poems of Sir Philip Sidney* (Oxford, 1962), pp. 500–501. For a discussion of my own views, see Appendix II. Quotations from the *Psalms*, and indeed
from all of Sidney's poetry, are from Mr. Ringler's edition, hereafter cited simply
as, for example: "Ringler, 500–501." I have also adopted Mr. Ringler's abbre-
viations as a convenient means of alluding to Sidney's works: OA = *Old Arcadia*;
CS = *Certain Sonnets*; and AS = *Astrophel and Stella*. Citations for individual lyrics
follow Mr. Ringler's numerical system, as: "OA 12," "CS 7," "AS 31."

   In addition to omitting any detailed discussion of Sidney's *Psalms*, the following
chapters also neglect the verse of Sidney's only masque, *The Lady of May*. That
verse is composed mainly in the stylized, formal manner which Sidney developed
for so many of the *Arcadia*'s lyrics. A full discussion of that manner, and of the
reasons for Sidney's use of it, can be found in Chapters Four and Five of this book.
It should be stressed, however, that the verse of *The Lady of May* is by no means
entirely uniform in style. Its very last lyric ("*Silvanus* long in love") is written in a
much more informal, conversational style that relates very closely to the style
which Sidney later employed in the *Arcadia*'s eclogues and in some of the *Certain
Sonnets*. Compare, for example, the closing lines of the second stanza of "*Silvanus*"
with the final couplet of CS 9 and CS 16.

CHAPTER I. *Sidney and Languet*

   1. *The Correspondence of Sir Philip Sidney and Hubert Languet*, trans. Steuart A.
Pears (London, 1845), p. 201. Nearly all quotations from Sidney's correspondence
with Languet are from this edition. Hereafter specific references are abbreviated
as for example: "Pears, 201."
   Since Pears's translation comprises, of course, only a selection from the complete Sidney-Languet correspondence, I have included relevant passages from the
untranslated letters whenever these seemed particularly illuminating. Inspection
of the untranslated letters revealed nothing to conflict with the argument of this
and the following chapters.
   2. The evidence for the *Old Arcadia*'s date of composition is, of course, not
utterly conclusive, but the years 1577 or 1578 to 1580 have no serious rivals. Most
of the work of composition seems to have been done between the early spring and
late autumn of 1580. For an excellent summary of the evidence on this point, see
Ringler, 365. Mr. Ringler also accepts Sidney's allusion to his "toyfull booke"
as a reference to the *Arcadia*. Feuillerat has the singular "booke" in place of
Pears's plural form (see F, III. 132).
   Sidney's visits to Wilton were, of course, intermittent. He was there from time
to time in the years 1577–1579, and then retired there for an extended sojourn
after the Anjou crisis of 1579. He left the court in February 1580, and did not
return permanently until October of the same year.
   3. Mr. Kalstone has recently done much to illuminate the conflict between
pastoral and heroic values in the *Arcadia*, although without reference to Sidney's
biography. See *Sidney's Poetry*, pp. 40–59.
   4. For a discussion of these factors, see Mona Wilson's *Sir Philip Sidney* (New
York, 1932), pp. 108–10, and Malcolm Wallace's *The Life of Sir Philip Sidney*

(Cambridge, 1915), p. 198. Neither writer considers the matter in very great detail, and both stress Sidney's desire to be actively engaged in court affairs.

5. This comes through particularly in Languet's replies, as: "But if your desire of fame and glory makes your present inactivity irksome to you, . . ." (Pears, 127).

6. On p. 176 of his *A Map of Arcadia* (New Haven: Yale University Press, 1965), Mr. Walter Davis comments:

> In this letter Sidney attributes to Languet the standard Stoic-Platonist view of retirement represented by his friend Lipsius, and pits against it, the Calvinistic insistence on self-examination, "the knowledge of a mans selfe, in the Ethike and Politique consideration, with the end of well doing, and not of well knowing onely," which he proclaimed in the *Defence* to be "the highest end of the mistresse knowledge." That is the problem *Arcadia* faces: the problem of moral improvement in the divided hero whose soul is rapt from his proper self in amorous contemplation. Sidney's response was to re-evaluate the nature of contemplative experience entirely, asserting that *contemplation was not merely a retreat, but a trial of the soul as well.*

The problems raised by such a reading are far too complex for summary discussion, particularly because they involve Mr. Davis' entire interpretation of the *New Arcadia*. But perhaps a few remarks may be helpful in making my own point of view clearer. Is Languet's position, when he urges that Sidney cultivate his "particle of the divine mind," really "the standard Stoic-Platonist view of retirement represented by his friend Lipsius"? Lipsius, according to Mr. Davis, believed that "the pursuit of contemplative wisdom necessitate[d] complete abandonment of the world" (*Map of Arcadia*, p. 172). It is difficult to imagine Languet—who was himself a diplomat, and who continually urged Sidney into the service of his country—advising his protégé to follow such a course; and it is equally difficult to imagine that Sidney would attribute such a view to him. Languet was not proposing "complete abandonment of the world" so that the soul might be rapt in contemplation of heavenly things (Lipsius' goal). The issue, as Sidney defines it, is whether or not the mind is cultivated by being "directed to *various kinds of knowledge*" (my italics), and these are clearly practical, useful kinds. Sidney mentions architecture and music, and previous letters have focused on his attempts to develop the good Latin prose style necessary for a diplomat. Languet believes such cultivation to be, in effect, good training; it is a way of keeping the mind alert, even if one ultimately never has the chance to use one's knowledge for "public advantage." Sidney (momentarily) disagrees and suggests that one might as well withdraw from affairs altogether. It is he, after all, who claims the role of Stoic for *himself* in the letter.

Sidney, then, argues for withdrawal, Languet for involvement. Whether one can legitimately characterize Sidney's notion of retirement in terms of a "Calvinistic insistence on self-examination" is another problem altogether. The tone of the passage, as I have suggested, does not seem to support so stern and programmatic a view. The words which keep recurring in this letter and those surrounding it are indolence, ease, leisure, relaxation, delight, and idleness. At the very beginning of the passage in question, Sidney notes that "my mind itself, . . . is now beginning, by reason of my indolent ease, imperceptibly to lose its strength."

This scarcely sounds like the beginning of a venture in serious Calvinistic self-scrutiny. Doubtless Sidney desired and found time for reflection and self-examination of a kind during his sojourn at Wilton—what intelligent and sensitive man would not? He wanted leisure to think, to read, and to write, but these were all to be done in the context of that life of "dignified ease" which he once told Languet he desired for himself (Pears, 184). Had Sidney really been proposing a serious program of self-examination, Languet surely would have replied more sympathetically to so sober an undertaking. Instead, his answering letter is full of friendly sarcasm and remonstrance:

> Is it not an insult, or at least a mockery of me, that while you have written to me but one letter since last October, you nevertheless in that letter complain that it is too much leisure that makes you neglectful? O happy ye, who may complain of too much leisure! I pray you may long be able to do so. But most men of high birth are possessed with this madness, that they long after a reputation founded on bloodshed, and believe that there is no glory for them except that which is connected with the destruction of mankind. . . . Make use then of that particle of the Divine Mind . . . for the preservation and not the destruction of men. And do not fear that you will rust away for want of work, if only you are willing to exert your powers. For in so large a kingdom as England, there must always be opportunities for the exercise of your genius, so that many may derive advantage from your labours.
>
> (Pears, 147–48)

Languet wants "many" to "derive advantage" from Sidney's labors, but Sidney is learning (with some pangs of conscience) to relax without reluctance.

7. See Sidney's letter to Leicester concerning the problems involved in returning to court (F, III. 129).

Languet's statement (in the quoted letter) that Sidney's retirement was "made most delightful to you by the society of your dearest friends" (Pears, 182) may throw some light upon the two lyrics designated by Ringler as OP 6 and 7. These are pastoral poems celebrating Sidney's friendship with Dyer and Greville (almost certainly the "dearest friends" mentioned in the correspondence). They sing the pleasures of a retired, pastoral life, and they may very well have been composed in 1580, just after Sidney's departure from Wilton. They give us a particularly vivid sense of Sidney's "delight" in life away from the court, and they bear further witness to Sidney's instinctive habit of associating Wilton with the pastoral mode. The second lyric (OP 7) is entitled "Disprayse of a Courtly life," and it laments the case of a man (acknowledged in the final stanzas to be Sidney himself) forced to leave the pastoral realm for that of the court. Both OP 6 and 7 might have been composed, of course, at almost any time in the late 1570's, although (judging from their style) probably not later than 1580–81. For further comments on these poems, see Morris W. Croll, *The Works of Fulke Greville* (Philadelphia, 1903), p. 3, and Ralph Sargent, *At the Court of Queen Elizabeth* (London, 1935), p. 70.

8. I am here indebted to Mr. Piers Lewis' excellent discussion of Sidney's political attitudes, particularly as they are revealed in the *Arcadia*. Mr. Lewis quotes those passages from the Languet letters which criticize "men of noble

birth," and he adds: "The issue is very clearly drawn; it is between the humanist who sees all men as members of a Christian society in which pride is disciplined and identities partly merged under the rule of law, and the aristocrat to whom civil law is merely an obstacle to his own heroic fulfillment and glory." See "Literary and Political Ideas in Sidney's *Arcadia*" (Unpubl. Doctoral Dissertation, Harvard University, 1964, p. 136, *et passim*).

9. See particularly the letter in which Sidney echoes Languet's opinions about Italy and insists that Robert furnish himself "with a knowledge of such things as may be serviceable for your country and calling" (Pears, 195–98).

10. Thomas Moffet's biography helps to illuminate these particular aspects of Sidney's character, and to suggest what qualities in him were at variance with the public, active life of the court. Although Moffet can never be taken quite at face value, the following passages do seem to be generally corroborated by what we know of Sidney from the letters and other sources:

> He so held letters in his affection and care that he would scarce ever sleep, still less go forth, without a book. . . . It was allowable, indeed, in view of his age, that he should give his mind to the pursuit of games, yet so rarely, so coldly, and so tamely did he play that he was judged not to hold sport in any great affection. . . . Yet a combative spirit was so far from being his that immediately he would receive a penitent adversary into favour, . . . He possessed a gentle, tender, disposition, . . .
> (*Nobilis*, trans. v. Hetzel and H. H. Hudson [San Marino, 1940], p. 71)

> Hence it twice occurred that, overstimulated by his prolonged studies in early adolescence, he fell ill of a fever attended by the greatest peril; and he was forced to slacken the reins in sports, until, the breakdown of his health having been repaired, more fit and more active he returned to the Muses. . . . And, to be sure, since he craved to be wise rather than to be strong, he would almost have failed in both had he not given himself over, though unwillingly, to recreation, and mingled, by way of spice, certain sportive arts—poetic, comic, musical—with his more serious studies. He amused himself with them after the manner of youth, but within limits; he was somewhat wanton, indeed, but observed a measure and felt shame. (*Nobilis*, pp. 73–74)

Sidney's love of learning, his mild disposition, and his delicate constitution all no doubt promoted his tendency toward withdrawal and retirement; and these were in turn reinforced by his love of "sportive arts" and his "somewhat wanton" nature.

A selection of passages from the untranslated portion of the Sidney-Languet correspondence (*Epistolae ad Philippum Sydneium*, ed. D. Dalyrymple [London, 1776]) may help at this point to shed further light on Sidney's temperament, as well as on his dilemma in the 1570's and early 1580's. Two passages, for example, reflect Languet's persistent worries about Sidney's "slacking":

> in court life, you will experience greater difficulties than your fellows, who already enjoy their father's resources: but to pursue leisure would scarcely be becoming of you ("sectari autem otium tibi parum esset decorum") . . .
> (*Epistolae*, p. 104)

If you accustom yourself to leisure for a long period of time ("si diu otio assuescas"), then later when tempests come and shake it from you, it will be more difficult for you to sustain them than if you had accustomed yourself to toils and troubles.

(*Epistolae*, p. 140)

One final passage, moreover, suggests how difficult it was for Sidney to relax with an easy conscience. He had written to Languet in 1578 that he was only "learning" to relax without reluctance (Pears, 143), and Moffet's account of Sidney's intense involvement in his studies stresses that Sidney gave himself over to recreation "unwillingly"; one of Languet's letters from 1579 adds:

You wrote to me that you had long struggled to attain a state wherein it would be possible for you to be lazy ("ut tibi liceat esse pigrum"), and that those who called laziness in you a vice were being unfair. (*Epistolae*, p. 213)

Sidney seems very much to have been one of those men who are strongly attracted by a whole range of leisurely pursuits and enjoyments which they have been schooled to regard with suspicion.

CHAPTER II. *The Letters and the* Old Arcadia

1. The Sidney-Languet letters are of course in Latin, but Pears's translation is faithful to the original in all the passages that I have drawn upon. For example, Sidney's important comparison of the age to a "bow too long bent, it must be unstrung or it will break" is a rendering of "ut arcum nimis diu intensum, aut relaxari aut frangi opportet."

2. All quotations from Sidney's *Apologie* are from *An Apologie for Poetrie*, ed. Evelyn Shuckburgh (Cambridge, 1891). Hereafter citations are abbreviated as for example: "*Apologie*, 6–7."

3. Sidney's phrase—"the often and free changing of persons"—is a puzzling one. Shuckburgh glosses it as "putting the words dramatically now into the mouth of one person and now in that of another" (*Apologie*, 82). This is certainly a possible reading, and one that makes sense in relation both to Sidney's own verse and to the Psalms, but it overlooks the fact that "persons" may bear its *grammatical* sense here: first person (I), second person (you), etc. Elizabethan rhetoric books sometimes use the word in this sense, and apostrophe was the figure of speech which most clearly involved a change of persons. Peacham, for example, defined apostrophe as "a forme of speech by which the Orator turneth suddenly from the former frame of his speech to another, that is, when he hath long spoken of some person or thing, he leaveth speaking *of* it, and speaketh *unto* it, which is no other thing then a sudden removing from the third person to the second." The passage occurs in Henry Peacham's *The Garden of Eloquence* (London, 1593), facsimile edition with an intro. by William Crane (Gainesville, Fla., 1954), p. 116. The Psalms, of course, are dense with apostrophe, and Sidney's own lavish use of the figure is ample testimony to his interest in it.

Prosopopoeia bears, in the *Apologie* passage, a meaning related to that which most classical and Renaissance rhetoricians ascribed to it. It was traditionally the figure by which direct or indirect speech was attributed to either historical or fictional persons. Hoskins defined it (in Sidney's era) as "feighning . . . the discourse of persons" (see Louise Osborne, *The Life, Letters, and Writings of John*

Hoskyns [New Haven, 1937], p. 162). The Psalms, of course, abound in prosopo-poeias, and Sidney himself, with his strong dramatic bent, made pervasive use of the figure. He seems, moreover, to have associated prosopopoeia instinctively with a whole set of devices which add vigor and immediacy to writing: "his notable *Prosopopeias*, when he maketh you as it were, see God comming in his Maiestie." The modifying phrase here does not suggest a simple attribution of speech or dis-course to God (although such speech will be part of the total effect); instead, emphasis is placed upon an almost visual realization of divine power and presence. Prosopopoeia makes one "see" God actively "coming" in majesty, and the term seems to take on the slightly more inclusive sense which sixteenth-century rhe-toricians sometimes attributed to it. It seems to contain the idea, not only of dramatized speech, but also of the entire vivid *impression* which such dramatiza-tion creates. Hoskins, for example, suggested in another passage that "to animate & giue life is *Prosopopeia*" (*The Life, Letters, and Writings of John Hoskyns*, p. 163); and Abraham Fraunce suggested that prosopopoeia is used "when the whole speach of anie person is *fully and liuely* represented" (*The Arcadian Rhetorike* [1588], ed. Ethel Seaton [Oxford, 1950], p. 86; my italics).

4. It is worth pointing out that Dorcas' speech from *The Lady of May* is closely related both to Pyrocles' defense of contemplation and to Sidney's defense of re-laxation and self-examination. On March 1, 1578, Sidney mentioned (in his letter to Languet) the possible danger of letting the mind be "drawn out of itself" by practical arts and affairs. If *The Lady of May* was indeed acted for the Queen sometime between May 6 and May 16, 1578 (see Ringler, 361–62), then Sidney must have been composing Dorcas' speech at approximately the time he wrote to Languet. Dorcas also praises a life free of distractions, in a place "where it is lawfull for a man to be good if he list, and hath no outward cause to withdraw him from it." Dorcas' version of that life is, of course, more rustic and conven-tionally religious than Sidney's own; but both versions were clearly the basis for Pyrocles' still different rendering, which Sidney must have written sometime during the next year or two: "but the workinges of the mynde I fynde muche more infinite then can bee ledd unto by ye eye, or imagined by any that distract theyre thoughtes wthowte them selves" (F, IV. 11–12).

The attitudes expressed by Sidney, Dorcas, and Pyrocles in these passages con-trast strongly, of course, with those of Pyrocles and Musidorus at the very begin-ning of the *Old Arcadia*. There, the young princes are described as "taking very tymely into theyre myndes, that the Devine parte of man was not inclosed in this body for nothinge"; they give "them selves wholy over to those knouledges, wch mighte in the Course of theyre lyfe bee Ministers to theyre well dooyng" (F, IV. 7). Taken together, this entire group of passages concerning the use of what Sidney once called man's "particle of the divine mind" (Pears, 143) demonstrates clearly the extent to which Sidney's fiction often served him as an imaginative means of illuminating, exploring, and distancing problems which engrossed him in the years 1577–1581.

CHAPTER III. *Love in Arcadia*

1. Some of the *Arcadia* verse offers the most explicit statements of this theme, although they are frequently accompanied by a good deal of wit and self-conscious strategy; see, for example, OA 7 and OA 16.

11*

2. OA 27, 14. The shepherds, of course, have a distinct point of view, for they represent Passion in the debate against Reason.

3. Kalstone, *Sidney's Poetry*, p. 122.

4. Baldassare Castiglione, *The Book of the Courtier*, trans. Sir Thomas Hoby (Everyman Library Edition), p. 322.

5. *The Comedies of Terence*, trans. Henry Riley (New York, 1887), p. 78. Sidney undoubtedly knew Ovid's *Ars Amatoria* and the *Remedia*; Terence he studied at school, and seems to have regarded as a particular favorite (there are several allusions to him in the *Apologie* and the letters to Languet).

6. Recent scholarship has tended to accept this and indeed all the *Arcadia*'s revisions as Sidney's own (rather than the Countess of Pembroke's). See Ringler's discussion (pp. 375ff.); Kenneth Rowe, "The Countess of Pembroke's Editorship of the *Arcadia*," *PMLA*, 54:1 (1939), 122–38; and William Godshalk, "Sidney's Revision of the *Arcadia*, Books III-V," *PQ*, XLIII (1964), 171–84.

The "Everlasting Justice" passage was revised in conjunction with several other, much larger alterations which Sidney was making: most notably, his omission of the seduction episodes—a change that made the narrator's harsh judgment of the heroes, at F, IV. 247, unnecessary.

7. Iacopo Sannazaro, *Opere*, ed. Enrico Carrara (Turin, 1952), p. 130. The translation is my own.

8. *Ibid.*, p. 128, n. 2.

9. Barnabe Googe, *Eglogs, Epytaphes, & Sonnettes*, ed. Edward Arber (London, 1871), p. 52.

10. George Turberville, *The Eglogs of the Poet B. Mantuan Carmelitan* (London, 1567), 21^f.

11. *Ibid.*, 17^v.

12. Googe, *Eglogs*, p. 45.

13. Consider, for example, the emphasis in OA 66 on "faithfull hart, cleane hands, and mouth as true," and the line "His good strong staffe my slippry yeares upbore," in relation to the following passage from Languet's letter of October 22, 1578: "I confess that in the splendour of a court, there are so many temptations to vice that it is very hard for a man to hold himself unspotted by them, and keep his feet on so slippery ground. But you must stand firm on your principle and strength of mind against these difficulties, knowing the harder the conflict the greater the glory of a triumph" (Pears, 155).

14. I am indebted to Mr. Lewis for having pointed out, in his study of the *Arcadia*, the connection between Musidorus and Euarchus: see "Literary and Political Ideas in Sidney's *Arcadia*," p. 74.

15. See Kalstone's excellent analysis of the entire episode: *Sidney's Poetry*, pp. 99–101.

16. Mr. John Buxton has called my attention to the fact that Fulke Greville's remarks about authorial irony are very similar to the practice of his friend Sidney. Greville, discussing his revision of his works, decided at one point

> to take away all opinion of seriousnesse from these perplexed pedigrees; and to this end carelessly cast them into that hypocriticall figure *Ironia*, wherein men commonly (to keep above their workes) seeme to make toies of the utmost they can doe.

The remark is to be found in Greville's *Life of Sir Philip Sidney*, ed. Nowell Smith (Oxford, 1907), pp. 153–54.

CHAPTER IV. *The* Apologie for Poetrie

1. Stephen Gosson, *The Schoole of Abuse* (1579), ed. Edward Arber (London, 1895), p. 22.
2. *Ibid.*, p. 34.
3. *Ibid.*, p. 24.
4. For a synopsis of the evidence concerning the *Apologie*'s date, see Wallace's *Life*, pp. 237–39.
5. Amphialus' defense of love in the *Arcadia* is clearly related to Sidney's defense of poetry: "then would he accuse, and in himselfe condemne all those wits, that durst affirme Idlenesse to be the well-spring of Love . . . am I now piping in a shaddow? or doo slouthfull feathers now enwrap me?" (F, I. 375). Both Sidney and Amphialus are at pains to deny the imputation of idleness and wantonness, and both insist that love (or poetry) is a formidable ally of heroic virtue.

CHAPTER V. *Ornament and Rhetoric*

1. *The Complete Works of William Hazlitt*, ed. P. P. Howe, 21 vols. (London, 1931), VI, 326.
2. *Ibid.*, p. 320.
3. See Theodore Spencer, "The Poetry of Sir Philip Sidney," *ELH*, XII (1945), 251–79.
4. William Empson, *Seven Types of Ambiguity* (New York, 1931), pp. 45–50.
5. John Crowe Ransom, *The New Criticism* (Norfolk, Conn., 1941), p. 112.
6. Kenneth Muir, *Sir Philip Sidney* (London, 1960), p. 26.
7. Robert Montgomery, *Symmetry and Sense: The Poetry of Sir Philip Sidney* (Austin: University of Texas Press, 1961), pp. 3ff.
8. *Ibid.*, p. 12.
9. Ringler, lvii.
10. Kalstone's recent discussion of the *Arcadia*'s verse in *Sidney's Poetry* is the first important departure from a long tradition of adverse criticism on the subject.
11. Kenneth Myrick, *Sir Philip Sidney as a Literary Craftsman* (Cambridge, Mass., 1935), pp. 180–91, *et passim*.
12. Anadiplosis is the figure in which the first word of one clause repeats the last of the previous clause, as: "*delaie, | (Delay,* the racke . . .*"
13. George Puttenham, *The Arte of English Poesie*, ed. Gladys Willcock and Alice Walker (Cambridge: Cambridge University Press, 1936), p. 159.
14. Girolamo Fracastoro, *Naugerius, sive de Poetica Dialogus* (1555), trans. Ruth Kelso (Urbana, Ill., 1924), pp. 68–69.
15. Spencer, "The Poetry of Sir Philip Sidney," pp. 251–52.
16. Kalstone, *Sidney's Poetry*, p. 88. See Mr. Kalstone's entire discussion of the *Arcadia*'s lyrics, pp. 83–101.

17. Julius Caesar Scaliger, *Poetices Libri Septem* (Lyons, 1561), facsimile edition with an intro. by August Buck (Stuttgart, 1964), p. 73.

18. See Osborne, *The Life, Letters, and Writings of John Hoskyns*, p. 126.

19. *Ibid.*

20. Puttenham, *The Arte of English Poesie*, p. 202.

21. *Ibid.*, pp. 202–203.

22. *Institutio Oratoria*, trans. H. E. Butler, 4 vols. (New York, 1933), III, 486–87.

23. *Ibid.*

24. Puttenham, *The Arte of English Poesie*, p. 208.

CHAPTER VI. *Style as Convention*

1. For Spencer's entire discussion of the *Arcadia* rhymes, see "The Poetry of Sir Philip Sidney," pp. 261–64.

2. See Empson, *Seven Types of Ambiguity*, pp. 48–50, and Kalstone, *Sidney's Poetry*, pp. 71–83. See also *Sidney's Poetry*, pp. 92–96, for some comments on the rhymes of the *Arcadia* sonnets.

3. See Ringler, lvi.

4. *Ibid.*, pp. 385–86.

5. Kalstone first pointed out this distinction; see *Sidney's Poetry*, pp. 66–67.

6. See John Thompson, *The Founding of English Metre* (London, 1961).

7. George Gascoigne, "Certayne notes of Instruction," *The Posies*, ed. John Cunliffe (Cambridge: Cambridge University Press, 1907), p. 468.

8. *Ibid.*, p. 38.

9. Thompson, *The Founding of English Metre*, p. 139.

10. *Ibid.*, p. 144.

11. See John Thompson's discussion in "Sir Philip and the Forsaken Iamb," *Kenyon Review*, XX (1958), 104–105.

12. The metrics of the *Certain Sonnets* are essentially the same as those of the *Arcadia*, and the available evidence suggests that both works were composed at approximately the same time (see Ringler, 423–24).

13. Thompson, "Sir Philip and the Forsaken Iamb," p. 99–100.

14. *Ibid.*, p. 106.

15. Inversions of the first foot, even of monosyllables, were of course relatively common throughout the sixteenth century. Surrey, for example, uses them with some frequency, although rarely with much sense of purpose. Sidney's inversions, by contrast, are more energetic, more pertinent to their contexts, and more carefully integrated into his style as a whole.

16. Thompson suggests very plausibly that Sidney's experiments with classical metrics raised in his mind the possibility of establishing in English a new relationship between metrical pattern and speech accent (see *The Founding of English Metre*, pp. 128–38). This proposal does not conflict with my own suggestion that Sidney may have first discovered how to create the effect of speech accent in sequences of monosyllables while writing passages like those quoted above.

Mr. Ringler, it should be noted, has also argued for a degree of irregularity in the *Arcadia*'s metrics, although the only examples he quotes are unfortunately not proof against Thompson's general theory. The first (OA 7, 42) is an example of dissyllabic inversion; and the second (OA 8, 5–6), while it involves monosyllables, is at best a matter of "weighting" rather than clear-cut metrical inversion. Mr. Ringler also suggests that Sidney's prosodic development was a gradual affair: "He introduced variations of this sort sparingly at first, but more frequently as he went on; until in *Astrophil and Stella* he resolved mechanical regularity to a controlled freedom" (p. lv). It is precisely this conception of gradual change, however, that is so difficult to demonstrate from the texts. The *Arcadia* lyrics, the *Certain Sonnets*, and the *Psalms* are all based upon the same metrical system, and the gap between them and *Astrophel* is very great indeed.

17. See Puttenham, *The Arte of English Poesie*, pp. xlviii–xlix, lxiv–lxv, and lxxi–lxxii.

18. *Ibid.*, p. 132.

19. *Ibid.*, pp. 133–34.

20. One might have supposed that Puttenham had learned about metrical counterpoint in English from *Astrophel and Stella*, which was probably written two or three years before the passages just quoted from the *Arte*. Yet Puttenham seems not to have seen *Astrophel*: at least he quotes from or alludes to Sidney six times in the *Arte*, and always in relation to the *Arcadia*. Sidney remains famous to Puttenham only for "Eglogue and pastorall Poesie" (p. 63).

CHAPTER VII. *The Drama of Philisides*

1. It is misleading, of course, to insist upon too close a connection between Philisides and Sidney himself, but it is perhaps still worth noting the extent to which Philisides' autobiographical sketch echoes Sidney's letters to his brother Robert. The most relevant passages in this regard are:

> I was suffered to spende some tyme in travell, that, by the Comparyson of many thinges I might rypen my Judgment: Synce greatnes, power, Riches, and suche like standing in Relation to an other (who dothe knowe no thing but his owne) dothe not knowe his owne. (F, IV. 313)

> so may I justly say, who rightly travels with the eye of Ulysses, doth take one of the most excellent ways of worldly wisdom. For hard sure it is to know England, without you know it by comparing it with some other country, . . . For you, that are a logician, know, that as greatness of itself is a quantity, so yet the judgment of it, as of mighty riches and all other strengths, stands in the predicament of relation; . . . (Pears, 196)

> And bycause the myndes Commaundement ys vayne withoute the body bee enhabled to obay yt, my strengthe was exercysed with Horsmanship, weapons, and suche other qualityes, as besydes the practize carryed in them selves some servisable use, wherein, so I proffited that as I was not excellent, so was I accompagnable. (F, IV. 312)

> At horsemanship, when you exercise it, read Crison Claudio, . . . When you play at weapons, . . . play out your play lustily, for indeed ticks and dalliances are nothing in earnest, for the time of the one and the other greatly differs, and use as well the blows as the thrust: . . . (Pears, 202)

Then beeyng home returned and thought of good hope (for the worlde rarely bestowes a better Tytle uppon yowthe) I continewed to use the Benifites of a quyet mynde, . . .   (F, IV. 313)

God bless you, sweet boy, and accomplish the joyful hope I conceive of you. . . . let no day pass without an hour or two such exercise: the rest study, or confer diligently, and so shall you come home to my comfort and credit.
                                                                                    (Pears, 202)

Sidney clearly had his own experience of travel and education in mind when he wrote to Robert, and the process of formulating his thoughts in the letters to Robert may well have crystallized finally in the passage on Philisides. In any case, the letters to Robert were both written while Sidney was bringing the *Arcadia* to conclusion.

2. Even Philisides' verse reflects to some extent the considerable stylistic variety of the *Arcadia* as a whole, and it would be a mistake to suggest too great a sense of uniformity in the poems Sidney composed for him. OA 24 is in a plaintive, measured style that matches the verse of Dorus' companion piece, OA 23. OA 66 is in a fittingly unaffected narrative style—proper for a beast fable—and OA 73 opens with a rich, heavy lyric passage which suits its "dream" atmosphere. In other words, Philisides' style, despite its relative homogeneity, also varies in accordance with the subject matter and occasion of particular lyrics.

CHAPTER VIII. *A Courtier's* Certain Sonnets

1. See Ringler, 423–24.

2. This variation is particularly apparent in the differences between the songs and sonnets of the sequence. The songs, as one might expect, are nearly always more formal, and sometimes more rhetorically elaborate, than the other lyrics, although they are rarely so highly patterned as the *Arcadia*'s ornate verse. CS 3, however, was sufficiently close to the *Arcadia*'s style for Sidney to transfer it there during his revision (he assigned it to Amphialus: see F, I. 442).

I have stressed throughout this chapter those of the *Certain Sonnets* which are clearly in a more private, informal, courtly style. This emphasis should not at all obscure the considerable stylistic range of the sequence—a range including some lyrics that were very likely intended for the *Arcadia* (or, perhaps, were simply experiments in the *Arcadia* manner). CS 15, CS 18–19, and CS 25 can all be intelligibly related to poems like OA 2, OA 23–24, and OA 77. CS 5 is apparently a very early poem (see Ringler, 423) in a Latin measure, and its rhetoric resembles that of several *Arcadia* poems. At the same time, there are a great many lyrics in the *Certain Sonnets* which have no stylistic analogues in the *Arcadia* (e.g., CS 2, CS 4, CS 8–11, and CS 16–17), and those few which do closely resemble *Arcadia* lyrics do so in a special way: they share the measured pace and tendency toward logical or schematic structure of so many *Arcadia* poems, but (excepting for CS 5) they avoid the heightened rhetoric—the operatic exclamations and apostrophes— and the most elaborate rhetorical schemes or figures characteristic of poems like OA 30, OA 70–72, etc.

3. I have throughout this chapter assumed that there is a single speaker or voice in the *Certain Sonnets*. This assumption is partly a matter of convenience, partly a reflection of the extent to which so many of the poems in the sequence do indeed seem to be expressions of a single persona. For further discussion of the unity of the *Certain Sonnets*, see the Appendix, p. 277.

CHAPTER IX. *Sidney and Ciceronianism*

1. Myrick, *Sir Philip Sidney as a Literary Craftsman*, p. 180.
2. *Ibid.*, p. 183.
3. *Ibid.*, p. 186.
4. *Ibid.*, p. 189.
5. Montgomery, *Symmetry and Sense*, p. 64.
6. See Montgomery's entire chapter, "The Theory of Artless Style," *Symmetry and Sense*.
7. Myrick, *Sir Philip Sidney as a Literary Craftsman*, p. 52.
8. *Ibid.*, pp. 151–52.
9. Ringler conjectures (p. 365) that Sidney had by this time sent his manuscript to a scribe for final copying.
10. See also George Williamson's account of Sidney and Ciceronianism, *The Senecan Amble* (London, 1951), pp. 66–70.
11. For Erasmus, Languet, Harvey, and others who were writing before the 1590's, "Ciceronian" almost always implied a particular method of imitation and a single-minded devotion to only one master—Cicero himself. Ralph Lever's association of Ciceronians with "sugar tongued fellowes" in his *Arte of Reason* (London, 1573) is unusual in its relative lack of definition. By the end of the century, the term had come to refer to a set of general stylistic qualities: ornateness, prolixity, rhetorical elaborateness, rhythmical fullness, etc. For a discussion of this change, see Wesley Trimpi, *Ben Jonson's Poems: A Study of the Plain Style* (Stanford: Stanford University Press, 1962), p. 28.
12. Erasmus, *Ciceronianus* (1528) trans. Izora Scott (New York, 1908), p. 23.
13. *Ibid.*, p. 27.
14. Gabriel Harvey, *Ciceronianus*, ed. Harold Wilson and Clarence Forbes, University Studies of the University of Nebraska, XLV (Lincoln, 1945), p. 77.
15. Erasmus, *Ciceronianus*, p. 123.
16. *Ibid.*, p. 80.
17. Harvey, *Ciceronianus*, p. 77.
18. Rhetorical and poetic invention were not, of course, considered to be identical, but they were both clearly concerned with the central activity of "finding" matter.
19. Sidney's relationship to Ramism has unfortunately never been fully explored; until we have a thorough study of this complicated subject, it will remain difficult to determine precisely what effect Ramist logic may have had upon his writing. That Sidney was interested in Ramism, that he had met and admired Ramus himself (as had Languet), and that he was closely connected with Ramists like William Temple and Abraham Fraunce—all of this is beyond doubt. But his university training at Oxford would certainly have been in classical rhetoric and Aristotelian logic (see Wallace's *Life*, pp. 97–107), and we have no evidence to

suggest that he ever repudiated that training in any significant way. Rather, he cultivated his Greek mainly in order to be able to read Aristotle easily, he took the trouble to translate Aristotle's *Rhetoric* (an unusual venture for a confirmed Ramist), and he remained sufficiently committed to classical rhetorical procedures to cast his *Apologie* in the form of a Ciceronian oration. The *Apologie* and the letters to Languet are full of allusions to Aristotle (as well as to Cicero, Demosthenes, and other classical rhetoricians); Ramus, on the other hand, is never mentioned once in either context. All of this is not, of course, to cast serious doubt upon Sidney's interest in Ramus, but only to suggest that his interest seems to have been a qualified one, and that it surely existed concurrently with a strong (and growing) interest in Aristotle. Distinguishing between what Sidney may have learned from Aristotle and what he learned from Ramus would be at the very least a delicate and highly speculative endeavor. What is perhaps clear is that Ramus would generally have reinforced Sidney's already strong opposition to Ciceronianism, with its preference for words over things. Ramus, like Aristotle, insisted upon the primacy of "invention" in persuasive discourse; in addition, the influence of Ramus must certainly have encouraged Sidney's fondness for tight logical argument and his free use of the disjunctive simile (see Chapters XII–XIV [pp. 331–410] in Rosemond Tuve's *Elizabethan and Metaphysical Imagery* [Chicago, 1947]). A careful study of Aristotle, however, might have produced essentially similar results. In either case, the logical density of Sidney's verse and prose remains a convincing testimony to his essential concern with the "matter" of his discourse. Far from producing mere symmetry of a decorative kind, his logical and rhetorical structures reveal his determination to "marshal" things "into an assured rancke."

Since the publication of Miss Tuve's book, there has been both support for and criticism of her general conclusions concerning Ramus' influence upon Renaissance literature. Father Walter Ong has partially corroborated her findings in *Ramus: Method, and the Decay of Dialogue* (Cambridge, Mass., 1958); for dissenting opinions, see A. J. Smith, "An Examination of Some Claims for Ramism," *RES* (New Series), 7 (1958), 348–59, and George Watson, "Ramus, Miss Tuve, and the New Petromachia," *MP*, 55 (1958), 259–68. A document such as William Temple's commentary on Sidney's *Apologie*, meanwhile, suggests what important differences Sidney must always have had with the Ramists. In this regard, see J. P. Thorne, "A Ramistical Commentary on Sidney's *Apologie for Poetrie*," *MP*, 54 (1956), 158–64.

20. For an interesting comment on this point, see P. Albert Duhamel, "Sidney's *Arcadia* and Elizabethan Rhetoric," *SP*, XLV (1948), 134–50. Miss Tuve's analyses of the logic in *Astrophel and Stella* are equally illuminating: see *Elizabethan and Metaphysical Imagery*, pp. 312–13 and 319–23.

21. For a useful account of Nizolius, see Quirnus Breen, "The *Observationes in M. T. Ciceronem* (1535) of Marius Nizolius," *Studies in the Renaissance*, I (1954), 49–58. Breen suggests, among other things, that Nizolius was far less narrow-minded and pedantic than his reputation would seem to imply.

22. See Williamson, *The Senecan Amble*, pp. 11–20.

23. Erasmus, *Ciceronianus*, pp. 84–85.

24. See Hoyt H. Hudson, "Jewel's Oration Against Rhetoric," *The Quarterly Journal of Speech*, XIV (1928), 383.

25. See Williamson's discussion of Harvey, *The Senecan Amble*, pp. 73–75.

26. Wilbur Howell, *Logic and Rhetoric in England, 1500–1700* (Princeton, 1956), p. 123.

27. Thomas Wilson, *Arte of Rhetorique*, ed. G. H. Mair (Oxford, 1809), Aii[f].

28. *Elizabethan Critical Essays*, ed. G. Gregory Smith, 2 vols. (Oxford, 1904), II, 263–65.

29. The most formal of Sidney's miscellaneous pieces is his epistle to the queen concerning the Anjou marriage. Its style is often rather stiff, and it is cluttered too much by rhetorical questions in series. Nonetheless, Sidney never sacrifices the stuff of his argument for the sake of elegance or a false formality; he begins by saying that he will set down his reasons "in simple & direct termes" (F, III. 51), and the letter as a whole makes good this promise.

30. See the remarks on p. 59 of the *Apologie*. "Natural" is, of course, a potentially misleading term: it means "unaffected" in Sidney's context, but not necessarily "plain" in the sense of lacking ornament, grace, or wit.

31. For a convenient account of some Renaissance comments on Pindar, see Trimpi, *Ben Jonson's Poems*, pp. 132–35. Sidney's various comments on Pindar are well worth attention, for they reveal a great deal about his general principles of style. In addition to praising Pindar's high style for its energetic and persuasive heroic quality, Sidney also takes Pindar to task for not observing decorum—for using the high style to dignify events and occasions which are unworthy of it: "And where a man may say, that *Pindar* many times prayseth highly victories of small moment, matters rather of sport then vertue: as it may be aunswered, it was the fault of the Poet, and not of the Poetry" (*Apologie*, 32). Finally, Sidney allows Astrophel to condemn *"Pindare's* Apes" (AS 3, 3); and the implication, clearly, is not that Pindar himself is unworthy to be imitated, but that his imitators have merely mimicked him as the Ciceronians had mimicked their own master.

Sidney, it should be noted, discusses Pindar in the context of lyric, rather than heroic, poetry (*Apologie*, 31–32). His comments show clearly enough, however, that it is a particularly martial, stirring kind of lyricism that he has in mind.

32. See Montgomery, *Symmetry and Sense*, p. 64, *et passim*.

33. One may forget how restrained and purposeful Sidney's own uses of alliteration are until one consults again the deadly and relentless "coursing" of Gosson (or even Lyly). Some critics (Montgomery, for example) have suggested that Sidney was, in the *Apologie* passage, criticizing the supposedly overdecorative uses of alliteration in his own *Arcadia*. This seems a very dubious view. What Sidney had in mind were the kinds of excesses he was satirizing as early as 1578 (in *The Lady of May*). His pedantic schoolmaster Rombus provides several examples of such alliterative excess:

> But what sayd that Troian Æneas, when he sojorned in the surging sulkes of the sandiferous seas, . . .

> a brace, a couple, a cast of yong men, to whom the crafty coward *Cupid* had *inquam* delivered his dire-dolorous dart.   (F, II. 331)

The *Arcadia* nowhere reveals the kind of alliterative "coursing" which Sidney detected in some of his contemporaries, which he satirized in Rombus, and which he himself scrupulously avoided. His own uses of the figure are invariably adjusted to suit the decorum of a given lyric or passage of prose.

34. In this regard, it is worth remembering that even so staunch an anti-Ciceronian as Languet encouraged Sidney to cull and imitate verbal flowers in an effort to develop his Latin prose style; and Sidney responded very willingly: see Pears, 2–5.

35. As is well known, Sidney rather disapproved of Spenser's "old rustick language" (*Apologie*, 51): farfetched words could apparently err on the side of plainness as well as that of fineness.

36. Myrick and Montgomery both take Sidney's confession that he is "sick among the rest" (*Apologie*, 59) as a tacit, perfectly serious indictment of the *Arcadia*'s style. This position has very recently been supported by Richard A. Lanham, *The Old Arcadia* (New Haven, 1965), pp. 342–44. But Sidney's remark hardly seems to warrant so broad an interpretation. In its context, it seems to be a gracious act of modesty—a natural inclusion of himself in his own criticisms. The remark also needs to be related to the air of diffidence and the tone of ironic self-deprecation which colors all Sidney's comments on his own writing:

> I wil give you a neerer example of my selfe, who (I knowe not by what mischance) in these my not old yeres and idelest times, having slipt into the title of a Poet, . . .   (*Apologie*, 2)

> But I . . . before ever I durst aspire unto the dignitie, am admitted into the company of Paper-blurrers, . . . Nowe, wherein we want desert were a thankeworthy labour to expresse: but if I knew, I should have mended my selfe. But I, as I never desired the title, so have I neglected the meanes to come by it. Onely, over-mastred by some thoughts, I yeelded an inckie tribute unto them.   (*Apologie*, 49–50)

This is courtly *sprezzatura*, and the faint haze of irony which floats over both passages tells us precisely how seriously we ought (and ought not) to take Sidney's statements. Undoubtedly he *was* dissatisfied by his own poetic achievements—what scrupulous poet is not? But to acknowledge that he may have felt some dissatisfaction with his writing is very different from suggesting that he repudiated that writing for its supposed Ciceronian excesses. Nothing in Sidney's work—as I have tried to demonstrate—would lend support to the second of these two alternatives.

37. It is perhaps worth mentioning at this point that the attitude toward literary style expressed in Sidney's early masque, *The Lady of May*, tends to confirm the general argument expounded in this chapter—that Sidney's work was all of a piece. *The Lady of May* was almost certainly written in the spring of 1578, long before the *Arcadia* was finished, or the *Apologie* undertaken. Yet the schoolmaster and pedant Rombus is there taken to task for his addiction to precisely those literary faults which Sidney attacked more explicitly, but no more vigorously, in later works like the *Apologie*. Like the Ciceronians (and like the "dainty wits" of *Astrophel*), Rombus invariably prefers fine words to solid things; like the logicians and philosophers of the *Apologie*, he relishes the apparatus of invention more than the serious ends which that apparatus was designed to serve:

> Now the thunderthumping *Jove* transfund his dotes into your excellent formositie, which have with your resplendent beames thus segregated the emnitie of these rurall animals: . . .   (F, II, 331)

First you must divisionate your point, *quasi* you should cut a cheese into two particles, for thus must I uniforme my speech to your obtuse conceptions; for *Prius dividendum oratio antequam definiendum exemplum gratia*, either *Therion* must conquer this Dame *Maias* Nimphe, or *Espilus* must overthrow her, and that *secundum* their dignity, which must also be subdivisionated into three equall *species*, . . . (F, II. 335)

Rombus' insensitivity to his audience (only one aspect of his total want of decorum), his equally great insensitivity to the problem at hand (a love problem, after all), his absurd conception of "high" rhetoric ("Now the thunderthumping *Jove*"), and his mechanical application of logical terms all mark him as one of those "qui dum verba sectantur, res ipsas negligunt." He "subdivisionates" the dignity of Therion and Espilus into "three equall *species*" very much as the uncongenial schoolmen of the *Apologie* strive to understand and define anger with their "*Genus* and *difference*" (*Apologie*, 18). Moreover, both Rombus and the schoolmen are ultimately incomprehensible. The "Philosopher, setting downe with thorny argument . . . is so hard of utterance, and so mistie to bee conceived, . . . that happie is that man who may understande him" (*Apologie*, 16–17). When Rombus is finished talking, meanwhile, the simple shepherd Dorcas exclaims rather endearingly:

O poore *Dorcas*, poore *Dorcas*, that I was not set in my young dayes to schoole, that I might have purchased the understanding of master *Rombus* misterious speeches. (F, II. 335)

The irony, of course, is that Dorcas (and other characters in the masque) are infinitely more eloquent than Rombus precisely because they are primarily concerned with the "matter" before them. They are the poets of the piece, and the lyric quality of their various speeches expresses very clearly that close dependence between words and things which constituted true rhetoric in Sidney's view:

O sweete hony milken Lommes, and is there any so flintie a hart, that can find about him to speake against them, that have the charge of such good soules as you be, among whom there is no envy, and all obedience, . . . (F, II. 335)

O sweet contentation to see the long life of the hurtlesse trees, to see how in streight growing up, though never so high, they hinder not their fellowes, they only enviously trouble, which are crookedly bent. What life is to be compared to ours where the very growing things are ensamples of goodnesse? we have no hopes, but we may quickly go about them, and going about them, we soone obtaine them; . . . (F, II. 336–37)

As early as *The Lady of May*, then, Sidney was parodying those who abused logic and rhetoric. As always, he demanded that manner be meaningfully related to matter. A great many of the stylistic points which he elaborated upon in the *Apologie* can be discovered in capsule form in *The Lady of May*, and the fact serves to underline once more the extent to which all of Sidney's work was generated and governed by the same set of stylistic principles and concerns.

38. Trimpi, *Ben Jonson's Poems*, p. 104.

39. *Ibid.*, p. 207.
40. Montgomery, *Symmetry and Sense*, p. 64.
41. Myrick, *Sir Philip Sidney as a Literary Craftsman*, pp. 183 and 189.
42. Trimpi, *Ben Jonson's Poems*, p. 31.

CHAPTER X. *Energia*

1. For Castiglione's entire dialogue on courtly styles of speech and writing, see *The Book of the Courtier*, pp. 50–72.
2. *The Rhetoric of Aristotle*, trans. R. C. Jebb (Cambridge, 1909), pp. 171–72.
3. See Osborne, *The Life, Letters, and Writings of John Hoskyns*, p. 155.
4. Scaliger, *Poetices Libri Septem*, p. 116. Scaliger's entire discussion of energia occurs in Book Three (Caput XXVII) of the *Poetices*. *Efficacia* is there defined as "vis orationis" and is identified with the Greek ἐνέργεια.
Scaliger's discussion of energia has never been translated. I am indebted to Mr. John Shea, of Harvard University, for the version which appears in my own text.
5. *Ibid.*, p. 117. The Latin for the quoted passages is as follows: "Maximam verò efficaciam prae se ferunt epiphonemata, aut Prosphonemata: *Tantae molis erat Romanam condere gentem.* . . . *vicisti tua est Lauinia coniunx.* . . . *hostis amare, quid increpitas?*"
6. *Ibid.*, p. 118. The Latin: "Est & in Apostrophe, & in interrogatione tanta efficacia: vt subsilire faciat animum auditoris. quae vbi coniunctae sunt: nihil deest ad summam vim Cùm enim lego illa ex secundo, caeteras omnes mihi excutiũt cogitationes, *Hocce erat alma parens, quod me per tela per ignes, Eripis?* . . . De Niso, *Quid faciat? qua vi iuuenem, quibus audeat armis Eripere?* Acclamationes vt diximus, & exclamationes simplices. *Latonae tacitum pertentant gaudia pectus, O térque quatèrque beati. O fortunati quorum iam moenia surgunt.*"
7. *Ibid.*, p. 119. The Latin: "Et ad inanimas maiore motu, *O nunquam frustrata conatus Hasta meos.* Et in duodecimo, *Túque optima ferrum Terra tene.*"
8. *Ibid.*, pp. 116–17. The Latin: "*Sagitta Acestae ignita.* Turnus inclusus in castris Troianorum. . . . Turni galea. ensis eius fractus. Imber ad nauium incendia."
9. *Ibid.*, p. 117. The Latin: "*Succedóque oneri.* Equidem videor patrem meũ virum fortissimum gestare.–*dextrae se paruus Iulus Implicuit, sequitúrque patrem non passibus aequis*: Hîc autem videor trahi. Nam quid est *Implicuit,* Certè me miseret. . . . Quis nõ animo Aeneã ibi comitetur?"
10. Scaliger alludes to Vergil frequently throughout all seven of the *Poetices Libri*, but his Third Book is given over entirely to a discussion of Vergil's excellences as a poet, and it includes an extensive, detailed analysis of the *Aeneid* from several points of view. Sidney's frequent references to the *Aeneid* throughout the *Apologie*—and he draws on Vergil more than on any other poet—seem generally inspired by Scaliger, and one or two passages are close enough to Scaliger to suggest direct influence. Scaliger's anatomy of energia, it should be noted, is also contained in this Third Book. A statement at the end of the *Apologie*, moreover, suggests very strongly that Sidney had in fact looked carefully into Scaliger's extended treatment of Vergil, for Sidney there urges his readers to "beleeve with *Scaliger,* that no Philosophers precepts can sooner make you an honest man, then the reading of *Virgill*" (*Apologie*, 62).

11. *Poetices Libri Septem*, p. 117. The Latin: "Etiam cum Venulum interbrachia Tarchontis audio, video quoque, *Volat igneus aequore Tarchon Arma virúmque ferens.*"

12. *Ibid.*, p. 119. The Latin: "Pudor in Deiphobo, *Pauit antem ac dira tegentem Supplicia.* Ira in Turno, *Totoque loquentis ab ore Scintillae absistunt, oculis micat acribus ignis.*"

13. Energia should be distinguished, of course, from enargia, which the rhetoricians usually define as vivid or clear *description* of people or objects or places. Enargia is primarily visual in its mode of operation: it aims simply to place clearly described objects before the reader, to engage him in the way that painting or photography does. Energia, by contrast, appeals to no particular sense, although visual effects are clearly among its most powerful.

14. See Buxton's discussion of this point, *Sir Philip Sidney and the English Renaissance*, pp. 113–16. Sidney certainly knew of the Pléiade experiments with verse and music; and he allows his shepherd Dicus to contend that "since verses had ther chefe ornament, if not eand, in musike, those which were just appropriated to musicke did best obtaine their ende" (Ringler, 389). There were also other important motives, of course, which must have prompted Sidney's experiments with classical meters. He undoubtedly felt that English prosody had very little of the rich expressive power of the Latin or Greek, and he wished—if possible—to find means of drawing upon that power. Although he gradually reconciled himself to the sweets of rhyme, he certainly regarded them with a good deal of skepticism for a long period of time. Like Campion, he was disposed to prefer more subtle harmonies—or at least he disliked the kind of musical crudity which unskillful rhyming so often produced in Tudor poetry. Spenser, when he wrote to Harvey about the so-called Aereopogus, said nothing about a program concerning the adaptation of classical meters to music, but he did proclaim "a generall surceasing and silence of balde Rymers"; and Sidney himself complained that so much English poetry was "a confused masse of words, with a tingling sound of ryme, barely accompanied with reason" (*Apologie*, 51). For a further comment on the subject, see John Hollander, *The Untuning of the Sky: Ideas of Music in English Poetry, 1500–1700* (Princeton, 1961), p. 142.

15. Hector Genouy, *L'Arcadia de Sidney* (Lyons, 1928), pp. 165–66.

16. See Thompson's *The Founding of English Metre*, pp. 128–38, and G. L. Hendrickson's "Elizabethan Quantitative Hexameters," *PQ*, XXVIII (1949), 237–60.

17. "Some Sonnets of Sir Philip Sydney," *The Works of Charles and Mary Lamb*, ed. E. V. Lucas, 7 vols. (New York, 1903), II, 218. Lamb is reading *Astrophel* as if it were autobiography; but although we may want to qualify his statement concerning the "historical thread" running through the sonnets, we can hardly disagree with him on the subject of their "full, material" nature. Indeed, it was that very fullness and circumstantiality which encouraged Lamb to believe that there was genuine "history" behind the poetry.

18. Nothing re-creates the sense of *éclat* which accompanied *Astrophel*'s appearance so well as Thomas Nashe's famous statement: "Put out your rush candles, you Poets and Rimers, and bequeath your crazed quaterzayns to the Chaundlers; for loe, here he cometh that hath broke your legs. . . . Sleepe *Argus*, sleep Ignorance, sleep Impudence, for *Mercury* hath *Io* & onely *Io Paean* belongeth to *Astrophel*" (G. Gregory Smith, *Elizabethan Critical Essays*, II, 225).

19. It is perhaps worth noticing here that the development of Sidney's prose parallels in certain respects the development of his poetry. For despite the effectiveness and appropriateness of the *Old Arcadia*'s prose, it seems clear that Sidney was striving in the revised version for a much greater intensity and amplitude—for a power and fullness consonant with his new heroic subject. Indeed, many of those passages which an earlier generation of critics considered most "curious" and conceited (and the "stucco decoration" of which Mario Praz pointed to as a sign of Sidney's stylistic decline) were in reality attempts to achieve a new kind of poetic vision in prose, a new largeness and grandeur infused with energy. This is true, not only of the particular portions of the *Old Arcadia* which Sidney rewrote, but especially of those sections which were composed specifically for the revision:

> but when they came so neere as their eies were ful masters of the object, they saw a sight full of piteous strangenes: a ship, or rather the carkas of the shippe, or rather some few bones of the carkas, hulling there, part broken, part burned, part drowned: death having used more than one dart to that destruction. About it floted great store of very rich thinges, and many chestes which might promise no lesse. And amidst the precious things were a number of dead bodies, . . . ful of grisly wounds, & their bloud had (as it were) filled the wrinckles of the seas visage: which it seemed the sea woulde not wash away, that it might witnes it was not alwaies his fault, when we condemne his crueltie: in summe, a defeate, where the conquered kept both field and spoile: a shipwrack without storme or ill footing: and a wast of fire in the midst of water.   (F, I. 9–10)

> Yonder my *Claius*, *Urania* lighted, the verie horse (me thought) bewayled to be so disburdned: . . . There shee sate, vouchsafing my cloake (then most gorgeous) under her: at yonder rising of the ground she turned her selfe, looking backe toward her woonted abode, and because of her parting bearing much sorrow in hir eies, the lightsomnes whereof had yet so naturall a cherefulnesse, as it made even sorrow seeme to smile; . . .   (F, I. 6)

> And now the often-changing Fortune began also to chaunge the hewe of the battailes. For at the first, though it were terrible, yet Terror was deckt so bravelie with rich furniture, guilte swords, shining armours, pleasant pensils, that the eye with delight had scarce leasure to be afraide: But now all universally defiled with dust, bloud, broken armours, mangled bodies, tooke away the maske, and sette foorth Horror in his owne horrible manner.
>   (F, I. 392)

Sidney's concern in each of these (and many other similar) passages is with the vivid creation of moving scenes that give us a feeling insight into terror, horror, or grief. Sights of a piteous strangeness are created primarily through the agency of energia: through the pervasive and extraordinarily compelling use of personification ("the wrinckles of the seas visage"); the demonstrative "placing" of people and objects ("There shee sate"); the ordered movement of the rhetoric toward powerful climaxes; and the use of forceful descriptive words in rhetorical and syntactical patterns designed to enhance that forcefulness ("part broken, part burned, part drowned"; "all universally defiled with dust, bloud, broken armours, mangled bodies"). This prose is far from "curious"; indeed, we shall have to go far to find its equal (Shakespeare excepted) in the entire Elizabethan era.

For further indications that energia was very much on Sidney's mind as he revised the *Arcadia*, see the descriptions of Zelmane's effective oration (F, I. 318) and Dorus' manner of composing a lyric (F, I. 356). In the latter very witty and revealing passage, Dorus acts as nervous self-critic:

> Here Sorow was not inough expressed; there he seemed too much for his owne sake to be sory. This sentence rather shewed art, then passion; that sentence rather foolishly passionate, then forcibly moving.

20. For a general account of the Camerata, see Gretchen Finney, *Musical Backgrounds for English Literature: 1580-1650* (New Brunswick, N.J., Rutgers University Press, 1962), pp. 126–138, and Hollander's *Untuning of the Sky*, pp. 141–43 and 180–94. Recent scholarship on the Camerata has qualified the revolutionary character of the Camerata's work, but it has not quarreled with the traditional view of the group's ideals and general program. See particularly two articles by Claude V. Palisca: "Girolamo Mei: Mentor to the Florentine Camerata," *The Musical Quarterly*, 40 (1954), 1–20, and "Vincenzo Galilei and Some Links Between 'Pseudo-Monody' and Monody," *The Musical Quarterly*, 46 (1960), 344–60; see also Nino Pirrotta, "Tragédie et Comédie dans la Camerata Fiorentina," *Musique et Poésie Au XVIe Siècle*, Coloques Internationaux du Centre National de la Recherche Scientifique (Paris, 1954), pp. 287–97.

There is no evidence that Sidney knew anything of the Camerata group and its program, although it is possible that he had heard something of them during his Italian tour. The Camerata was just beginning to hold its periodic meetings in the early 1570's, and Sidney visited Florence for a short time in the spring of 1574.

Sidney also knew, of course, about the Pléiade experiments uniting music and poetry; but de Baif's circle, unlike the Camerata, never reached the point of fully subordinating all other factors to the dominant role played by a dramatic speaking voice, and it was just this achievement (in essence, the creation of recitative) which seems so strikingly parallel to Sidney's.

21. Finney, *Musical Backgrounds*, p. 128. Sidney had reflected on the problem of the relationship between text and music: Lalus, in his *Arcadia* debate with Dicus, argues that "musicke is a servaunt to poetry" (Ringler, 390).

22. Finney, *Musical Backgrounds*, p. 129.

23. Vincenzo Galilei, *Dialogo della musica antica e della moderna* (1581), *Source Readings in Music History*, ed. Oliver Strunk (New York, 1950), p. 318.

24. Finney, *Musical Backgrounds*, p. 130.

CHAPTER XI. *The Styles of* Astrophel

1. The song, by John Daniel, is printed in *English Madrigal Verse*, ed. E. H. Fellowes (Oxford, 1929), p. 405. For a discussion of Daniel's lyric, see Hollander's *Untuning of the Sky*, pp. 188–89.

2. Montgomery, *Symmetry and Sense*, p. 88.

3. Puttenham, *Arte of English Poesie*, p. 262.

4. See Montgomery's excellent discussion of this point (*Symmetry and Sense*, pp. 100ff.) as well as Kalstone's entire discussion of *Astrophel* (*Sidney's Poetry*,

pp. 133–78). Any critic of Sidney necessarily owes a great deal to Montgomery's and Kalstone's studies, as well as to Richard B. Young's "English Petrarke," *Three Studies in the Renaissance* (New Haven, 1958). My own study is particularly indebted to Young's elucidation of the general structure of *Astrophel*.

5. Tuve, *Elizabethan and Metaphysical Imagery*, p. 243.

6. See Kalstone, *Sidney's Poetry*, pp. 124–30.

CHAPTER XII. *The New Poetry*

1. Kalstone makes this point, *Sidney's Poetry*, p. 140.

2. See, for example, OA 39 and OA 41–43.

3. Thompson, "Sir Philip and the Forsaken Iamb," pp. 110–12.

4. *Ibid.*, pp. 108ff.

CHAPTER XIII. *Astrophel as Poet*

1. This is, of course, Montgomery's view, and it has been recently restated by Trimpi, *Ben Jonson's Poems*, pp. 104 and 206.

2. See Mario Praz, "Petrarch in England," *The Flaming Heart* (Garden City, N.Y., 1958), p. 272, and Young, "English Petrarke," *Three Studies in the Renaissance*, pp. 6–7.

3. The subject is too complex for summary discussion; the essential point of difference, however, is that the anti-Petrarchan criticisms of Ronsard and du Bellay are far less "technical" than Astrophel's. Sidney permits his hero to discourse informally on the subjects of invention and imitation to such an extent that the *Astrophel* sonnets demand to be read as serious, substantive criticism informed by a good deal of classical rhetorical theory.

4. Kalstone, *Sidney's Poetry*, pp. 126–28.

5. Erasmus, *Ciceronianus*, p. 75.

6. *Ibid.*, p. 123.

7. *Ibid.*, p. 81.

8. Astrophel, of course, does not discuss the methods of proper imitation, but chooses to stress his own originality and his reliance upon his "inward tuch." Sidney reveals a similar emphasis in his discussion of the matter in the *Apologie*. Imitation had in general become so closely identified with simple copying or "aping" that it was far more important in 1580 to mock abuses and to stress the importance of a writer's individual, personal response to experience than to state again the quite legitimate uses of imitation—uses which no one would have questioned.

9. *Institutio Oratoria*, III, pp. 189 and 191.

10. See Kalstone, *Sidney's Poetry*, pp. 128–30.

CHAPTER XIV. *Dialogue and Debate*

1. For some passages that relate closely to the tone and spirit of OA 66, see particularly Pears, 2–5, 29–30, and 46–49.

2. This is demonstrated in a very striking way by Janet Scott: see *Les Sonnets Elisabéthains* (Paris, 1929), pp. 15–53.

CHAPTER XV. *Astrophel in Love*

1. Fraunce, *The Arcadian Rhetorike*, p. 63.
2. Wilson, *The Arte of Rhetorique*, p. 210.
3. *Ibid.*, p. 208.

CHAPTER XVI. *The Campaign Pursued*

1. Young, "English Petrarke," *Three Studies in the Renaissance*, p. 62.

CHAPTER XVII. *Two Closing Songs*

1. See Ringler, 484.
2. See Montgomery, *Symmetry and Sense*, pp. 116–17, and Kalstone, *Sidney's Poetry*, p. 207.
3. AS 107 shows Astrophel trying to return to the public world of action, but he is scarcely successful in his attempt.
4. Astrophel's tone, of course, as well as his character and conduct as a whole, preclude any characterization of him as a heroic lover in the way that the poet of Shakespeare's *Sonnets* is heroic: we will find in Sidney no deep struggle against time and mutability, no final triumph over vicissitude. Astrophel's protestations of enduring love are obviously in another key altogether; they reflect his weakness in the face of overpowering desire rather than any determination on his part to assert the strength of the human spirit in the face of absence and change. Yet, in spite of this, Astrophel's final expression of love remains significantly different from and more moving than Stella's.

Index

❧❧